THE BATTLE FOR
HEARTS
AND MINDS

THE BATTLE FOR
HEARTS
AND MINDS

CHANGING FORTUNES AT HEARTS OF MIDLOTHIAN FC

CRAIG WATSON

BLACK & WHITE PUBLISHING

First Published 2005
by Black & White Publishing Ltd
99 Giles Street, Edinburgh EH6 6BZ

ISBN 1 84502 046 4

A CIP catalogue record for this book is
available from the British Library.

Printed and bound by Creative Print and Design

CONTENTS

PART 4 – TWO TURBULENT SEASONS

ACKNOWLEDGEMENTS

My thanks go to Shirley and Maisie: Shirley, for her patience and support as I put in the hours of research and writing; and Maisie, as a potential Hearts fan of tomorrow. For a while, it seemed as though there might not be a Heart of Midlothian Football Club for her to support in future years. Credit must go to Peter for coming up with the idea for the book although, during the more difficult moments, I felt less charitable towards him for doing so. Thanks for proof-reading to Peter and Shirley as well as Gordon, who also had to bear many hours discussing the contents over a pint or two of 80 shilling. Thanks also to Kenny for his input – surprisingly generous for a Hibs supporter. And of course, there would be no book at all without the backing of Bob and everyone at Black & White.

I am extremely grateful to the many contributors, although Donald Ford should get a special mention for his time and wisdom. I would have struggled without his help. Freddie Glidden and Jack Alexander provided valuable insight into Hearts during two of their more memorable eras. And those connected with the running of Hearts over the years – Wallace Mercer, Leslie Deans, Chris Robinson and George Foulkes among them – also gave up their time to make important contributions.

Finally, the improving fortunes at Hearts are a tribute to all those who fought to ensure the survival of the club, particularly Save our Hearts. Without the likes of Derek Watson, Martin Laidlaw, Peter McGrail, Robert McGrail, John Borthwick, Gary

ACKNOWLEDGEMENTS

Mackay and all the other individuals who gave their time, effort and money to secure the club's future, this may have been a book without a happy ending.

INTRODUCTION

The maroon balloons bobbled around the touchline – at least, the ones that had not been burst by the ground staff using garden forks did. Six thousand had been released by fans at half-time, all stamped with a cheeky, defiant message aimed at the chief executive: 'Get this balloon out of Tynecastle.' The demonstration created a bizarre spectacle, as the balloons were batted around by supporters in the stands before drifting down towards the pitch in waves. The chief executive, Chris Robinson, sat impassively in the directors' box as the second half was delayed to allow ground staff to clear the touchlines. The supporters booed as each insult was popped although a handful escaped the boots and the garden forks and continued to waft around in the bright sunshine in small bunches.

Motherwell had gone ahead with the last move of the first forty-five minutes and should have made it 3–1 at the start of the second but Hearts cleared off the line. The home team clawed its way back into the game and equalised with a tap-in. The decisive goal for Hearts bounced into the net fifteen minutes before full-time and some fans ambled down and along the passageways towards the exits soon after. The characteristic fight and determination shown by the team was not universally matched by those in the stands.

The ball was blootered up the park and a blast of the referee's whistle signalled the end of the game and season 2003–04. The players raised their arms in relief and triumph at their achievement. Most fans stood to applaud, some cheered enthusiastically,

1

others sat and stared and clapped gently. This was, after all, a cause for celebration as another entry had been logged in the record books – Hearts had become the first team to finish third in successive seasons in the Scottish Premier League (SPL). They had finished with one more point than they had had in 1997–98, the season they challenged for the league and won the Scottish Cup.

On both occasions, the key to their success was an impressive home record. As had been the case six years before, the side was unbeaten in the league, at Tynecastle, by teams outwith the Old Firm. Hearts would be playing in Europe again the follow-ing season, hopefully making it through the first round to the revamped – and potentially money-spinning – group stage of the UEFA European Cup. Yet none of those European games would be played at Tynecastle which at that time had been the home of Hearts for 118 years. The ground, and the atmosphere it helped to create, had led Hearts into Europe but it was not deemed suitable for European football. The widely admired stadium had recently been refurbished to the tune of £12 million but, according to a report by Hearts, it was 'not fit for purpose' because the pitch no longer complied with new UEFA regulations.

Those inside Tynecastle were aware of this report and that perhaps explains the oddly muted reaction of the fans. No doubt the team deserved recognition for its achievement yet the stadium, its greatest asset in many ways, had been put up for sale. There would be no more European nights at Tynecastle; there would be few Saturday afternoons left either if the plans of the board were given the go-ahead. The sale of the old ground would be used to pay off soaring debts of more than £18 million; Tynecastle would be bulldozed and luxury flats built in its place.

Even the most optimistic of fans could not fail to be reminded of this financial plight as three first team players – Scott Severin, Steven Boyack and Andy Kirk – made a valedictory appearance on the pitch at the end of the game. They waved farewell to the fans as the remainder of the squad strolled around the park in a leisurely lap of honour. Coach Craig Levein had been forced to release the three players in an effort to reduce the crippling wage bill. The coach took the microphone and walked to the centre circle to address the fans. He thanked all the players for their effort during a long, hard season and paid tribute to those who were leaving, expressing his frustration and disappointment that they were being forced out because of the club's predicament.

In contrast to the defiance evident during the balloon release demo and an earlier protest rally and march by 5,000 fans, Levein's words of doom actually prompted sporadic applause from fans still in the ground. The supporters reacted out of sympathy for the coach's difficulties and admiration for his achievement in those circumstances. But it also reflected a shared understanding of the depth of the problems at the club.

The break between seasons 2003–04 and 2004–05 had begun. The former would go down in the record books as a success for the consecutive third place finish. The latter would go down in the history books for a memorable European campaign and not just because of Hearts' chosen 'home' venue – it was also half-time in a struggle for the very heart and soul of the club. The questions were posed in 2003–04. Would the sale of Tynecastle go through, despite the opposition of supporters? Should the increasingly unpopular Chris Robinson remain in office? Could Hearts survive the crisis? Season 2004–05 would provide the answers. The clues were in the club's colourful history.

PART 1

EARLY HISTORY

1

FORMATION AND FIRST CRISIS

The group of lads who kicked a ball around the cobbled streets of Edinburgh's Old Town and loitered in the dark closes off the High Street and the Canongate could never have known that they were to form what would become a Scottish sporting institution.

Tradition has it that the actions of a local policeman, concerned at what today would, no doubt, be described as anti-social behaviour, set in motion a chain of events which led to the establishment of Heart of Midlothian Football Club. The group of young men were regulars at the Heart of Mid-lothian dance club in Washing Green Court, as it was called in the early 1870s. The area is better known now as the site of the Dumbiedykes flats by the new Scottish Parliament building. Their interest in dancing appeared to amuse the policeman, who suggested their spare time would be better spent playing the emerging sport of association football at the Meadows parkland rather than hanging around street corners. An alternative theory suggests that there was no gentle persuasion and they were ordered to stop playing football outside the Tolbooth because it was causing a nuisance. Whatever the truth, it is thought that, during a meeting at the city's Tron Kirk, the dancers then decided that they would form a team playing under local rules, which were an amalgam of football and rugby codes.

Perhaps inspired by the first ever international match the previous year – a 0–0 draw between Scotland and England on St Andrew's Day 1872 – they bought a new football at Percival King's shop in Lothian Road. A headquarters was then established at Mother Anderson's Tavern on West Crosscauseway and it was decided to use the name of their favourite dance hall and the city's old Tolbooth. The name, whether taken from the venue for their other pastime or the place where they had been banned from playing football, was apparently suggested by the club's first captain, Tom Purdie. It would later become associated with the romance of a club which was to experience enviable highs and shattering lows. The fact that it also described the jail which once provided the final night's rest for the condemned man before he was led to the gallows in the Grassmarket was to serve as a more ominous warning for the football club.

In his 1959 book, *The Hearts*, Albert Mackie said:

> Tom Purdie, if it was he who chose it, had a stroke of genius when he selected Heart of Midlothian as the name of a sport club. It outdazzles New York Yankees, Boston Braves and even Queen of the South. Football teams around Edinburgh were fond of such floral names as Thistle, Primrose, Bluebell, Violet and Rose, and there were occasional excursions into the literary such as Ivanhoe and into the royal with Balmoral and Royal Albert, but no-one ever thought of another name to match Heart of Midlothian. It is a proud name, and a graceful one, even if it did at one time adorn a fetid prison, and it has demanded in its players a standard of football and of conduct in keeping with its grand sound.

Purdie claimed that these events took place in the autumn of 1873 after the founding of the Scottish Football Association and before a groundbreaking exhibition match involving the best players from Glasgow the same year. Queen's Park FC, the pioneers of the sport in Scotland, organised the showpiece as a 'missionary game in Edinburgh to popularise the sport there'. The regulars from the Heart of Mid-lothian dance hall must have been impressed because they adopted association rules early in 1874, the year that is now given as the one when the football club was officially formed.

Queen's Park officials were less optimistic, considering the Edinburgh exhibition match more as the 'invasion of a rugby stronghold'. It was a comment which is still made of the capital city and one with even more resonance as Hearts recently faced the prospect of becoming tenants at the home of the sport of rugby in Scotland.

However, Hearts were at the forefront of developing the game in the east of Scotland, joining the Edinburgh Football Association and first entering the Scottish Cup in 1875. The first two cup games both ended 0–0 against the 3rd Edinburgh Rifle Volunteers, who were credited with pioneering the sport in the capital. Both teams progressed to the next round, as was the rule of the day, with Hearts losing 2–0 to Drumpellier of Coatbridge in the next round. At this time Hearts, who played in an all-white strip with a maroon heart on the chest, boasted forty-five members and appeared to be thriving. Unfortunately, a year later, the club faced its first crisis when it informed the authorities that it was disbanding. Albert Mackie's book described how the decision was taken after an earlier defeat by another Meadows-based team, St Andrew Boys Club, although other accounts suggest it was because of a shortage of players. Mackie's version is based on the recollections of John Cochrane, who played first for St Andrew and then Hearts. Cochrane's story, told in 1939 when he was eighty-three years old, may indicate some truth in both versions of events. It also explained how the name, Heart of Midlothian, was retained. Mackie recalled that three Hearts players turned up at a regular St Andrew meeting and asked to join the team, cleverly arguing that the club name may get confused with the Fife University town. Cochrane said a motion was put to the meeting and duly carried – the name was changed to Heart of Midlothian Football Club.

Cochrane also explained that, by now, Hearts were playing in white, red and blue, while St Andrew wore maroon. He claimed credit for suggesting that the new team should wear the St Andrew colours and described how the mother of one player sent both teams' strips off to be dyed and personally cut out heart shaped patches to sew on to the jerseys. By 1877, a new-look football club had emerged.

The last survivor of the original Hearts team at the time, Cochrane then went on to give an account of what he said was the first game against city rivals, Hibs, a recently formed club founded by Irish immigrants. He said the match in 1875 finished 3–1 to Hearts, despite the best efforts of Hibs fans to make their own team's goalmouth smaller by pushing the posts together when Hearts attacked. A more epic encounter between the rivals took place in the final of the 1878 Edinburgh FA Cup, with Hearts eventually running out 3–2 winners after four previous matches were drawn. The game, which ended with Hearts captain Tom Purdie taking refuge in a house in Causewayside after being chased by a group of Hibs fans, helped to fuel a rivalry that generated increasing interest in association football in the capital.

The Glasgow area remained the heartland of the game in Scotland but it was becoming ever more popular in Edinburgh. As well as staging cricket matches, the Meadows was now crowded with around a dozen rival football teams and their supporters. With this in mind, Hearts – a nickname which emerged around this time – exerted pressure on the local council to provide a 'proper field'. They soon started playing many of their first-team fixtures at Powburn, near Blackford, in the south-east of the city. By 1879, they were also using the superior facilities at Powderhall, in the Broughton district.

The team was improving at this time, recording its record victory (21–0 against Anchor FC in the Edinburgh cup) in 1880 and becoming the first Edinburgh club to play in England, despite losing to both Aston Villa (4–2) and Blackburn Rovers (2–0) in 1881. It was also during that year that the club took over a private field in Gorgie, the area which would be the focus of so much controversy more than 120 years later. The club did not, however, occupy the site of the current stadium; instead the ground was across the road on land that now includes Wardlaw Street. In an echo of language associated with more recent financial problems, there were concerns that the new site was not viable for the football club.

At the time, the population of Gorgie–Dalry was smaller than it is now and the area was regarded as too far from the city centre to attract large crowds. But, after the official opening of Old Tynecastle on 9 April 1881, when they beat the Edinburgh team Hanover 8–0, Hearts undercut their other city rivals with half-price admission charges. An extension to the tram system soon allowed supporters to travel to the ground more easily. Hearts at least had a ground of their own. There were around 40 clubs in Edinburgh at the time, most of which played their football in public parks and were lobbying the local council for better facilities. But the Gorgie club's financial problems were far from over.

2

PROFESSIONAL PLAYERS, BUSINESS BEGINNERS

By this time, basic commercialisation had already taken place in football but the sport was to face its first major challenge over the issue of the introduction of professionalism. The fight to wrest the sport from the public schools in the south of England began with the formation of clubs in urban areas throughout Britain in the 1870s and 1880s. Workers were benefiting from higher wages and more time off, particularly on Saturdays, and, as a result, football teams formed from industrial, social and religious groups. The need to organise fixtures increased as the sport's popularity grew, followed by a demand for suitable stadiums and facilities. The natural next step was to charge those watching matches a small fee to cover the cost of paying for those facilities, although this often amounted to a donation with extra money given to charity. The expectations of spectators rose in these new surroundings, resulting in pressure to produce a winning and entertaining team. As a result, more demands were placed on players' time to train and prepare for matches. The players, in turn, sought compensation for their efforts, particularly if they faced the possibility of losing earnings from their full-time jobs as a result of their football commitments.

Clubs in the north of England were at the forefront of the fight to introduce professionalism but faced stiff opposition from those in the more affluent south who could afford to play the game 'for its own sake'. They argued that, if players were dependent on football for their livelihood, they might be more inclined to cheat.

No doubt they also feared the masses organising and gathering together in large numbers to follow pursuits which might involve drinking and gambling.

Despite the opposition, payments were made to players unofficially during the 1870s, often under the guise of a full-time job offer outwith football. In 1885, inevitably, professionalism was formally legalised in England and the first football league was set up by twelve teams from the north and midlands three years later. Not for the first time in their history, Hearts were to pay the price for wider changes taking place in the game of football as English clubs raided the Scottish leagues for new talent. For instance, the promising team which won the first Roseberry Charity Cup in 1883 was systematically dismantled by teams from down south. This was illustrated the following year when the SFA issued a list of players who had been banned from playing north of the border because they moved to England – ten of the fifty-seven names were former Hearts stars. The same year the club even wrote to Johnny Gair, after he had moved to Burnley, urging him and fellow former player Will Ronaldson to return north for an upcoming cup tie against Hibs. The letter urged him to 'get your men from Lancashire . . . let it cost what it will' and claimed they would 'receive the thanks of all the football followers – if we could just snuff out the Hibs'.

Perhaps the greatest individual loss was that of Hearts' first truly great player, Nick Ross. He had been outstanding for Hearts in the early 1880s and went on to become the club captain. The versatile fullback, who was to be lured south to play for the Preston North End 'Invincibles' that won the first English league title in 1889, was even credited with 'inventing' the pass back to the goalkeeper. In his 1920s book, *The Story of the Hearts*, William Reid wrote:

> A present-day famous team manager, asked his opinion of Ross, said: 'Today he would be worth the Bank of England.' He knew every trick in the game, and it is said of him that he was the first back who ever, as a matter of tactics, passed the ball back to his own goalkeeper.

Reid also recognised the fact that payments were made in an attempt to retain and attract the best players by compensating them for the loss of other earnings, adding:

The offence of paying a man sub rosa (secretly) was regarded as a venial one, and men of the greatest probity in private life thought nothing, in their capacity of members of this club or the next, of contributing a small stated sum each week towards the fund out of which 'broken time' was paid and other surreptitious payments were made.

Hearts were to pay a hefty price for this practice when they became the first team to be investigated and suspended by the SFA for fielding professional players during the 11–1 defeat of Dunfermline in the cup in October 1884. Other teams were guilty of the same offence but Hearts had been caught paying two players more than £2 a week. The club admitted the irregularity, Dunfermline were awarded the tie, a new committee was formed and Hearts were re-admitted to the SFA within a month. The clubs continued to put pressure on the SFA to allow professionalism but the governing body was to hold out for a further nine years before giving in to the demands in a belated attempt to regulate the practice.

Clearly, football was outgrowing the local clubs which pioneered the organised game. Local traders and businessmen had become involved in their running, although they remained private organisations. But the need to pay wages and running costs led to further commercialisation of the sport, with the first English teams converting to limited companies – owned by shareholders but run by directors – in the late 1880s. The move allowed directors to borrow money from banks without being personally liable for any debts incurred.

Hearts were keen to develop as a business and so played their last game at Old Tynecastle on 27 February 1886, beating Sunderland 2–1, and moved across the road to the new Tynecastle Park. The improved facilities, which included two pitches and cost

£200 to build, reflected the ambitions of the club. Another victory over English opposition, this time 4–1 against Bolton Wanderers, marked the official opening of the new stadium on 10 April. Trams were now running to Dalry and around 6,000 spectators turned up for the game. The first scorer at the new ground, Tom Jenkinson, went on to become the club's first international when he was capped for Scotland in the 4–1 defeat of Ireland ten months later.

That season and the next, the southern connection continued with Hearts taking part in the FA Cup. They failed to progress and the SFA banned participation in the English competition from 1887. But, despite Hearts' ambitions, the crowds were disappointing perhaps because Hibs remained the top team in Edinburgh. That was soon to change. First, Hearts defeated their adversaries 3–1 in an 1887 cup derby which William Reid described as 'the turning point in the club's history; henceforth the Heart of Midlothian were one of the leading clubs in the country'. Then, a year later, another team with Irish roots arrived on the scene, this time in the industrial heartland of Glasgow. The formation of Celtic was to have a huge impact on football in the capital, with the Glasgow club poaching the best players from Hibs, just as the Edinburgh team had beaten English champions Preston to become self-styled 'champions of the world'. The Scottish League was established in 1890 and the enterprise Hearts had shown in previous years, which included building a 10,000-capacity stadium with two stands and a pavilion, started to pay off. They soon added a new committee room, facilities for the players, a press box and even refreshment stalls.

The following fifteen-year period was to prove the first of two golden eras for the club. Between 1891 and 1906, helped by the signing of the great Bobby Walker, Hearts won two league championships and four Scottish Cups. The first cup win, in 1891, was notable as much for its notoriety as for the silverware itself. On that occasion, the Hearts defender Jimmy Adams fisted out what looked like a certain goal in the 3–1 defeat of East Stirlingshire. The SFA investigated the sixth-round tie and it was decided to award a penalty kick in such circumstances in an effort to stamp out the 'growing evil' of this type of behaviour. Also in this period was the only final ever to be played outside Glasgow – a satisfying 3–1 victory over rivals Hibs at Logie Green, by Powderhall in Edinburgh, in 1896. Hearts also registered a record Edinburgh derby scoreline during this period, beating Hibs 10–2 at Easter Road during 1893–94.

Professionalism was finally introduced during this period of success on the pitch for Hearts and the club continued its attempts to develop as a business. But the limitations which were to surface in later years also first came to light at this time. In 1896, the club responded to claims that there had been 'looseness about the management' with the insistence that the critics failed to recognise the difficulties in running a football team. The club cited travel to cup ties in 'outlandish parts' (Blantyre, Ayr and Arbroath) as one of the reasons for a downturn in profits, although it should have been some concern that, in the previous season, expenditure, at £5,200, was outstripping income of almost £4,900. Already, payments to players made up 40% of costs. Wages continued to rise as players faced the lure of playing down south towards the end of the century and efforts were made to increase income.

Hearts had considered buying Tynecastle from the local council in 1893 but the deal did not go through and Edinburgh Corporation was accused of 'forestalling' the club. Nevertheless, a cycle track was constructed at the ground to rent out and Hearts hosted a variety of events, such as sports meetings. An annual concert was staged, trackside advertising was also introduced and prize draws were held. The first international match at Tynecastle was played on 26 March 1892, with Scotland beating Wales 6–1. The need to increase revenue was obvious. It was in part to fund the erection of a new covered stand and the almost constant improvement work but also because of mounting financial difficulties in the new century.

Most clubs, at this time, were run by directors who sought to contribute to the local community and boost their own reputation in the process rather than make a profit. They were also responsible for all team affairs – at least they were until Peter Fairley was appointed Hearts' first 'manager' in 1901, although he acted more as a club secretary than a modern-day coach. Hearts were undoubtedly proving a success on the pitch but the members of its organising committee were becoming increasingly concerned that they may be exposed to financial loss as a result of their football connections. Hearts responded to this concern in 1903 – the same year that Fairley was replaced by the more hands-on William Waugh – by following the example of the big English clubs and forming a limited liability company. Writing two decades later, William Reid explained that:

> By and by certain members began to be dubious as to their position.
> The question of liability was beginning to agitate the public mind,
> so a departure was made, the club being converted into a limited
> liability company in 1903. The capital was £3,000.

But the ploy proved a failure as financial pressure continued to build and the club was 'wound up voluntarily' in 1905. It was replaced by a new company which took on debts of £1,600, while assets – 'the erections on the ground' – had not been valued but cost £2,500. Shareholders of the old company received new shares for old ones they held and a further 4,542 of the 5,000 £1 shares were offered to the public. The prospectus issued at the time of the deal remained upbeat, while also carefully targeting potential investors. It said:

> The directors confidently appeal to the public of Edinburgh and
> district for their assistance in providing the necessary capital. Many
> thousands are brought into the city through the medium of football
> and, as a consequence, shopkeepers benefit largely.

Unfortunately, the public failed to answer the call and the take-up was slow. The fact that they were reluctant to subscribe should have provided an early lesson for those who would later seek to attract investment into the club, eventually floating it on the stock exchange. However, the situation was rescued by the intervention of local businessmen, including the manager of the Edinburgh and District Tramway Company and the proprietors of the *Edinburgh Evening News*. The chief newspaper owner, Robert Wilson, became the chairman of the reconstituted organisation and promised it would be run in a more business-like way.

The popularity of, and affection for, Hearts was not in question. The team's potential was obvious, with new items of silverware displayed regularly in the Tynecastle trophy room. In an early example of 'speculate to accumulate', the directors had spent money on the stadium to improve facilities and upped wages to retain the best players possible. But this was a difficult time in the new business world of football and Hearts faced challenges which still exist 100 years on. Reid described the club's demise and its subsequent revival:

> Season 1904–05 was one of the most precarious in the history of the club. The Glasgow clubs were paying their players a bigger wage than was current in England; the players remained. The Hearts were paying less, and were plundered right and left . . . The clouds were gathering over Tynecastle, the finances were running low, and a process of reconstruction had to be engaged in the late spring . . . In these latter days when over £5,000 has been paid by a Scottish club for the transfer of a single player, it is hardly believable that as recently as nineteen years ago the reconstructed company could hardly go to allotment (assigning shares), the public being so fearful that the minimum sum required by law was only realised through the good offices of a number of local public men . . .

There were almost immediate signs of improvement. Annual figures for 1905–06 showed that income (£5,800) was above expenditure (£5,500), with almost half of that (£2,500) spent on wages. At the same time, 'several new players were engaged, an effort being made to secure uniform strength the team over', according to Reid. The introduction of an incentive and bonus system appeared to have the desired effect on the players and the team ran Celtic close to the league championship, eventually finishing six points behind them in second place and, of course, winning the Scottish Cup by defeating Third Lanark 1–0. Boardroom changes the following year, unfortunately, led to what Jack Alexander in *McCrae's Battalion* described as 'financial slippage'. Wages had soared, players had to be sold and the team slumped. However, that would be remedied by the appointment to the board of the club's Russian-born auditor, Elias Furst, who had expressed concern about the original flotation. Alexander, who carried out meticulous research into the period, wrote:

> Harry Rawson's departure seems to have been followed by a certain amount of financial slippage. The new director discovered that the club was once more being run from a tin box in the boardroom. No receipts were kept and players were paid on demand, often direct from gate money on match days The *Evening News* announced that Furst had instituted immediate accounting changes – which implied that there had been some accounting in the first place. The club finished ninth in the league. It was a poor year.

The following four seasons were even worse, with Hearts finishing twelfth three times and then fourteenth – the lowest league placing to date. Guided by Furst, the club had been stabilised off the field, helped by record crowds, but a number of key players, such as Charlie Thomson, were also sold. The missing piece of the jigsaw – success on the park – remained elusive. Ex-Hibs player James McGhee had replaced William Waugh in 1908 but his disciplinarian style of management was unpopular and he resigned after the board refused to back his decision to suspend the legendary Bobby Walker for missing a game.

The appointment, in 1910, of John McCartney after six years in charge at St Mirren was the first step towards improving team performances. His attitude was summed up in a story told by Alexander:

> On his first day in charge he found a framed notice above the door to the boardroom – 'YOU MUST ALWAYS CUT YOUR COAT ACCORDING TO YOUR CLOTH!' It was probably Furst's, and it

may have been intended as ironic. Whatever, the new manager tore it down and replaced it with a paper scroll of his own design – 'YOU MUST ALWAYS GIVE THE PUBLIC WHAT THE PUBLIC WANTS!' It would stay up there for nine momentous years.

Through a series of astute signings, his bold attitude was to help build a promising team which finished fourth once and third twice between 1911 and 1914, registering a record fifty-four points in season 1913–14. But his outspoken manner and the uncompromising approach he appeared to have taken over the board's call for financial prudence did not result in major confrontation. In fact, McCartney had spent only moderate amounts of money on new players and was in charge when a number of others left the club – these included Percy Dawson, who went to Blackburn Rovers for a then world-record fee of £2,500. The manager seemed to understand the board's ambitions as well as its limitations, particularly its vision of much-improved stadium facilities.

During McCartney's period at Tynecastle, a new covered enclosure for 4,500 fans was built at the distillery side of the ground, crush barriers were introduced for the first time and 'telephonic extensions' were even fitted in the press box. By now, the capacity had reached 60,000. In 1914, an even bigger gamble was taken when it was decided that the cramped and uncomfortable old pavilion and grandstands were to be demolished to make way for a new 4,000-seat grandstand with a boardroom and offices, which would eventually cost £12,000 to build – double the original estimate. The stand, designed by sporting architect Archibald Leitch and based on a similar structure at Sheffield Wednesday, was intended to be the ultimate modern facility but the soaring cost would cripple the club in the years ahead.

However, the effects of that were not felt at the beginning of season 1914–15 when an atmosphere of optimism surrounded the club and the team. The positive outlook appeared well founded when the team beat champions Celtic 2–0 in the first game and went on to record eight victories in a row. It was even suggested that this may have been the best Hearts side ever to pull on the maroon jerseys. But that promise would never be properly tested. The outbreak of the First World War and the reaction of the Hearts players to Britain's involvement in the conflict were to ensure that their potential would never be fulfilled.

3

THE TEAM THAT SAVED
THE GAME

The heroic actions of Hearts players, shareholders and season ticket holders in enlisting for the war have been well documented. But the fact that, in doing so, they set in motion a chain of events which led to the intervention of the then Prime Minister, Herbert Asquith, and the defeat of a vociferous movement which argued that football was a distraction during war-time and should be banned, has gone largely unnoticed. It was said then and since that, in quelling that campaign, Hearts actually saved the game of football in Britain, the hub of the sport even in global terms. It is a bold assertion but one which deserves overdue recognition.

The outbreak of the war at the end of July 1914 and Britain's declaration that it would join the conflict a week later raised questions about the manpower required for the massive military operations planned for the months ahead. One of the issues under scrutiny was the role of organised sport, with critics claiming it was harming recruitment efforts.

At the same time, the charismatic Edinburgh civil servant, Sir George McCrae, had volunteered for the army, on the condition that he would be permitted to raise and command a battalion of local recruits. Author Jack Alexander, in his book *McCrae's Battalion*, said that McCrae's aim to achieve that within seven days looked unlikely – until eleven Hearts players enlisted followed by two more the next day. Others did likewise. The players, intent on redeeming the game's reputation, were the first British senior footballers to sign up en masse and it caused what became known as the 'Edinburgh sensation'. Recruitment snowballed when the news broke of the actions of the Scottish league leaders, one of the most attractive football sides in the country. Sir George successfully formed the 16th Royal Scots – McCrae's Battalion. The sport's critics had been silenced.

The actions of the Hearts players and those who followed had ensured that it could no longer be said that football was damaging the recruitment of the country's young men. The Prime Minister of the day, Asquith, said as much in parliament the day after the Hearts players' decision. Hansard, the official parliamentary record, recorded the exchange between the Unionist MP for Mid Armagh, Sir John Lonsdale, who called for professional football to be suspended, and the prime minister. Lonsdale opened:

> [Is the Prime Minister] aware that recruiting meetings held in connection with assemblies of men to watch football matches have produced disappointing results: and in view of the gravity of the crisis and the need for recruits, will he introduce legislation taking powers to suppress all professional football matches during the continuance of the war?

Asquith responded:

> Communications are taking place with those who are responsible for the organisation of football matches from which I hope for good results. I do not consider that a case exists for such legislation as the honourable member suggests.

Lonsdale:

> Is the right honourable gentleman aware that on Saturday last, notwithstanding the most strenuous efforts at a number of football grounds attended by many thousands of people, only one recruit to the colours was obtained?

Asquith:

> Yes, I saw that in the papers; but, on the other hand, I am glad to say that in Scotland there was a very different response.

That evening, 26 November 1914, Sir George attended a meeting of various local sports clubs to discuss the latest developments. A report of that meeting in the *Edinburgh Evening News* the following day said:

> Had the players not taken the step that they had taken it might have been that the exercise for the good of their sport would have been prejudicially affected forever . . . [Sir George] believed they had, at Tynecastle, struck a note which would reverberate over the length and breadth of the football land and he did not think he was going too far to say that they had saved the situation as far as football was concerned.

The tributes poured in from figures such as the commander-in-chief of the allied armies, Marshall Foch, the King of the Belgians, the commander-in-chief of the French army, Marshal Joffre, and the commander-in-chief of the Italian army, General Diaz. The tributes were brought together in *The Hearts and the Great War* in 1918. William Ward, Scottish Football League (SFL) president between 1911 and 1914, wrote to the club with the message:

> You have indeed given a splendid lead to the other clubs, and I hope your example will be immediately followed by others. Your action is a proper answer to the stop-the-game croakers and will enlist for the game, and those who take part in it, the goodwill of all right-thinking people. Hats off to the patriotic Hearts.

Former Scottish international, Dr John Smith, wrote:

> Your players have set an example to others that they must follow, and then the risk of our good old game becoming as a stink in the nostrils of the nation will be swept away.

And, writing in the same booklet, the then *Edinburgh Evening News* columnist Diogenes told how he had been asked by the then Hearts manager, John McCartney, to pen an article on how 'the Hearts saved football'. He summed up the feelings of many when he wrote:

Other men in like circumstances sheltered themselves under the sacredness of their contract with their clubs – the clubs pleaded the sacredness of their contract with their players. The Heart of Midlothian club and its players scouted the sacredness of a football contract, their contract was with their country. The country needed the men, the club and its players stood out as professional football's first big contribution to the common cause. Incidentally they 'saved the game'. It had been resolved that the game should be 'carried on'. The soundness of the decision is not disputed now, and need not be debated. But whereas indoors entertainments might be expedient, out-of-doors sports were more or less under taboo, and football, the most popular of all British sports, was singled out for criticism and abuse. It seemed, from what one read and heard, that it was almost as important to 'stop football' as to win the war. Its value as a soothing influence on over-wrought human material had not yet been recognised, its potentialities as a hindrance to recruitment were ridiculously over stated. But the point was that a sport which had assumed the dimensions of a legitimate industry was in danger of being ruthlessly cast out to placate a noisy minority. The actions of the Hearts altered all that. It forestalled by a single day a question in parliament having for its object the summary stoppage of the game, and, happily, Mr Asquith was well posted up, the then Prime Minister, giving a reply which silenced the critics. It was felt that what Edinburgh was doing today the rest of the country would do tomorrow.

Almost 600 Hearts shareholders and season ticket holders also enlisted in Sir George's sportsmen's battalion, along with 150 supporters from Hibs and contingents from other clubs, particularly Raith Rovers and Falkirk. Two years later they took part in the costly Battle of the Somme, suffering heavy losses despite fighting bravely. In fact, a number of Hearts players were among the C Company men who made the deepest penetration of enemy lines on the first day of the 'Big Push' in July 1916. By the end of the war, the roll of honour was a lengthy one. The players killed in action or died in service were: Duncan Currie, John Allan, James Boyd, James Speedie, Ernest Ellis, Harry Wattie and Thomas Gracie. Many others were wounded or suffered from the rigours of training and fighting in the war. The popular Bob Mercer was gassed and injured, leading to his death from heart failure in 1926. He collapsed and died on the pitch after turning out for Hearts in an exhibition match against his old club, Selkirk. Paddy Crossan, one of the stars of his era, also died at the young age of thirty-seven after being gassed during the war.

It was estimated that a £12,000 team was lost because of the war and, needless to say, the league campaign, which had begun with such promise, ended in disappointment. The men who enlisted increasingly suffered the physical effects of inoculations and exhausting training, contracting illnesses and turning up for games not long after gruelling marches and manoeuvres. The team which had led the league in thirty-five of the thirty-seven weeks of the season lost their last two games and were overtaken by Celtic for the championship. In the coming seasons, Hearts slumped to as low as fourteenth position and, once again, began to rack up debts. Crowds fell because of the lack of munitions works to keep men in the Edinburgh area and there were even moves to exclude the club from the league because of the difficulty it had in fulfilling its fixtures.

Also writing in *The Hearts and the Great War*, Sir George paid tribute to the players:

> In the closing months of 1914 much recrimination was hurled at the devotees of the world of sport, and they were freely charged with reluctance to do their bit in the great world war. Much of that criticism was ungenerous and unfair, made without knowledge of what had been done by the individual . . . The 'Hearts' company has earned never-dying fame in a battalion which embraced some of the finest material that the British army has ever seen . . . The battalion has given a good account of itself in many a hard-fought engagement, and where danger has been greatest and the shells falling thickest – there has the 'Hearts' been – all 'forwards' then. Their losses, like that of the battalion, have been severe . . . We are proud of our fallen heroes. They have made the supreme sacrifice willingly, gladly, for a great cause.

Despite the devastating impact of the war, Hearts did start to rebuild the team when peace broke out; the club's cause was assisted by rising gate receipts from the huge crowds which were filling football grounds across the country, with a number of new records set at Tynecastle. By 1919–20, Hearts had even managed to clear their war debts. However, some poor business practices returned after Elias Furst decided to take a less active role due to ill health and the team continued to struggle on the park, finishing a new low at sixteenth in the league. This post-war slump was not helped by the departure of manager John McCartney to Portsmouth after a dispute with the board over interference in team affairs. McCartney went on to take Portsmouth from the Third Division to the First within seven years. His son, William McCartney, took over at Tynecastle and there was some respite in 1920–21 when Hearts finished third behind Rangers and Celtic. But it was a false dawn and the side flirted with relegation by ending up in a lowly nineteenth place the following year.

However, a fund-raising campaign did allow the Haymarket War Memorial to be unveiled in 1922 and plans to create a 'Greater Tynecastle' to ensure lockouts – times when the ground is full and some fans wanting to attend a game are locked out – were kept to a minimum also emerged. The authorities rejected a proposal to rebuild the main stand at the school end but other improvements were made, including better entrances and exits. Then in 1925, the club bought Tynecastle from Edinburgh Corporation for £5,000. Once again, the team was forced to sacrifice while attempts were made to balance the books, with star striker Jock White sold to Leeds United for £5,700 – around a third of the cost of the ongoing ground refurbishment. Burgeoning attendances helped to ensure that on-field performances at least stabilised during the late 1920s, though without looking likely to win any silverware.

The post-First World War years had been an extremely testing time for Heart of Midlothian but they had survived. Other British clubs survived too – a fortunate fate they may unwittingly have owed to the Tynecastle players for their actions some years before.

Jack Alexander explains:

A lot of clubs were carrying big debts around this time and that is why those in England wanted to carry on playing the game as normal during the war. But that attitude caused a lot of resentment and led to the campaign to have football suspended. It is not over-stating the case to say that the Hearts players stopped that happening. The game continued in Scotland and a new regional system was introduced in England. There was less money in the game but there was enough to keep some clubs going. If the game had been banned completely, it is difficult to imagine what football would have been like when it re-started at the end of the war. I suspect a number of the big clubs would have had to re-form or would not have re-started at all – given the financial implications of not playing for a number of years. Clubs like Celtic, Rangers and even Manchester United and Liverpool might have Hearts to thank for the position they find themselves in today. Football as we know it would be very different if it had not been for the sacrifice of the Hearts players and supporters, as well as those from other clubs. It is no exaggeration to say that the Hearts players and supporters saved the game.

4

PLANS TO MOVE FROM TYNECASTLE

Like the Hibs it was as a club playing in the public parks that the Hearts came into existence, but for 40 years the home has been at Tynecastle; and, taking a look at the enclosure today, at the abundant terracing, at the spacious grandstand, and well-equipped accommodation for teams, it looks something like a romance to read of the modest beginnings.

The big crowds kept on turning up at Tynecastle in the 1930s, with the popularity of the ground among Hearts fans apparent in the passage above from the *Tales from Tynecastle* booklet produced for the 1928–29 season. In fact, the record attendance, which stands to this day, was set on 13 February 1932 when 53,396 watched Hearts go down 1–0 to Rangers. But, despite this healthy revenue source – that record-breaking game alone brought in more than £3,400 – the club faced the ongoing capital cost of ground improvements.

The solution proposed and some of the reasons behind it would sound familiar today. Hearts should move into a massive new super-stadium with a much-increased capacity and improved facilities. Tynecastle could be redeveloped further but it would be awkward, not least because its tight confines provoked fears that construction work would encroach on surrounding land. Plans for a new 5,000-capacity enclosure at the school end were blocked because it was thought the structure would block light from the nearby classrooms. The adjacent child-care centre was also concerned at the expansion plans of its big neighbour. With that in mind, the nearby open spaces at Sighthill or possibly Saughton were earmarked as potential new stadium sites in the 1930s. Sighthill and Saughton, where Hearts used to train, were two of the options considered again during the recent debate about a new home for Hearts and may yet emerge as possibilities in the future.

It is also true that, like today, the board of seventy years ago realised that something must be done to bring rising debt levels under control. But that is where the similarities end. In the 30s, debts were a concern but the level remained manageable, not least because the sport was booming and crowds were at an all-time high. Supporters were likely to fill the steep new terraces then, bringing in much-needed extra cash. In contrast, current debts have spiralled and attendances, while levelling out in recent years, are still much lower than during the club's heyday. Then, the move to a 100,000-capacity ground would have been made through choice, ambition even. In more recent times, the sale of the club's major asset was the proposal put to a bank understandably seeking to recoup at least some of its significant financial outlay. There was one further fact that linked the decades – scepticism that such a plan was wise or workable. Albert Mackie outlined the dream and the doubts:

> The Sighthill dream – with grandstand seating for 15,000 to 20,000, covered accommodation for at least 30,000, and terracing for 25,000 at each end – continued to be discussed at meetings throughout the late thirties. The stand was visualised as accommodating all the equipment featured at first-class grounds – baths, gymnasium, recreation room, library, reading room, offices, boardroom, trainers' and doctors' rooms ... But councillor Adam Miller said very wisely, 'There is such a thing as goodwill even in football, and I think Hearts would lose if they deserted Tynecastle, which is now a tradition.'

The fact that the club's historic home was already regarded as 'a tradition' three generations ago explains the depth of feeling that has been aroused by the twenty-first century proposals to sell it to a housing developer. Others also questioned the costs involved in the Sighthill plans, estimated by the club to be up to £130,000. The sceptics included Elias Furst, who had turned the fortunes of the club around during the financial difficulties at the beginning of the century. Like today, those seeking a solution turned to the possibility of joining forces with the local corporation or council. Mackie described how Furst backed an early forerunner to today's stadium working party when he called for a thorough examination of all available options, which he said should include remaining at a redeveloped Tynecastle. Even the scope was uncannily familiar:

> [Furst] moved that the special ground committee should investigate the probable costs of extending the stand at Tynecastle and possible ground extensions and improvements and that they should go forward to the corporation to obtain an option on ground at Sighthill.

As Mackie wrote twenty years later, of course, the decision to move was not taken and improvements were made to Tynecastle, including floodlights and a new press box. The role of the corporation, like today, was also central as it was considering building a municipal stadium for the Empire Games, although the only British city to host the event during this period turned out to be London in 1934. Edinburgh would have to wait until 1970 to stage the now retitled Commonwealth Games.

Mackie also put the financial difficulties of the club in some context and gave credit to Alexander Irvine, who became chairman in 1935, for adopting a policy of 'achieving solvency'. When Irvine joined the board in 1932, debts stood at £23,000 yet the sale of just two players, Alex Massie and Dave McCulloch – however unpopular with fans – brought in almost half that amount three years later. A series of profits were then recorded and a further share issue took place in 1937. With the club's finances improving, the latter move was designed to involve more people in the running of its affairs. The directors explained that 'the proceeds of this issue are not required at present for any specific purpose, but will be used as the directors think fit from time to time'.

The coffers were further swollen by some massive crowds, including the record 102,661 who watched the 1935 cup semi-final against Rangers at Hampden and the Tynecastle league record of 49,904 against Celtic three years later. The boardroom changes had resulted in the resignation of manager William McCartney and the appointment of former Celtic player David Pratt. But, perhaps because of the loss of some key players, he lasted just two years to be replaced in 1937 by the first Hearts boss with control over team selection, ex-England and Arsenal goalkeeper Frank Moss.

As had happened in the period before the First World War, Hearts were overcoming their financial difficulties – and showing the ambition to further improve the situation – at the same time as an attractive team was playing on the park. The crowds were flocking to watch free-scoring stars such as Barney Battles and Tommy Walker knock in almost ninety goals a season and, although the club did not win any major honours, it was clearly improving. The team challenged Celtic for the league title in 1937–38, eventually finishing three points behind in second place. It was the highest league position since 'the team that saved the game' also finished runners-up to Celtic more than twenty years before.

Improvements continued to be made off the field as well. It was announced at the 1939 AGM that all debts had been cleared and a dividend would be paid to shareholders for the first time in the club's history. It was also around this time that the fans began to organise, notably when the newly formed shareholders association made a bid to elect their own representative to the board. The move failed to find favour but reflected a desire to become more involved in the running of the club.

But, despite the promising signs, the spectre of the First World War would return to Hearts once again. The club had recovered from that first conflict and was once again challenging for honours. However, a second and even more devastating world war had been brewing from the moment the peace treaties were signed in 1919. Not only had the Great War failed to resolve the European power struggle, it had actually created the climate which led to the second. On 1 September 1939, Hitler's armies marched into Poland, drawing allies Britain and France into the war two days later.

The Scottish football season had started the month before and Hearts began reasonably well but, after just five games, it was abandoned, with Hearts in fifth place on six points. The game seemed to have suffered the fate Hearts had rescued it from twenty-five years earlier. In reality, however, the main reasons behind the ban were very different to those put forward in 1914. The new threat was aerial warfare and there was a real and understandable fear that it would be too risky to allow football stadiums to pack tens of thousands of spectators into such a confined space.

In the end – and perhaps with a backward glance at events in 1914 and the subsequent discovery that football could boost morale rather than hinder the war effort – a compromise was reached and the authorities relaxed the ban, albeit under a new league structure and rules. The regional league system allowed some football to continue but the teams would not challenge for recognised major honours for seven years until the 1946–47 season kicked off. Wages were capped to the bare minimum and many joined up for the services, leaving guests and youngsters to fill the gaps. Hearts' best finish was second in 1940 but attendances had been restricted to 8,000 because of the threat of air raids and crowds slumped to little more than 3,400. The following year, they reached the final of the wartime League Cup, only to be defeated by Rangers.

Unlike their experience with the First World War, Hearts did not suffer disproportionately. There were those connected with the club who had again lost their lives but, this time, the other clubs were forced to share the burdens of war on a more equal basis. The result was that Hearts emerged from the conflict in a reasonable position. The pre-war league structure was re-established in 1945–46 but the season was considered a transitional period and official honours were not awarded until 1946–47. A post-war boom allowed crowds to quickly reach 1930s levels. A canny and well-respected manager, Davie McLean, had been appointed in 1941 after Frank Moss returned home when war broke out. And he made a number of crucial signings even as war continued to rage. The first of the famous Terrible Trio, Alfie Conn, broke into the first team towards the end of the war. Then, in 1946, he was joined at the club by Jimmy Wardhaugh and Willie Bauld – the man who would be crowned King of Hearts. The three stars of the future had reputedly been signed for just £200. It would take time, manager McLean pointed out, but a blend of these and other signings – including Bobby Parker from Partick Thistle – and youngsters already on the books would build a successful team to 'last for years'.

There would be disappointments – the sale of Hearts legend Tommy Walker to Chelsea – and difficulties – the need to carry out further renovation work on the terracing following the death of thirty-three fans in a crush at Bolton's Burnden Park. And the team endured some disappointing league campaigns. But the public remained enthusiastic about the club's fortunes.

They were given more reason to be optimistic when the Terrible Trio played together for the first time in a 6–1 thrashing of East Fife in October 1948, with Bauld getting a hat-trick. Hearts continued to record some impressive results and draw massive crowds such as the 65,840 who watched the 1950 New Year derby against Hibs at Easter Road, a record for a Scottish match outside Glasgow. The team went on to finish third that year and would remain in the top five for the following ten years, ending the long wait for silverware in the process.

The first and most favourable opportunity to place Hearts at the top of Scottish football had been relinquished but a second chance was approaching. Unfortunately, this time, Hearts did not have the benefit of the privileged position they occupied at the turn of the century. The challenge of capitalising on this new opportunity would be as testing. But there were clear signs that this crop of exceptional and exciting players would be up to the challenge.

OVERVIEW

The birth of Scottish football provided Hearts with an opportunity to cement their place at the very top of the sport. Despite the fact the game was dominated by teams from the west of Scotland, in the country's industrial and urban heartland, Hearts rose to the challenge. As the establishment club in the second biggest centre of population, they were well placed to do so, regardless of the capital's reputation as a rugby city. Hearts responded to the early demands of providing appropriate facilities, charging entry fees and eventually the legalisation of professionalism and the payment of wages to staff. The football side which began as a pastime for a group of dance-hall regulars was developing as a fledgling business. And that process allowed the team on the park to flourish.

Aside from Queen's Park, who remained amateur and won their last Scottish Cup in 1893, Hearts were the most serious challenge to Celtic and Rangers during this early era. In the period from the formation of Hearts to their 1906 cup victory, Celtic won ten major trophies, Rangers nine and Hearts six. The nearest other challengers were some distance behind with three senior honours to their name. And that sustained challenge by Hearts would not be bettered for almost eighty years when the Edinburgh club's overall tally of silverware was overtaken by the great Aberdeen side of the early 1980s. But Hearts were not only successful – they were also popular. The fact that they drew sizeable crowds was clearly essential if the club – as both a football team and a business – was to thrive.

An analysis of attendances at the sport's showpiece match, the Scottish Cup final, again shows that Hearts were closer to the Old Firm than may be imagined. In the thirty or so years from the first competition to 1906, finals and replays involving Rangers drew the biggest average crowd at almost 24,700 fans. Those in which Celtic played attracted just over 24,000, while the average attendance at Hearts finals was around 21,500. It is also worth bearing in mind that, the 1896 final aside, Hearts fans had to travel to Glasgow to support their team. By the turn of the twentieth century, Scottish football was dominated by the big three rather than the big two we are familiar with today.

It was not only Hearts who were in a favourable position at this time – Scottish football itself was in the ascendancy. Having developed alongside the game south of the border, football in Scotland had a head start on the rest of the world. A number of countries – such as Denmark, Holland Switzerland, Austria and Hungary – soon shared the British obsession with football but Scotland and England were considered the birthplace of the game and their teams were revered as ambassadors wherever the sport was developing.

Despite securing this relatively favourable position in Scottish and world football, Hearts' fortunes did dip several years into the new century. The club may not have been as far behind the Old Firm as would be expected but there was no disguising the fact that it was not as big or as successful as Celtic and Rangers. The introduction of professionalism, strongly supported by the Old Firm, and the demands of developing a successful business allowed Hearts to prosper at the expense of other teams.

But there was a cost to competing with more powerful rivals within Scotland and south of the border. Hearts' attempts to keep up with the bigger clubs led to the ill-fated formation of a limited liability company in 1903 – a step undertaken by Celtic in 1897 and Rangers two years later. The change in status proved troublesome and Hearts were rescued by an injection of cash two years later. Signs of improvement in the boardroom were then followed by yet more 'financial slippage' and performances on the field slumped, the cup-winning season being an exception.

Once again, though, Hearts' difficulties must be considered alongside the mixed fortunes of the Old Firm. Internal bickering and financial problems were said to push Rangers close to insolvency during the 1880s. Celtic's boards were also faced with a number of challenges in their early years, which led to some severe cutbacks. The east-end club also developed a reputation for thriftiness akin to the more recent accusations of 'biscuit tin' financial management.

Hearts' slump, however, coincided with a surge in the sport's popularity around the globe. The game was now being played in every country in Europe and was beginning to take off in South America. The governing body, Fédération Internationale de

Football Association (FIFA), was formed in 1904, although it initially only represented European associations. By the First World War, the challenge to British dominance was well under way. Hearts' progress had stalled at an unfortunate time. Attempts to achieve predominance in the future would not just involve challenging the ever-strengthening Old Firm – it would mean taking on the giants of European football.

But at least the club was revived on and off the field in the pre-war period due, in large part, to the combination of an astute board, led by Elias Furst, and a shrewd manager, in John McCartney. Several intelligent signings helped the team on the park and, aided by an upsurge in crowds, the board sought to place Hearts at the forefront of Scottish football by building a main stand that would be among the finest in the country. Through in Glasgow, Queen's Park had recently cleared their debts by constructing the world's biggest stadium at Hampden Park. The financial benefits of drawing huge crowds were obvious to onlookers. Celtic and Rangers were also cashing in – particularly in games against each other – because they had developed large, impressive stadiums.

Unfortunately, before Hearts' ambitious project could be completed, Europe's political leaders embarked on a struggle which would create tens of millions of military and civilian casualties. It had a catastrophic global effect. But the consequences of the conflict would also prove a pivotal event in the history of Heart of Midlothian Football Club.

The team which showed such promise was torn apart by men enlisting and training for war. The potentially lucrative Scottish Cup was suspended. Crowds fell and income slumped as the financial hardships of war became apparent. The timing could hardly have been worse. Not only was the team dismantled just as it was beginning to fulfil its promise but the club now also had to find the cash to pay for a state-of-the-art grandstand, the cost of which had doubled since the original estimate. And this was at a time when fewer people with less money were available to fill the structure. In a matter of months, Hearts had gone from an exciting team capable, even likely, of winning major honours to one in the process of slumping to a new low in the league. The development of first-rate new facilities as part of an ambitious plan to position the club among Scottish football's elite had, instead, created a massive financial burden. The team that saved the game was broken, the club broke.

It is a matter of speculation how Hearts' fortunes might have turned out if world events had taken a different twist but there is no doubt the club would have been ideally placed to take advantage of its position at a key stage in the development of the game. As it turned out, the Old Firm – with their bigger crowds, higher revenues and fatter wage packets – withstood the war-time austerity and post-conflict disruption better than every other club and, thereby, tightened their stranglehold on Scottish football during its infancy.

The unique social and religious culture surrounding Rangers and Celtic today was not as apparent in the game's formative years as may be expected. Irish immigrants did face discrimination and antagonism – mainly over the perception that they provided competition for local jobs – and sectarian sentiment was common at the time. But Hibs, rather than the big Glasgow teams, was the club that was established along sectarian lines when it was decided that players must be practising Catholics. In fairness, it was common at this time for clubs to be formed by church organisations. Yet Hibs were not allowed to join the SFA or, initially, to compete in the Scottish Cup because they were regarded as an Irish team. Hibs would go on to become the major Catholic team in Scotland and the Edinburgh derby – fuelled by the social divisions of the day (based on religion, incomers against established population and, to some extent, class) – was the tie that was, according to *The Heart of Midlothian Football Club: a Pictorial History 1874–1984*, associated with 'racial and sectarian bitterness' during this period. The Catholic press, too, had been as critical of Hearts and Queen's Park – as pillars of the establishment – as it had of any other club. As Queen's Park would opt to remain amateur, it is conceivable that the Edinburgh sides could have gone on to form the major rivalry in Scottish football. After all, in England, Arsenal aside, it was the teams from the north, latterly Manchester United and Liverpool, which went on to dominate football rather than those from the more heavily populated south-east of the country. The arrival on the scene of Celtic, their successful bid to poach the best Hibs players and the subsequent reaction of Rangers to the challenge from the other side of Glasgow would eventually put paid to the possibility of Scottish football being dominated by clubs from the east.

Celtic's Irish roots and Rangers' Protestant ethos are well documented and fans were well aware of those differences at the time. Yet the first recorded sectarian reference by a player was not until 1898, when one of the Rangers team hurled abuse at a Celtic rival. The clubs enjoyed a good relationship at the time, with officials attending social functions together and inviting their opposite numbers to each other's ground to watch English opponents. It is also true that a number of Catholics played for Rangers in the early years – admittedly, only four between 1904 and 1908. The truth was that the Glasgow teams recognised the benefits of developing along commercial rather than religious lines. According to historian Bill Murray, it was this policy that led to them being described as 'The Old Firm of Celtic and Rangers Ltd' in the *Scottish Referee* publication in 1904. The co-operation of the clubs helped to force first the formation of the Scottish League and then the introduction of professionalism. There were even accusations of games being drawn to ensure lucrative replays. It seemed the lure of healthy profits was more powerful than any religious differences. But that would change in time.

There is no justification for the sectarian hatred which has resulted from the Glasgow rivalry but it is the foundation on which the Old Firm dominance was to be built. It was in the period immediately before the First World War – as the Hearts recovery was under way but had not yet been realised – that these religious divisions became more apparent.

Hibs had abandoned their sectarian policy when the club was re-formed in 1893 but Celtic's success in the new century's early years demanded a response from the Protestant establishment. Celtic's connections with nationalist politics in Ireland developed further and Rangers showed signs of responding to this stance with a more sharply focused Protestant ethos. By around 1910, Rangers had stopped signing Catholics, although few had played for the team in any case. Then, Belfast shipbuilders, with a previous reputation for sectarianism in their home country, arrived in Govan, perhaps encouraging workers to join Orange and Masonic lodges. The growth in those organisations continued, fuelled by the advance of the Irish home rule movement. The Easter Rising in Dublin in 1916, or at least its suppression by the British authorities, further aided the nationalist cause and led to the Irish Revolution. In Scotland, full funding for Catholic schools, an issue which remains controversial today, was granted in 1918. It was then against a backdrop of the partition of Ireland and creation of the Irish Free State in the early 1920s that the unique and unyielding nature of the Old Firm hostility became firmly entrenched.

The Great Depression in the 1930s intensified the sectarian divisions in Scottish society, leading to the formation of Glasgow street gangs, such as the Billy Boys, and extreme Protestant groups such as John Cormack's Protestant Action and Alexander Ratcliffe's Scottish Protestant League. Followers were accused of directing abuse and sometimes violence at Catholics, while some of the latter were blamed for openly siding with militant Irish republicans. The divisions in society were reflected in Scotland's national sport and the Old Firm sides were rare beneficiaries. Historian Bill Murray aptly described Rangers and Celtic as the 'standard bearers for a divided society'.

Certainly, the period during which the sectarian divide took hold in Scotland, from before the First World War to after the Second, was one of almost complete Old Firm dominance in the league – and one of relative obscurity for the Edinburgh clubs.

Indeed, between 1905 and 1948 Motherwell were the only side outwith the Old Firm to win the championship when they did so in 1932. That dominance may have been likely but it was not inevitable.

As Scotland's biggest clubs, Celtic and Rangers could pay higher salaries than their rivals, especially as they were not constrained by the maximum wage system which existed in England. However, without the need to compete beyond Scotland's borders, there was no pressure to pay excessive wages and costs were, therefore, kept to a reasonable level. Perhaps more importantly, the roles the clubs had adopted in Scottish society allowed them to lure players to 'sign for the jersey' as much as for any cash incentive. Despite their difficulties, Hearts had remained closer to the Old Firm in a football sense than many would suspect. Hibs did likewise up to 1903 but faded as a force thereafter, failing to rise above mediocrity for almost half a century and even suffering relegation in 1931. But both clubs would struggle to disrupt a dominance which had gone beyond issues of sport and business to embrace the impassioned realms of religion, culture and nationality.

In Europe too, Hearts were in danger of falling further behind rival teams. The position of British teams was not helped by the persistent bickering of the home nations' football associations with FIFA. Unconcerned by the politics of football in Britain, the game boomed in Europe and then South America. Crowds soared and, with that, players' wages shot up, leading to the creation of the first foreign superstars as early as the 1920s and 30s. The process was further spurred on by the development of popular media outlets, particularly radio and newsreel.

Hearts had won national honours before some of the great European teams had even been established but the balance of power was swinging towards these continental upstarts. Soon they would compete with Hearts and others for players and attention. Eventually they would form a sporting aristocracy of their own.

Hearts may have saved the game – and, indeed, helped to export it to parts of France and Belgium – with their response to the Great War but they would not reap the rewards of those players' unselfish actions. Celtic and Rangers would go on to dominate Scottish football in the years ahead, representing the country in Europe and attracting bigger crowds than the national team. The First World War sealed Hearts' fate – the big three had become the big two. The team that saved the game had been sacrificed in the process.

PART 2

THE GOLDEN YEARS

5

NEVER HAD IT SO GOOD

Despite the lack of silverware since their glory days at the turn of the century, Hearts had at least looked promising before the outbreak of the Second World War. There was some dismay in west Edinburgh, then, when Hibs emerged as the capital's main challengers after the war, winning the league three times and also finishing runners-up on three occasions and third once. The turning point appeared to be when Hibs 'lost' the league on goal average to Rangers in 1952–53 – a fate which would single Edinburgh football out twice more in the years ahead, although it was to be Hearts who were the victims on both occasions. Before goal difference – where the number of goals conceded is deducted from the number of goals scored – was introduced as a means of separating teams that were tied on points, a system of goal average was used. Goal average is arrived at by dividing the number of goals scored by the number of goals conceded. Hearts were to lose out on being league champions under both systems.

Sadly, Hearts manager Davie McLean died in February 1951 but he was replaced by Tommy Walker who had returned from Chelsea and taken up the assistant manager's post a year earlier. Walker ushered in a new management style at Tynecastle, actually spending time with the players in the dressing room rather than simply picking the team as his predecessors had done. Although Walker's approach cannot be compared with today's emphasis on detailed tactics, he would at least have a quiet word with each player before the game and, at half-time, he would perhaps offer a simple word of advice. The team embarked on a consistent run of three fourth-place league campaigns under Walker who continued McLean's policy of promoting young players and backing them up with quality coaching staff.

In 1953–54, Hearts mounted a serious championship challenge, eventually ending up five points behind a Celtic team which celebrated its first title in sixteen years. The following season, on 23 October 1954, Hearts finally ended their forty-eight-year trophy drought. With the Terrible Trio now in rampant form, the team scored thirty-four goals in the League Cup, eventually overcoming Motherwell 4–2 in the final at Hampden. The 30,000 or so Hearts supporters in the 55,640 crowd boisterously acclaimed the team and particularly hat-trick hero Willie Bauld before heading back to celebrate in the pubs and streets of Edinburgh. Albert Mackie, writing in *The Hearts* five years later, recalled how the welcome home had been likened to citizens acclaiming a liberating army. Describing the return of the team and their triumphant parade through Edinburgh, he went on to suggest they had not been as demonstrative since the lynching central to Walter Scott's novel, *The Heart of Midlothian*. And, helping to create the folklore connecting Hearts with Gorgie, he added:

> Gorgie is believed to derive its name from an old Celtic word meaning 'beautiful place', and it has some beautiful corners, but on the whole it is drably workaday. Nevertheless it is a district with a great friendly heart, and it certainly showed it that night . . . The old grey-stone walls, the smoke-blackened walls, reverberated with the wave after wave of cheering. Women threw maroon rosettes to the team as if to Spanish toreadors. At McLeod Street, where part of the Saturday crowd surges into Tynecastle, there were crowds of people singing outside the public-house where the fans have their last hurried pint on their way to the match and their first to celebrate victory or drown their sorrows afterwards. This time it was undoubted and crowning victory, and the foaming pint tumblers of good strong Edinburgh ale slopped over as they were raised in salute . . . The noise was like Hell let loose, but this was Gorgie in Heaven.

That season, the team went on to notch up a couple of emphatic victories over Hibs in the league and Scottish Cup (5–0 and 5–1) but otherwise their challenge for honours faded, at least until the following season.

Hearts supporters had wondered after the recent League Cup victory when – or, indeed, if – they would ever experience such celebrations again. As Mackie said, they did 'with embellishments, the following season'. Hearts made a good start to the 1955–56 league season and remained in touch for most of the campaign but faltered towards the end, eventually finishing in third place. But it was the Scottish Cup which was to thrill the fans, with up to 60,000 making the trip through to Glasgow for the final against Celtic on 21 April 1956. It was Hearts' first appearance in the final since 1907 but they had reached it with style. The 3–1 victory – inspired by John Cumming and Dave Mackay and courtesy of two Ian Crawford goals and one from Alfie Conn – concluded a run which had seen eighteen goals scored with only one conceded.

Cup-winning captain Freddie Glidden – the first Hearts player in half a century to get his hands on the old trophy – recalled the moment of triumph:

> I just sagged when the final whistle went at the end of that 1956 final. Everybody was congratulating each other but all the tension had dropped away. The next thing, I was walking forward with the boys behind me, and the crowd howling all around us. It was fifty years since anyone from Hearts had won the thing and all I could think was, 'Well it's ours now.'

The subsequent celebrations in Gorgie, Edinburgh and the players' villages have gone down in the club's folklore. This time, Mackie said, 'Gorgie went mad in maroon.'

A runners-up spot in 1956–57, after being pipped at the post by Rangers, set Hearts up for even more glory the following season. The cup victories of 1954 and 1956 may have sparked wild scenes but the league results of 1957–58 must surely have marked the club's finest hour. The team scored 132 goals, more Division

One goals than ever before, and only conceded twenty-nine. It is a record that stands today. The end-of-season statistics showed Hearts with their highest points tally – sixty-two from thirty-four games and thirteen ahead of second-placed Rangers. With all other competitive and friendly games taken into account the total reached a staggering 243 goals scored. Hearts had waited sixty-one years for the league title and, with that league win, another famine had ended in the fabulous 50s. The directors bragged, 'The winning of the league championship in such decisive manner was a fitting climax to one of the best seasons in the club's long history.'

And the trophy hunt was not over yet. In 1958–59 Hearts added another League Cup to their roll of honour, with a 5–1 victory over Partick Thistle, but fell at the final hurdle in their attempt to regain the championship. The following season they achieved the club's only double, winning both the league championship and the League Cup when they beat Third Lanark 2–1.

The 50s were and remain today the most successful decade in the club's history. And the on-field glory had a significant knock-on effect in the boardroom. After the Scottish Cup victory, the club announced a profit of more than £5,400 and paid a 20% dividend to shareholders. The 1957–58 season brought records off the pitch as well as on it, with a near-£13,000 profit. In fact, the club had only recorded one season of losses since the end of the Second World War. This financial success was possible because of the large crowds common in football of that era but the good times would not last forever.

6

THE SEEDS OF DECLINE

It is worth noting that average attendances at Tynecastle in the late 50s, Hearts' most successful spell, hovered between around 20,000 and 24,000; impressive but still nowhere near the guaranteed sell-outs enjoyed by the Old Firm over the years. Games could attract up to 50,000 people but, equally, it was common for only around 10,000 to attend. The gate even dipped to four figures when, in March 1958, just 9,000 supporters witnessed Hearts overtaking Motherwell's goal-scoring record of 119 in a victory over Raith Rovers. Cup matches – including a first competitive foray into Europe against Standard Liege – and a share of away gates further boosted the coffers but, as in the club's early years, sound financial management combined with astute man management were also required. Albert Mackie recognised just that in *The Hearts* when he paid equal tribute to both the hard work of chairman Nicol Kilgour and the 'wise management' of Tommy Walker. He also commended the 'sportsmanship and team spirit and common sense of the players' as well as 'the generally happy atmosphere at Tynecastle' – something that is difficult to achieve but utterly invaluable at any football club.

The achievements of the boardroom should also be set against a number of budgetary challenges. Further improvements had been made to provide better facilities for everyone connected with the club – covered areas for fans, showers for players, dugouts for management and a new press box for the media. In 1957, a £14,000 floodlight system was installed. Yet, despite this upgrading of

Tynecastle, the 1930s debate about moving to a larger stadium once again resurfaced. Remarkably, this time the proposal was not only to move to nearby Murrayfield but actually to buy the rugby stadium. As in the thirties, the huge ground would at least have been utilised, albeit only sporadically. And, of course, the football club would have owned rather than rented it. However, it is still astonishing that fifty years before the recent controversy, this revolutionary suggestion, however speculative and low-key, received little attention. Indeed, it took the launch of Dave Mackay's autobiography in 2004 to bring it to public notice. Mackay said:

> We were getting between 30,000 and 40,000 for games at Tynecastle and the board looked into the possibility of buying Murrayfield. People turned up because they were seeing a good side, and with Conn, Bauld and Wardaugh in the team they were guaranteed goals. The idea fizzled out, but there was none of the fuss surrounding it as there is now.

In *The Real Mackay*, the former Hearts star recognises the role Tommy Walker played in the club's success when he explained that the manager's 'personality and ethos had been stamped on us . . . he had taught us to believe in ourselves without slipping into arrogance or complacency'. However, the captain of the league-winning side also acknowledged that the team, with its blend of youth and experience, peaked in the late fifties. He was right. Alfie Conn was the first of the Terrible Trio to leave when he was sold to Raith Rovers in 1958. Mackay followed a year later, despite setting his sights on captaining Hearts to a treble and proving they were 'the finest Scottish team in history'. Walker's renowned man-management skills appeared to be failing him. Mackay was told that Spurs were interested in his signature and he was also given the impression Hearts wanted to sell him, despite the fact they did not appear to need the money. Mackay left Tynecastle reluctantly, not even increasing his £20-a-week maximum wages. In his autobiography, Mackay said:

Did they need the money? I doubted it. Crowds were high. Not a lot of money had been spent in the transfer market. It was baffling . . . Fans were up in arms and the papers were full of it. Most people, like myself, could not understand the logic of selling me at a time when the championship was still within grasp and they felt that my sale was tantamount to surrendering to Rangers. Sadly, that was to happen and Hearts ended the season as close runners-up to the Glasgow club.

In reality, of course, the huge £32,000 fee must have been tempting – particularly as the club that year spent £23,000 on a new enclosure at the distillery side of the ground.

Amid claims that their pace was failing, the remaining two from the Terrible Trio were next to go. Jimmy Wardhaugh moved to Dunfermline later that year and Willie Bauld retired after playing his last game for Hearts in 1962. Man-management flaws once again let the club down, however, when the 'King of Hearts' was told that the price of the match ball and other expenses would be deducted from his testimonial proceeds. He refused to return to Tynecastle for the next twelve years. The terrifying threesome had scored an incredible 950 goals during their time at Hearts.

After finishing in the top four throughout the 50s, Hearts dropped to eighth in 1960–61. They finished sixth in 1961–62 and were beaten by Rangers in that season's League Cup final. Discontent among the Hearts supporters was voiced at games as the team in transition slipped backwards. The board was left in no doubt about their anger when forward Alex Young, who had slotted in alongside the Terrible Trio since making his debut in 1955, and defender George Thomson were sold to Everton for £58,000 in November 1960. Certainly, the sale of those two players was highlighted by Dave Mackay as a turning point for the club. The long-serving former skipper Freddie Glidden also remembers sensing that the club was changing as his Hearts career drew to an end:

It was a great team in the 50s and up to the 60s but if they had real foresight they would have replaced one or two players with new lads before the likes of Willie Bauld and Alfie Conn were allowed to leave. The progression of the team didn't happen after the late 50s.

There were also concerns that the 4–2–4 formation favoured by Tommy Walker around this time was too defensive. In defence of Walker, who, by this time had been awarded an OBE, a record fee of £15,000 was spent bringing forward Willie Wallace to Tynecastle from Raith Rovers. However, if there was some slippage in the stewardship of Hearts, the team did at least go on to claim another trophy. They beat Kilmarnock 1–0 in the League Cup final in 1962 after a late 'goal' for the Ayrshire team was chalked off. It was to be Hearts' last trophy for thirty-six years. But the team's league form improved sufficiently to finish fourth the following season and mount a serious, if ill-fated, challenge in 1964–65.

Apart from a stumble at the turn of the year, Hearts had looked like title contenders throughout the season but the championship nevertheless remained closely fought. Kilmarnock – the team so aggrieved at Hearts' previous trophy success – had pushed them all the way and the destination of the league flag would be decided in dramatic style on the final day of the season. The two main challengers, Hearts and Kilmarnock, squared up at Tynecastle on 24 April 1965, with the home team needing only a draw or even a single goal defeat to take the title. Kilmarnock had to win by two clear goals to triumph on goal average. By half-time, Kilmarnock were two up, with the second scored amid appeals for offside. Despite some dramas in the second half, the score remained 2–0 and Kilmarnock had won the league by a goal average advantage of only 0.042.

The directors lamented, saying, 'Never in the history of the Scottish league has a club finished so near to the actual winners as Hearts did on 24 April.' It remains the closest finish in Scottish football and Hearts later argued to alter the system to one where goal *difference* would decide the title in the event of a points tie. But they would struggle to recover from the trauma, failing to finish in the top three again until they lost the league in remarkably similar circumstances twenty-one years later – ironically, on the goal-difference system they had championed.

Some commentators have pinpointed this cruel 'loss' as the beginning of a long period of decline. In *The Boys in Maroon*, life-long Hearts fan and journalist John Fairgrieve blamed the lack of success on 'unimaginative tactics', adding, 'If they had lost it well, the reaction among the fans might not have been so drastic. They lost it badly. They lost it without regard for the great Tynecastle tradition which insists on real football.' Morale was damaged, crowds dropped by a quarter, a number of players tabled transfer requests and the board lost faith in the club's most successful-ever manager, Tommy Walker. After guiding Hearts to seven trophy wins, Walker resigned in 1966. A reluctant replacement was found in trainer Johnny Harvey, perhaps because it would have been more expensive to attract a proven manager. More star players left, the team was not adequately strengthened and the club continued to slip backwards. With little more than a losing Scottish Cup final appearance in 1968 to capture their imagination, the supporters stayed away and Hearts drifted aimlessly into the 1970s.

7

THE SORRY SEVENTIES

Bobby Parker – a Hearts player, captain, coach, board member and chairman between 1946 and 1993 – later identified Harvey's appointment as an error. Parker's assessment of Harvey was correct. The burden of managing the club proved troublesome – something Harvey himself may have recognised as he unsuccessfully attempted to bring Dave Mackay back from Spurs as player-manager – and he stepped down. Harvey reverted to his previous role as trainer, to be replaced in the top job by former Preston North End boss Bobby Seith in 1970.

In Mike Aitken and Wallace Mercer's book *Heart to Heart*, Parker also recounted a telling boardroom anecdote after he became a director in 1970:

> I was sitting at the end of the table, opposite the chairman, not really sure what was expected of me. I looked up and saw two of the older directors snoozing. Their eyes were shut, and being charitable I wondered if they were just gathering their thoughts. But after watching them for a bit I knew they were asleep.

In the same book, ex-club secretary Les Porteous revealed how aloof and distant the directors had become, refusing, for instance, to allow anyone beyond the reception area other than themselves. He even recalled how one player was 'put out for no good reason other than it had been decided that he had no right to be there'.

A diverting run to the 1971 final of the Anglo-Scottish Texaco Cup aside, Hearts made little impression in the major competitions.

Worse was to come. On New Year's Day 1973, Hearts suffered the humiliation of a 7–0 drubbing by Hibs at Tynecastle. It was a result that appeared to damage morale even further and the team finished tenth in the league.

Despite reports that Hearts were interested in signing Manchester United and Scotland star Denis Law, in reality, little was being invested in the playing staff. The club website describes Bobby Seith as a 'fine tactician' but adds that 'the club struggled financially and could not find the funds to help him strengthen the weaknesses in the side'. But there were some hopeful signs. Goalkeeper Jim Cruickshank was continuing to prove an able replacement for Gordon Marshall, while centre forward Donald Ford was emerging as a goal-scoring talent who benefited from the arrival of £35,000 record-signing Drew Busby and winger Rab Prentice in 1973.

Hearts started well in 1973–74, even topping the league early in the season, but the challenge faltered and the club approached its 100th birthday with little to celebrate. Early in 1974–75, the club suffered League and Texaco Cup exits to Second Division Falkirk and Oldham respectively. By October 1974, Hearts had still failed to record a league win. Following protests by fans, Seith resigned, to be replaced by coach John Hagart after an unsuccessful bid to woo Dundee United's Jim McLean.

Average attendances had remained static since the late 1960s and the Safety at Sports Grounds Act – introduced to improve safety for large crowds following the Ibrox Disaster in which sixty-six fans were killed during a staircase crush in 1971 – had reduced the capacity to 30,000 in any case. But revenue was suffering, not least because of a series of poor cup runs. No doubt with this in mind, Hearts were supportive of league reconstruction in the belief that it would favour the country's biggest clubs. Amid threats of a breakaway, the smaller clubs caved in and it was agreed to set up a ten-team Premier Division from season 1975–76. The aim was to give the top clubs more control over their destiny and boost crowds by increasing the number of big, competitive games rather than playing out meaningless end-of-season matches against relegation strugglers.

But the danger of this new league structure must have been obvious to Hearts. In the decade since the eleventh-hour league championship disappointment, the team had finished outside the top eight places four times. On three of those occasions they did not even make it into the top ten. So, in other words, they could be likely to be relegated under the new set-up. The new league would clearly prove tough for Hearts and it was no surprise when they struggled to qualify for the first Premier Division championship, eventually finishing the final Division One in eighth place.

The first Premier Division campaign got off to the worst possible start, with a 1–0 defeat to Eddie Turnbull's high-flying Hibs. That first season proved extremely tight and Hearts finished fifth, albeit just three points ahead of relegated Dundee. However, they also had the prospect of a Scottish Cup final against Rangers. Unfortunately, Hearts were up against it from the start, with a goal scored by Derek Johnstone reputedly before 3 p.m. as the referee had kicked off a fraction early. Rangers eventually won 3–1 but there were some consolations.

Thanks to their cup-final appearance, season 1976–77 at least provided memorable European Cup Winners' Cup matches against Lokomotiv Leipzig and SV Hamburg; the former included a 5–1 comeback at Tynecastle after a 2–0 defeat in the first leg. But, in reality, it was to be perhaps the grimmest season in the club's history. John Hagart had recognised the competitive nature of the league and how a team could quickly slide down the table but still little was being invested in quality players. Worse was to come when star player Ralph Callachan was sold to Newcastle United for £90,000. The board, under chairman Bobby Parker, defended the decision but it was clear the team was struggling, which led *Sunday Mail* journalist and Hearts fan John Fairgrieve to claim, 'No doubt the board are good men and true but they are strongly lacking in imagination and are presiding over the decline of a great club.'

After a dismal run-in, the club was relegated for the first time in its 103-year history, with chairman Bobby Parker describing the time as 'our darkest days'. As the club prepared for life in the First

Division, players left in their droves and John Hagart was forced to resign. The misery was compounded by news of the death of former Hearts favourite Willie Bauld. Hearts had been the only team apart from Rangers and Celtic still playing in the top league since its inception in 1890 and they would kick-off in 1977–78 against lowly Dumbarton, the first winners of that title who had since fallen on hard times.

In his autobiography *All Heart*, Jim Jefferies, a skipper from the 1970s who went on to manage the club and end its trophy drought in 1998, pinpointed that the Cup Winners' Cup exit signalled a change in fortunes. He said:

> That European experience seemed to be a major turning point in the club's fortunes. From then on, the club seemed to deteriorate rapidly; there were clear financial problems which were harming the club and things were not going as well as they should have. A lot of new players were brought in, on the playing side, but it was a big gamble to bring in players from a lower division. They were a great bunch of lads but, as time would prove, just not good enough to play at the higher level. It was downhill all the way after that – very depressing times for those who had a real feeling for Hearts. The inevitable eventually happened: Hearts were relegated.

Former Scotland and St Johnstone manager Willie Ormond was given the task of returning Hearts to the Premier Division. His track record as a player and manager was impressive and hopes were high that he would succeed in revitalising Hearts, although his previous associations with Hibs did cloud the judgement of some fans. Nevertheless, several key signings were made and Hearts went on to finish in second place, finally winning promotion (two teams were promoted and demoted each season in those days) with a nervy 1–0 victory over Arbroath on the last day of the season. It was significant, too, that, while crowds had dipped, the supporters generally remained committed to the cause, even setting a First Division record attendance of 19,720 against Dundee. But it was clear there were problems in the dressing room. The players threatened to go on strike over bonus payments during the season and Hearts did themselves few favours when they refused to allow Jim Cruickshank to train at Tynecastle while he was with Dumbarton. Perhaps even worse was the fact that Cruickshank, who then held the record for number of appearances, was not even granted a testimonial. Jim Jefferies summed up the mood of the club after the strike threat in *All Heart*. He said:

> It should never have happened in the first place, but this confrontation really illustrated just how serious the problems were at Tynecastle at the time. I hate to say it, but I have to be honest and say that Hearts were not a happy club or a good place to be. The money problems were starting to bite in a big way; cuts were being made all over the place and it did not take a genius to appreciate that the club was on the way down. We, in the dressing-room, of course, could do nothing about it, but for a man like myself who has a great love for Hearts it really hurt very badly.

The fans responded to promotion by turning out in reasonable numbers in 1978–79 but, by now, they were developing a reputation of a different kind. A number of unsavoury incidents had taken place in recent seasons and matters boiled over at the first derby game of the season. Hibs scored late in the match to equalise and deprive Hearts of their first derby win since 1973. Hearts fans invaded the pitch, the referee was attacked by a supporter and dozens of arrests were made. The club was fined £5,000 by the SFA and a perimeter fence was hastily erected. The fans were also becoming more vocal about the performances on the pitch, threatening a boycott after a series of losses which included a 7–2 aggregate defeat by Morton in the first round of the League Cup. Shareholders, too, were concerned and they were given no reassurance when star youngster Eamonn Bannon was sold to Chelsea for a new Tynecastle record of £215,000, although, with debts creeping upwards and rumours that the club was nearing closure, his sale at least helped to balance the books. But the transfer did nothing to help the team on the pitch. An appalling run of ten successive defeats at the end of the season ensured that Hearts were once again bound for the First Division, finishing eleven points adrift of eighth-placed Partick Thistle. Once again relegation resulted in a clear-out of players, including former favourites such as Drew Busby and Rab Prentice.

The club had survived one season in the lower leagues but the prospect of a second gave rise to concerns about the real financial difficulties which no doubt lay ahead. Revenue would suffer in the First Division and there were already signs that gate receipts could nosedive, with as few as 2,700 fans turning up for the final home game of the previous season. Parker and Ormond remained in post but new directors Archie Martin and Ian Watt joined the board promising to improve the club's fortunes. It was to prove a significant appointment in the years ahead but signs of improvement were not immediately obvious to those on the terraces.

Few new players arrived for season 1979–80 and, before long, the team was knocked out of the League Cup by Ayr United, while remaining unconvincing in the league. Morale appeared poor and the mood of the supporters turned ugly, particularly when they ran riot in Kirkcaldy after a late defeat by Raith Rovers. The inevitable happened in early 1980 when Ormond was sacked because of the under-par performances on the park. His parting shot was to describe the board as the worst he had known and threaten them with the possibility of taking his case to an employment tribunal, although that never happened.

Ormond was replaced by Carlisle manager and former Scotland defender Bobby Moncur who promptly stated the obvious when he described how the atmosphere at Tynecastle suggested the club had slipped into serious decline. He later told the monthly magazine *Hearts*:

> When I walked into Tynecastle I couldn't believe my eyes. The place itself was rundown and tatty – there was even grass coming out of the gutters in the stand. It was clear that the club was in some state. I realised that, while the team was doing really well, a lot of work was needed to make Hearts a threat to the bigger clubs. I accepted

that it was going to be a long, hard slog and the only way I could see it progressing was to start the youth policy.

The board obviously recognised the need for improvements, with chairman Bobby Parker writing to shareholders that year outlining a £1 million five-year refurbishment programme. He added, 'The intention is that at the end of that period we will have an all-seated stadium with modern facilities.' However, it was not clear where the money to achieve this would come from. The plan was well intentioned but would not be realised.

Despite the bad feeling surrounding the club, Moncur managed to steer the team back into the Premier Division, even winning the First Division championship in a final-game clincher against title rivals Airdrie. It was a double celebration for many fans when Hearts passed Hibs on the way up as the Easter Road side now tasted the indignity of relegation. But others bemoaned the fact there would be no derbies to look forward to in 1980–81.

Hearts were champions but it had come at a cost. The core support was being eroded, with the final home game of the season against Airdrie the only one to attract a five-figure attendance. Money was tighter than ever, not least because new seats had been installed in the enclosure – or Shed as it was now known – at Tynecastle. A now familiar clear-out took place and it contributed to Hearts' worst season yet. A dismal run of results in 1980–81 condemned the team to the only last-place finish in the league in the club's history, with a miserly eighteen points from thirty-six games.

Behind the scenes, Moncur had been as good as his word and introduced a promising youth policy which convinced up-and-coming stars Gary Mackay and Dave Bowman to remain at Hearts rather than move south. He also signed future legend and head coach John Robertson but the fans would have to be patient to witness the benefits of his policy. Moncur told the club magazine, 'People will look at my record and say that I was the man who got Hearts relegated. I'd like to think that I set the basis for the club to get bigger and better.'

For now, it was clear that their team was second-rate and many were not prepared to play a waiting game. Average crowds had dropped to four figures, a pathetic 5,700, for the first time in 1979–80. Although that increased by a couple of thousand in their following Premier season, it was still worryingly low. One game against Kilmarnock late in the season, for instance, drew just 1,800 people. It was clear the club's financial difficulties were continuing to mount.

Season 1981–82 would prove perhaps the worst in the history of Hearts as average crowds fell to a new low of just 5,200, hooliganism intensified and the team failed to win promotion. Hearts were to languish in the lower leagues for another year. It was a fate which would almost prove ruinous. The need for radical change was obvious.

In an interview for this book, former striker Donald Ford concludes:

> The principal reason for the decline was very poor direction from the boardroom and the complete absence of a solid financial structure at the club. Money must have been the motivation for selling players such as Dave Mackay, probably the best footballer in Scotland at the time, and Alex Young, who was arguably as good as Willie Bauld. From the early 60s to the late 70s, signings were made but only really to keep supporters happy for a few months. No outstanding players were brought in because no real money was made available to spend on them. The club was undercapitalised and the answer was to put more capital in but the directors failed to stabilise the position by doing that. They took the easy option and sold players instead.
>
> The situation was not desperate then because it wouldn't have taken huge amounts of money to turn the situation around but it didn't happen. It was nonsense for a club like Hearts but that was the way it was handled by the directors. At the same time, the reserve side at Tynecastle was terrible. There were poor young players coming through and they couldn't replace those moving on. The Hearts scouts had done a terrific job bringing in the 50s team but maybe they lost a couple of key scouts or got complacent.

There's no doubt that when people start winning they start to get complacent. The decline was progressive, steady and obvious. In the end, Hearts were like an alcoholic. Just like an alcoholic, they didn't know they were in the gutter until they got there. Hearts were in the financial gutter by 1980.

OVERVIEW

The outbreak of the Second World War may have thwarted Hearts' ambitions but ironically its conclusion would provide them with the best opportunity since before the Great War to mount a serious challenge to Old Firm domination.

By the 1940s, Celtic and Rangers were entrenched as Scotland's big two as the unique cultural, religious and geographical factors which allowed them to rise to prominence continued to work in their favour. Consequently, they continued to pay the highest wages in Scotland, remaining on a par with the big English clubs in this respect. However, the end of the war in 1945 at least partially wiped the Scottish football slate clean.

The professional game had been suspended for understandable reasons – concern over public safety during air raids – but pre-war attendances had ensured the clubs were generally in better financial health than during the First World War. Rangers and Celtic still emerged from the conflict in a strong position but the hiatus and a relatively stagnant transfer system presented the other senior teams with the best chance to threaten their superiority since the game's very formation.

The fans flocked back to grounds around the country. Huge six-figure crowds packed into Hampden for Scottish Cup finals, including those involving teams outwith the Old Firm. For instance 136,300 attended the Motherwell–Dundee showpiece in 1951–52 and almost half that figure was recorded even at Scottish Junior Cup finals. The 65,860 crowd at the 1950 New Year derby between Hibs and Hearts topped the Old Firm attendance on the same day.

On the one hand, supporters were buoyed by the prospect of a relatively level playing field and enticed by a government order to keep admission prices low to restore morale. On the other, post-war austerity and limited choice prevented people seeking out alternative leisure pursuits. The city teams outside Glasgow were in pole position to take advantage of this renaissance and it was no surprise then that Hearts, Hibs, Aberdeen and Dundee quickly emerged as serious challengers. But it was also a golden era for Scotland's provincial clubs, with Motherwell, Clyde and East Fife all winning major honours in the decade after the war, the latter an incredible three League Cups during the period. In the early 50s, there were even two seasons (1951–52 and 1954–55) when the Old Firm finished with nothing – something which had only happened once since the league was formed when, in 1894–95, Hearts won the championship and St Bernard's lifted the Scottish Cup. It has never been repeated.

The boom allowed Hearts – aided by Davie McLean, Tommy Walker and a network of effective scouts – to embark on the most successful period in the club's history. But, despite winning seven trophies in ten years, the chance to stake a claim at the forefront of Scottish football was to prove much more limited than it had been half a century beforehand. A number of factors, many beyond the confines of Scottish football, conspired to restrict Hearts and the other challengers to a relatively brief assault on the Glasgow giants rather than an all-out war of attrition.

Britain's place at the epicentre of world football had been gradually eroded since the turn of the century while the European and South American games in particular continued to grow. Despite its image as an era of comfortable conservatism and homely solidity, in reality, the 50s witnessed the birth of a revolution in football. It was the beginning of a process which would transform the game from an accessible mass spectator sport to an international corporate phenomenon.

Just four months before Hearts won the first of their 1950s trophy haul, UEFA was formed to 'work on behalf of Europe's national associations to promote football and to develop unity among the European football community'. The new organisation's first priority was to establish international competitions for clubs and the European Champion Clubs' Cup between the winners of domestic leagues was established in April 1955. The same month it was followed by the Inter-Cities Fairs Cup. The former tournament was to become the Champions League while the latter has developed into today's UEFA Cup. A third club competition was added when the Cup Winners' Cup was introduced in 1960–61, although this merged with the UEFA Cup in 1999. UEFA also sought to expand competition between national teams and the European Nations' Cup – later the European Championship – commenced in 1958, with the finals taking place for the first time in 1960.

In short, the game was transformed at exactly the same time as Hearts went on the rampage at the domestic level. But, while European football had arrived on Scotland's doorstep, the sport here was slow to embrace some of its tactics and innovations, such as the all-powerful coaches who soon became commonplace. This failure to learn and modernise would prove damaging to Scottish football in general and to Hearts in particular.

Yet this football revolution was not the only change beginning to take place in the 1950s. Technology and its increasing availability took vast leaps forward in the post-war period. Previously, mass media had been restricted to radio, newspapers and, to a certain extent, cinema. Now televisions were becoming increasingly common in people's homes. By the 1960s, football was the main sports attraction on TV and a handful of players were emerging as stars to rival those from the worlds of music and film. The long-term effects of television and its love-hate relationship with football were difficult to foresee but already its fascination with celebrity was encouraging top players to demand the rewards enjoyed by other entertainers.

This inflationary pressure on wages was then aggravated by the abolition of the maximum wage in England in 1961 and the collapse of the old 'retain and transfer' system two years later. Both created more movement of players between clubs and they acted as a lure south to those plying their trade north of the border. (Under the retain and transfer system, players had to put in a transfer request if they wanted to move clubs. But the club holding the player's registration could refuse the request and keep him as long as his wages remained at least the same as they had under his previous contract.)

Average earnings for top professionals in England more than doubled in several short years yet they remained relatively low in Scotland, particularly for those outside Celtic and Rangers. However, even the Old Firm lost players because of their salary demands – most famously when Jim Baxter left Ibrox and moved to Sunderland in 1965 to double his weekly wage to £80. Such prudence would not always be practised by the big Glasgow two. In time, they would be forced to abandon that policy in order to challenge for the international club competitions.

While it is difficult to establish the exact reasons players left Hearts for England, it is nevertheless apparent that significant numbers did so at this time. Among them was 1956 Scottish Cup hero Ian Crawford who went to West Ham in 1961. He was followed by the dependable Bobby Blackwood who went to Ipswich Town for a similar fee of around £10,000. Then, in 1963, Gordon Marshall, virtually ever present in goals for the past six years, was sold to Newcastle United for £18,000. In the second half of the decade, Roy Barry moved to Coventry City and popular winger Johnny Hamilton switched in Watford. Then, in 1968, there was uproar when fullback Arthur Mann went to Manchester City for £70,000.

The effect of these changes in the football 'marketplace' was to increase the pressure on clubs to maximise revenues. The commercialisation of football was gathering pace. The 'branding' of the World Cup in England in 1966 successfully led to the sale of souvenirs and other spin-offs. Later, the Texaco Cup, which Hearts took part in, was an early example of competition sponsorship. Shirt sponsorship followed in Britain in the late 1970s. Yet this upsurge in commercial activity was not accompanied by any meaningful attempt to market the actual product on offer or improve the sport's facilities to an appropriate standard. In fact, in an effort to boost income, the reverse happened and admission prices were hiked upwards with an assumption that fans would turn up regardless. Not surprisingly, the result was a further downturn in attendance levels. A spiral of decline had begun and not only had lessons from abroad been ignored but the competition from elsewhere was also eroding the status of the game in Scotland and Britain.

In addition, the advance of commercialisation was polarising football. The biggest clubs could meet the demands of the bold new era but others increasingly found themselves on the fringes of club competitions. It is telling that Third Lanark, one of the founders of the Scottish game and former league and cup winners, folded in the 1967 amid claims of boardroom corruption – ironically, it was the same year that their fellow Glasgow team Celtic went on to become the first British side to win the European Cup.

The smaller clubs were not helped by massive improvements in transport. Car ownership surged, encouraged by a motorway building programme, and a comprehensive network of bus transport also began to develop. The habit of the football enthusiast turning up, for instance, at Tynecastle one week and Easter Road the next was dying. By the 60s, the away fan had been born – it was yet another development which would benefit the elite at the expense of the many as more and more supporters were drawn to the most successful teams.

Crowds across the country had begun to dwindle from the mid 1950s and this continued more markedly in the 60s. One effect of this was that the boom years after the Second World War failed to provide Hearts with an adequate safety net. There is a perception that the club must have made enough money from the large crowds of its trophy-laden era to sustain it in the longer term. However, this was not the case in reality. Also, while Hearts recorded some massive crowds at Tynecastle, with only a few notable exceptions, these were for a handful of games against the Old Firm and Hibs or the later stages of the cup competitions. Matches against lesser lights could draw as few as 10–15,000. Average attendances, even at this peak, still remained below 30,000 and fell to a little over 20,000. Even at that, the money from gate receipts then is almost incomparable with today's inflated prices. The benefits, therefore, were limited. For instance, the near £10,000 from a bumper 40,000 crowd which packed into Tynecastle for Hearts' first game in Europe against Standard Liege in 1958 is dwarfed by the £1 million reported to have been netted from the more recent match against Schalke. To put the proceeds from the Liege game into perspective, up until that point, Hearts had made a total profit of £76,000 since the Second World War – the equivalent of around £1.13 million today. Compare that with the £8 million investment into Hearts by SMG in 1999 – and the speed with which that disappeared.

The immediate post-war era also saw substantial redevelopment work at Tynecastle so much of the revenue generated went on capital expenditure. Pitch improvements cost almost £5,000 and concreting work was carried out on the terraces at a cost of almost £17,000. Then a floodlight system was installed for £14,000, while a new distillery-side enclosure to 'ensure our faithful supporters of greater comfort during inclement weather', as the club's annual report put it, made a £23,000 dent in the coffers when it was built in 1959. Further improvements were made to facilities for staff and the press.

There are also those who claim that money was diverted away from the taxman or that certain turnstiles were not included in the attendance figures and the cash from those gates found its way into directors' pockets. These practices may indeed have occurred in the Scottish game but there is no evidence to prove that they did at Hearts. What is true is that Hearts' most successful years resulted in a recorded profit which would barely top £1 million today – hardly enough to buy a decent international player yet it is a sum that can now be made from a single European tie. It is fair to say that the low-cost, relatively egalitarian football of the 1950s was very different to the game today which offers vast riches to a fortunate few.

By the time Hearts won their last trophy of the golden era, in 1962–63, the average home crowd was just 15,000. From this time onwards, the club fluctuated between profit and loss. This inconsistent financial performance was not helped by attendances which sometimes dropped below 5,000. Increases in admission charges were starting to have an effect but supporters also faced more competing demands for their cash. Home ownership became fashionable, foreign holidays were possible and alternative leisure pursuits emerged. Football was losing its stranglehold over the masses and was doing little to reverse the trend.

Shortly after the sapping league 'loss' of 1965, Tommy Walker resigned. His replacement, Johnny Harvey, undoubtedly a fine trainer who had played his part in the Hearts' earlier triumphs, failed to revive the club's fortunes and a number of top players put in transfer requests. Some, such as Willie Wallace, were sold for what were regarded as cut-price fees. The absence of a genuine youth development system, as opposed to a simple scouting network, failed, at this stage, to rear the stars of the future and performances suffered as the club entered a new decade.

The board of directors, meanwhile, did nothing to arrest this decline. Not only that, they also allowed continuing financial decay to take hold and, by the 1970s, losses were commonplace.

Credit should be given to the board in 1977 for buying out the council's remaining 'right of pre-emption' over Tynecastle, which would have allowed the local authority to purchase the land if it was put up for sale. The deal cost the club £10,000 but provided it with a valuable asset which could be used as security for borrowing. It was also, effectively, the first step in a process which eventually led to the recent plans to sell the ground, by this time, with a price tag of £22 million. That aside, the slump continued.

This downward spiral, followed by the collapse of traditional industries and economic decline in 1970s Britain, created the conditions for hooliganism to flourish. While a hardcore of fans continued to follow their clubs with a new fanaticism to home and away games, that violent intensity of the hooligans proved a turn-off to the bulk of supporters. Some Scottish Cup finals attracted as few as 30,000 spectators and, at a number of League Cups, even fewer turned up. Scottish football also experienced outbreaks of high-profile crowd disorder in the 70s, such as the Rangers fans battling with the Spanish police at the 1972 Cup Winners' Cup final and the Wembley pitch invasion by Scotland fans in 1977.

In Scotland, however, the situation regarding football in general and hooliganism in particular was once again complicated further by the presence of Rangers and Celtic. The religious and cultural divide between the two had continued to grow during the 1940s and 50s – the row over Celtic's right to fly the Irish tricolour at Parkhead was just one example of the mounting tension. But the enmity was pushed to new levels when the sporadic, sectarian violence in Northern Ireland suddenly escalated in 1969. Some fans had genuine connections with the warring communities in Northern Ireland but others crudely adopted the language and symbols of the conflict with little understanding of current or historical events. Tensions spilled over at the 1980 Scottish Cup final riot when the sight of warring Rangers and Celtic fans being challenged by mounted police on the Hampden turf was caught in the full glare of prime-time television. Hearts and Hibs were tainted by a similar, if diluted, upsurge in sectarian animosity and remain so today. But the die had been cast – there was no room for any more clubs in Scottish football's sectarian niche market.

Internal inertia and external events were threatening to overpower Hearts. By 1980, income had plummeted and the club recorded a huge £308,000 loss. The overdraft, meanwhile, had reached £175,000. The club had quickly gone from a golden era of more trophies, bigger crowds and record profits to one of repeated relegation, haemorrhaging crowds, sickening hooliganism and financial decay. It was clear that radical change was needed.

PART 3

HEARTS IN THE MODERN DAY

8

ENTER WALLACE MERCER

Chairman Archie Martin arrived at Hearts promising to take the club forward. In May 1981, encouraged by the Federation of Hearts Supporters Clubs set up nine years earlier, he persuaded shareholders to agree a change in the Articles of Association. The idea was to allow 350,000 shares to be put on public sale in a bid to raise desperately needed cash. Effectively, the club was being auctioned to the highest bidder. Edinburgh bookmaker Kenny Waugh, who later took control of Hibs, put in a bid of £255,000, prompting a rival consortium to enter the fray. Significantly, it was a player from the tail end of a successful Hearts era who intervened at a crucial moment when the club was at such a low ebb. Former centre forward and Scotland international Donald Ford, who was also a respected accountant, contacted Edinburgh property developer Wallace Mercer and told him the club needed a 'saviour'.

Mercer was originally a Rangers supporter and had little initial interest in running a football club. But his Edinburgh base brought him to take an interest in Hearts' fortunes and soon he became a nominal shareholder. The ongoing crisis persuaded him to invest a more substantial sum of around £30,000 but it was not until Ford picked up the phone that events gathered pace. Caught up in the emotion of a 1–0 Scotland victory over England at Wembley, Mercer decided to answer Ford's SOS call.

He quickly stepped up the war of words, accusing previous regimes of mismanaging the club over the past ten years. Mercer then, with the support of a group of shareholders, upped the bid to £350,000. Waugh responded by forming an alliance with a rival group of shareholders and matching Mercer's offer. Eventually, it came down to a vote among board members, with Mercer winning by three votes to two, although only after presenting the board with a cheque for his share of the bid.

By June 1981, Mercer had a controlling interest in Hearts. He looks back on the takeover for this book:

> The cupboard was bare. [The club] just had insufficient funds to pay the wages and to keep the business going and there was no money there. Apart from one or two ageing decent players, the rest probably wouldn't have got into a junior team. Hearts were doing the best they could within limited budgets and it was just getting poorer and poorer and poorer. And the quality of play was getting worse and worse and there just was a complete lack of direction in terms of developing the business. Hearts were dying a death. It needed a complete renaissance.
>
> Up until then Hearts was really a closed business with a limited number of shareholders. They needed to get new money but the directors were frightened because they knew that, by issuing new shares, effectively they would lose their position and the club may fall into the hands of one individual. And the one individual it fell into the hands of was Wallace Mercer.

Archie Martin resigned and further boardroom changes followed with Edinburgh publican Alex Naylor taking over as chairman. Mercer famously recalled manager Bobby Moncur, saying, 'I didn't like the cut of his jib and I was delighted when he resigned.' Tony Ford was appointed in Moncur's place – it was later admitted to be a 'stop-gap' move – after unsuccessful attempts to woo the highly-rated Jock Wallace and Jim McLean.

It is little known that Mercer turned down an invitation to join the Masons at this time but it was a move which would help in overhauling the playing squad. He recalls:

> My father had been in them and I was invited within a week of taking over at Hearts and I turned them down not because I have a

74

disrespect for them but I just did not want to be identified, I wanted it to be seen to be a family business and we weren't just a Rangers off-shoot. That's why, ironically, in the first year or so we got more support in players from Celtic Football Club than we got from Glasgow Rangers. It was important that this was going to be a family business – we would hire and fire from both sides of the community.

Indeed, a number of players were brought in, including Roddy McDonald from Celtic for a then record fee of £55,000. But results remained disappointing during 1981–82. The team and management were criticised for the cautious style of play adopted and for failing to capitalise on the recent investment. Ford was sacked in December.

Former skipper Jim Jefferies was damning of Ford's management style. In *All Heart*, he said:

While Tony was a nice fellow and all that, I could not see him being an answer to what was needed at the club in the time of change. For me, he did not have a good attitude as a coach. He knew a bit about the game, but had a terrible job in getting it over to the players . . . [His] attempts at being funny had that sarcastic ring and did not endear him to the players. He used to get some terrible stick from a lot of the lads who had been around the game for a long time and who were very streetwise. He just could not cope with it.

Journalist John Fairgrieve was also not overly impressed by the recent managers – he described Moncur as 'more of an administrator than a manager' and said Ford believed that 'if anything went wrong, it could be put right by more hours of training' – but he endorsed the new man at the helm. Alex MacDonald, who signed from Rangers the previous year, was handed the job of improving performances in the role of player-coach. The truth was that the innovative new role had been created at least partly for reasons of cost – the club could simply not afford the luxury of a dedicated manager.

The prospect of an upturn was dashed when the team recorded one of its worst defeats – a 1–0 home loss to Second Division side

Forfar in the Scottish Cup in February 1982. The cup exit led Fairgrieve to suggest, in anger, that Tynecastle should be turned into a car park. Results did not improve sufficiently and Hearts finished third in the First Division, out of the promotion places. It was a new low for the club. They had been relegated in the past but at least bounced back instantly. This time they were condemned to yet another potentially crippling year outside the top flight. The anger and frustration boiled over on the final day of the season when Hearts were beaten 1–0 by Motherwell despite needing just a point to go up. Violence erupted on the Tynecastle terraces which led to a number of arrests and injuries to three policemen. Wallace Mercer, who left the directors' box to appeal for calm, later recalled that the events of the afternoon made him question whether he should ever have invested in the club.

Mercer had provided the club with loans of £75,000. He had given a personal guarantee for a further sum of £100,000 and this meant his business and even his home were on the line. The club would struggle to pay back the money he was owed – fewer than 100,000 spectators had attended Tynecastle during the entire league season.

As well as the purchase of Roddy McDonald from Celtic, Willie Pettigrew and Derek Addison had been signed from Dundee United for a new record transfer fee of £165,000. Unfortunately, these signings had been made, at least partially, on the 'never-never' as Mercer later admitted. Hearts failed to pay their transfer debts, even passing the money to the bank when Addison was sold on to St Johnstone, and were banned from buying players by the authorities. In desperation, Hearts even offered to sell Gary Mackay and Dave Bowman to United but the Tannadice board only offered £30,000 each so the offer was retracted. The incident also led to the resignation of chairman Alex Naylor but it did at least give Mercer an opportunity to rebuild from scratch. The depth of feeling displayed by supporters after relegation persuaded Mercer to remain committed to the cause and also to keep the club full-time despite the perilous financial situation. Former Scotland defender Sandy

Jardine was brought in as assistant player-manager from Rangers and new faces were also added to the boardroom.

Hearts' precarious position suggested that season 1982–83 would be a roller coaster, with the fear that failure to win promotion would lead to part-time football. Cuts had already been made among the backroom staff but MacDonald and Jardine did manage to build a team combining youth, such as promising young striker John Robertson, and experience, in former Scotland winger Willie Johnston, for example. Basic wages were set at a low level but bonuses were increased significantly. MacDonald also set out to introduce a new culture at the club. He later told the *Daily Record*:

> The place was a glorified disco at first. There was music in the dressing room and the players wore string vests and bleached denims to their work every day. All they talked about was the parties they had been to the night before. It was a joke environment, more like a junior club than anything else, and I knew I had to change it. I got rid of the music and I binned the guy who used to sell the players crisps and Coca-Cola at the end of training. We started to wear Hearts gear, with proper collars and ties, and that gave us a reminder of who we were and what we represented.

Off the field, Mercer and his commercial staff were making strides in levering cash into the club. The club was re-registered as a public limited company in 1982, allowing shares to be traded publicly and providing access to capital markets. Other initiatives included attracting a shirt sponsor for the first time and even staging a lottery for a free house and car. Cut-price season tickets and cheap away travel deals were also introduced and, around the time of the miners' strike, which started in 1984, the unemployed would be allowed into Tynecastle for free. The creation of a corporate viewing area was a first at the time, as was the recently established family area and junior club. There was even the innovative appointment of a director, Pilmar Smith, to represent the fans. There was some optimism that Hearts had turned the corner.

The team made the latter stages of both cups and eventually won promotion behind St Johnstone. Mercer recalls:

> We were up to lots of high jinks at the time. We used to run it by the seat of our pants. Pilmar Smith used to say to me, in the early days, 'Wallace, you were having press conferences once a month in the boardroom and Les Porteous and I were looking after the sheriff's officers in the secretary's office next door to try and get a delay on the payment of VAT and National Insurance contributions.' We sailed fairly close to the wind for a few years but it was always in the right direction. In the first two seasons at Tynecastle with young ownership and management we tried to be quite radical in our approach to the business of football which was conditioned by our need to improve revenue both from commercial and gate income and radically rid ourselves of the public perception as to the club's social problems induced by many years of non-performance.

9

THE ROAD TO DENS PARK

Such were the hardships at the club that volunteers painted and repaired Tynecastle to save money before season 1983–84. But more experienced players were somehow brought in, earning the team a 'Dad's Army' reputation. The ban on buying players was lifted and initially led to the board agonising over splashing out paltry fees such as the £1,000 spent on Malcolm Murray. But it also allowed Craig Levein to make the move from Cowdenbeath for just £30,000. The blend of youth and experience, along with the intense team spirit, was soon to prove a difficult-to-beat formula. Hearts won their first five games, including victories over Hibs and Rangers, and found themselves top of the league.

That level of achievement could not be maintained but, unbeaten against Hibs, the team finished a creditable fifth and clinched a place in the following season's UEFA Cup. Average crowds had doubled to 12,000 and there were suggestions that the 'sleeping giant' was finally awakening.

Hearts failed to live up to their billing in 1984–85 but, for many fans, the double-header against Paris Saint-Germain, the team's first game in Europe for eight years, was memorable enough in itself. Around 4,000 made the trip to the French capital for the first leg in September 1984 and, although the team was soundly beaten 4–0, the club had returned to the biggest stage available. And the fans, who had developed such an unwelcome reputation – because of bad behaviour that included a mini-pitch invasion at the Hibs derby just a month before – behaved impeccably. They cheered for their team long after the final whistle had gone and even swapped hats with the French riot police on their way out of the stadium. The second leg ended 2–2 and Hearts regained some pride, although they were out of the cup.

Another disappointment followed when midfielder Dave Bowman was sold to Coventry City for £170,000 but, importantly, players such as Kenny Black, Brian Whittaker, Sandy Clark and Neil Berry had settled into the side and shown promise. Hearts finished a disappointing seventh but at least had the consolation of winning the popular Tennent's Sixes indoor competition at Ingliston.

That summer was a memorable one for English football, for the most tragic of reasons. The tragedy would have consequences for teams in Scotland and throughout Europe. In the space of less than three weeks in May 1985, the game south of the border suffered a double disaster. First, on 11 May, fifty-six supporters were killed when a discarded cigarette set fire to rubbish under the main stand at Bradford City's Valley Parade ground. Then, eighteen days later, thirty-nine people died and hundreds were injured when Liverpool and Juventus fans clashed at the Heysel Stadium in Brussels before the European Cup final. UEFA promptly banned all English clubs from playing in European competitions indefinitely. The ban would last for five seasons and, while the circumstances behind the exclusion were tragic, it would provide Scottish teams with an opportunity to make some advances. None of this, of course, could be foreseen at the time. Indeed, no one could possibly anticipate what would happen to Hearts in the season ahead.

The squad was further strengthened in the close season with the purchase of Celtic winger John Colquhoun for just £75,000 and there was some expectation that Hearts could improve on the previous season. The league campaign began with a decent 1–1 draw with Celtic at Tynecastle but that was put into perspective by a 6–2 embarrassment at the hands of St Mirren a week later. A mixed spell of results followed before Hearts embarked on an extraordinary run of games. It started with a mundane 1–1 draw against Dundee at Tynecastle and would end against the same team in the most agonising of circumstances thirty-one games later. Hearts were unbeaten in the league over twenty-seven matches, including notable victories over the top four teams – Celtic, Aberdeen, Rangers and Dundee United – as well as Hibs of course. The run to the Scottish Cup final had also included defeats of Rangers and Dundee United.

It was a sensational story – the team that, five years before, had been close to extinction and had only come up from the First Division three seasons ago was sweeping all before it. Leading newspapers and commentators pleaded 'give them the flag' before the fixtures had even been completed. One of two books which were published at the end of the season, *Glorious Hearts*, by Mike Aitken, even described the stunning 3–0 victory over title rivals Dundee United at Tannadice on 12 April as 'the day Hearts tied up the championship', presumably because it was being written as events unfolded and was not corrected. But Celtic, who had been nine points behind two weeks before, had won their two games in hand and beaten Aberdeen at Pittodrie the same day to almost halve the gap to just five points. Hearts stumbled through the next two games, with a late equaliser in a 1–1 draw against Aberdeen in Scotland's first league game to be shown live on television and a narrow 1–0 defeat of Clydebank six days later. If Celtic defeated Motherwell in midweek, which they did, Hearts would need only a draw or possibly even a narrow defeat against Dundee at Dens Park to win the championship. It was 1965 all over again.

Part of the reason behind Hearts' unbeaten record had been their ability to field an almost unchanged side from week to week. There was dismay, then, when rumours spread on the morning of the crunch match, 3 May 1986, that a mystery illness had hit the Hearts camp. The rumours proved to be true. John Colquhoun, Kenny Black and Neil Berry missed training early in the week with a bug and were still struggling at the weekend. Brian Whittaker and George Cowie were hit by the illness later in the week and Craig Levein called in sick on the day of the game.

The magnitude of the match and the problems revealed in the build-up finally appeared to sink in among the 10,000 Hearts fans who made the trip to Dundee and the apparent nervousness of the players during the first half did little to ease their fears. News of a flurry of goals from Celtic, giving them a 4–0 lead over St Mirren at half time, left a growing number of supporters ashen-faced. The possibility of winning the championship on goal difference despite suffering a narrow defeat appeared to have vanished. As the minutes dragged by, Hearts would have to hang on for the draw or find goals from somewhere.

The deadlock was finally broken, with just seven minutes to go but it was Dundee's Albert Kidd who put the ball in the net. Hearts fans were simply stunned. A pitch invasion followed the goal, although it came out of bewilderment more than malice. Supporters and players alike were still dazed when order was resumed but there was little surprise when Kidd, a substitute who had failed to score all season, knocked in the killer second goal with two minutes to go. Some fans seemed to barely even notice the second goal as they drifted aimlessly around Dens Park or sat with heads in hands. A 2–0 defeat to 'lose' the league on goal difference on the final day of the season – it was an almost exact repeat of Kilmarnock in 1965. Almost – if Hearts had not argued so strongly for a change from goal average (dividing goals for by goals against) to goal difference (calculating the margin between the number of goals scored and those conceded), they would have won this title, albeit by just 0.024 goals. Equally, in 1965, with their plus-twelve goal difference over Kilmarnock, they would have triumphed under the new system.

The Hearts supporters cheered for the team at the tunnel entrance and outside the main stand after the final whistle but the spirit of the players had been broken. Alex MacDonald later admitted in *Ten of Hearts* that he had struggled to cope with the trauma and had found it impossible to console the players. He said:

Three times I tried to go in and say something that would lift them, but there was just no way. There was nothing that could be done to relieve the most hellish pain I had experienced in over 20 years in the game.

In a bitter twist, it later emerged that Dundee pushed forward so forcefully only because they wrongly thought a spontaneous surge in noise levels around the stadium meant Rangers were dropping points against Motherwell. If true, it would have meant that Dundee could qualify for Europe by winning the match. There was also no consolation in subsequent reports that referee Bill Crombie admitted he should have given Hearts a penalty when Sandy Clark went down in the box. In *The Boys in Maroon*, writer and Hearts supporter John Fairgrieve, described his feelings as he watched the title dream end at Dens Park:

> At the full-time whistle, at the end of all this trauma, at the final trumpet, the only emotion left is drained, stunned despair. The fact that we had, perversely, thought it might happen anyway didn't matter any more. Some Hearts fans weep. They should not be ashamed. There is nothing wrong with honest emotion. There is nothing wrong with giving way, after a day of exceptional ambition, to the realisation that the dream is shattered.

John Robertson and Ian Jardine were hit by the same bug as their colleagues in the coming days, although they recovered for the cup final the following Saturday. The prospect of the first league and Scottish Cup double in the club's history had disappeared a week before but in reality there was also an inevitability about the 3–0 defeat that day, particularly after early goals from Aberdeen in both halves. To add to the misery, captain Walter Kidd was sent off for throwing the ball at an opponent. The players, several in tears, collected hats, scarves, banners, even a sombrero, which had been thrown onto the pitch by the 40,000 Hearts fans that remained behind to hail their heroes. The scenes were repeated when the squad arrived back at Tynecastle and a crowd of 3,000 had even gathered at the Caledonian Hotel in the city centre, knowing that the club's post-match reception would be held there.

The season had ended in disappointment but there were a few crumbs of comfort for Hearts. The club had re-asserted its right to be considered among the elite of Scottish football by a remarkable series of performances, which resulted in qualification for Europe. Sandy Jardine was the first and, to date, only Hearts star to be named Player of the Year, when he picked up the Scottish Football Writers' Association award. Earlier in the season, he became the first player in Scotland to make 1,000 senior appearances when he turned out against his old club Rangers on 16 November. Meanwhile, Craig Levein won the Scottish Professional Foot-ballers' Association Young Player of the Year title and Alex MacDonald was the Scottish Brewers' Manager of the Year. The management team had proved a talented combination, particu-larly for the spirit of determination and teamwork which had been fostered at Tynecastle by such innovations as the opening of a players' lounge at the stadium.

Crowds had soared to an average of more than 16,000 – the high-est level since the previous doomed title challenge in 1964–65. As in later years, the basis of Hearts' success was put down to their impressive record at Tynecastle, where they remained unbeaten. And the financial mess associated with the club for the past fifteen or so years appeared to have been sorted. The increase in gate receipts and heightened commercial activity had led to a pre-tax profit of almost £384,000, while £254,000 was also spent on improving the stadium and facilities.

But the season also had unforeseen consequences which would leave Hearts trailing in the years ahead. Rangers had finished a distant fifth in the league, fifteen points behind Hearts, and with an average of under a point per game for the first time in the club's history. Decisive action had already been taken at Ibrox to ensure such a 'failure' would not be repeated. Not long after Hearts com-fortably disposed of Rangers 3–1 at Tynecastle at the end of March 1986, former Scotland, Sampdoria and Liverpool star Graeme

Souness succeeded Jock Wallace as manager at Ibrox. Soon he would be handed a massive multi-million-pound budget to revive Rangers' fortunes. The Ibrox revolution had begun, Celtic would attempt to keep up and the rest of Scottish football would struggle in their wake. In fact, no team would again come as close as Hearts had to wresting the championship from either half of the Old Firm.

10

GOODBYES AND GLORY NIGHTS

Inevitably, Hearts struggled to live up to expectations in 1986–87, slumping out of the League Cup at the hands of Montrose (2–0), falling at the first UEFA Cup hurdle to Dukla Prague on the away goals rule (3–3) and losing a Scottish Cup semi-final to St Mirren (2–1) with the Old Firm and Aberdeen already out of the tournament. Some convincing results were recorded in the league, such as the 7–0 demolition of Hamilton, but inconsistency cost the injury-plagued side, which failed to qualify for Europe. To make matters worse, star young defender Craig Levein suffered knee ligament damage which would result in a lengthy lay-off. But the 50% increase in the wage bill, which brought it to £767,000, may have been a sign that the financial prudence of the past was giving way to a more risky transfer strategy – one that was influenced, perhaps, by events in Govan.

The board also made cash available for new signings and Rangers defenders Dave McPherson and Hugh Burns were brought in for around £500,000. The £350,000 fee for McPherson was a new Tynecastle record and it breached the club's cost-control policy simply because the opportunity of obtaining a top-level professional at that price came up so rarely.

There was a marked improvement in performances in season 1987–88, with the team even topping the league early on in the campaign. Hearts reached the quarter-final of the League Cup, only to be beaten 4–1 by Rangers, and made it to the semi-final of the Scottish Cup, losing two late goals to go down 2–1 to Celtic. The Hearts team, half of whom had won Scotland honours, finished second in the league behind Celtic and had clearly made progress.

Average crowds of 16,600 exceeded even the nail-biting championship race two years before and the financial situation at the club was stronger then ever. In his own book, *Heart to Heart*, which was published in 1988, Wallace Mercer called the 1987–88 season 'the most successful business-wise since I assumed control'. He added:

> In the last seven years Hearts have become one of the most financially sound football clubs in Britain. We've made a trading profit for the past six years. And at the time of writing, the club has no debts and assets involving the team and the stadium is worth approximately £6 million. Since 1981 we've spent something like £2.5 million on new talent and in the region of £750,000 on improvements to our stadium. All these positive developments have been achieved thanks to the revenue we've earned and the commercial support we've enlisted.

But there were concerns at the club – key players Craig Levein and Gary Mackay had suffered serious injuries and John Robertson's future was a matter of considerable speculation. It was not the first time Robertson had been linked with a move south – he had been tipped to sign for Spurs several years before – but, this time, there appeared to be more substance to the rumours. His contract was due to expire at the end of the season and chairman Wallace Mercer insisted Hearts would not meet demands for a signing-on fee of £100,000 plus £1,000 a week in wages. The wage bill was already on target to jump by a further 20% and Mercer was concerned that Robertson's stance would further disrupt the salary structure at the club. With the possibility of him moving for a cut-price fee in the summer, Hearts accepted a £750,000 offer from Newcastle United for their star striker, although the figure is sometimes given as £625,000. The player, who had just scored a personal record of thirty-one goals in a season with a handful of games still to go, felt he had little choice but to accept the deal if Hearts would not meet his terms. He was comforted by the fact that he would be playing at a top English club while based not far from Edinburgh. Despite the fact the money was re-invested in players – £325,000 for Iain Ferguson and £225,000 for former Tynecastle favourite Eamonn Bannon, both from Dundee United – the fans were devastated. The evidence was that the board was being more ambitious rather than less but there were signs that the tide was turning. Mercer, the man widely credited with rescuing the club from ruin, was considered, by some fans at least, to be losing his winning touch.

This was reinforced early in the 1988–89 season when Sandy Jardine, who had been made co-manager with Alex MacDonald two years before, was sacked as Hearts lay third bottom of the table. There was no question that it had been a disappointing start to the league, with only two wins – both against relegation favourites Hamilton – in their first eighteen matches. One explanation for the poor league form may have been the distraction of the cup competitions as the team reached the League Cup semi-final, only to be beaten 3–0 by Rangers, and had already embarked on what would prove a taxing but memorable UEFA Cup run.

The reason behind Jardine's dismissal seemed to be that the co-manager system was not working well. But Jardine may also have been frustrated at the financial restraints he was forced to work under. In his 1987 autobiography, *Score and More*, he admitted that Celtic, Rangers, Aberdeen and Dundee United all had an 'enormous advantage over us financially' yet he also declared his desire to win trophies despite that handicap. Whatever the truth, he appeared to recognise the vulnerability of his own position, perhaps even anticipating what was to come when he said:

It is a fact of life in this sport that you can work damn hard for five or six years in order to achieve a base, make one or two wrong moves, and then watch the pack of cards collapse all around you. It takes a long time to bring a club up to a certain standard, but no time at all to slip back.

It was a message which the board would also do well to heed. To most Hearts fans, who still held Jardine in high esteem after the thrills of 1985–86, it seemed a harsh move. The resignation of Douglas Park from the Tynecastle board at the same time only served to fuel speculation about what was happening behind the scenes at Tynecastle.

Performances did pick up in the second half of the season, although 1988–89 will be remembered by most fans for the thrilling UEFA Cup run which saw the club progress further than ever before. It began in Dublin in September with a relatively low key 2–0 defeat of St Patrick's and the victory was followed by a repeat of that scoreline in the return leg at Tynecastle. Hearts met Austria Vienna in the next round, managing only a 0–0 draw at home but then going on to record a memorable 1–0 victory in the Austrian capital. A convincing 3–0 win over Bosnian side Velez Mostar allowed Hearts the luxury of a 2–1 defeat in the intimidating return leg. The team had reached the quarter-final, further than Hearts had ever progressed in Europe. The reward could hardly have been more mouth-watering – a double-header against German giants Bayern Munich.

With John Robertson brought back from Newcastle after an unhappy time in England's north-east for a club record of £750,000 and left back Tosh McKinlay signed from Dundee for £300,000, there was a surge of optimism among supporters. There was some discussion about moving the potentially lucrative UEFA tie to Murrayfield but, in the end, 26,000-plus fans crowded into Tynecastle for the occasion in February 1989. And they were not disappointed when Iain Ferguson cracked home a 25-yard drive from a free kick outside the box to give Hearts a 1–0 lead which they held until full-time. To the frustration of their 3,000 supporters watching from the stands, Hearts went agonisingly close in the return leg at Munich's Olympic Stadium. Twice John Colquhoun looked to have scored, hitting one just wide and another against the post, but the team eventually went down 2–0 and the Germans progressed to the last four.

It had been a season of mixed fortunes. The impressive run had given the club a taste for European competition, although a sixth-place finish would mean there was no return to the big stage in 1989–90. And the failure to make an impact on the domestic scene had proved costly. The board had invested heavily in the team, spending £1.8 million on players and signing-on fees and recouping only £450,000 from those who moved on to new clubs. Wages showed another big rise this year, up by a quarter, and a £100,000 fine by UEFA for the unauthorised live coverage by a German television company during the European run had dented the accounts. Despite increased gate receipts and turnover, the club suffered a loss of just over £1 million, the first trading deficit in six years. The overdraft and bank loans shot up from almost zero to £1.4 million.

Hearts had taken a gamble with the sale of Robertson and sacking of Sandy Jardine and had been forced to spend big money to bring the star striker back to Tynecastle and make further additions to the playing staff. The team may have been struggling to keep up with Rangers in particular but they had to at least cement themselves as the 'best of the rest' and secure regular European appearances to sustain the ongoing levels of expenditure. Wallace Mercer made it clear in the 1989 annual report that failure to meet that target could result in cutbacks. He said efforts were being made to increase commercial activities, particularly corporate hospitality, but added, 'To maintain its player base and commitment to salaries the club must participate in European football.'

11

HIBS TAKEOVER, STADIUM MAKEOVER

League performances did improve as the club entered the 1990s and the team finished third, behind Aberdeen in second on goal difference. But off-the-field events would soon divert attention once again. Wallace Mercer realised that Rangers were beginning to surge ahead in Scotland and he sought to keep Hearts as close to them as possible. The books had almost been balanced in 1989–90, although, with the 'high cost of money', interest payments of around £260,000 led to a small loss and fans were buoyed by the availability of a transfer budget which allowed Scotland international Derek Ferguson to be signed from Rangers for £750,000 in the close season.

But even that was overshadowed by the announcement that Mercer planned to launch an audacious takeover bid for cash-strapped Hibs. Fans from both clubs were stunned. Some Hearts fans regarded the very suggestion as getting one over on their rivals and confirmation that the Gorgie club was Edinburgh's dominant force. Others were concerned about the implications for Hearts' future. The move had been described as a merger that would see the new super team playing in a purpose-built out-of-town stadium but that cast doubt over everything the supporters held dear – the club's name, colours, home and history.

Hibs fans refused to accept the notion that it would be a merger of the clubs, insisting it was a takeover which would result in their club being closed down and the assets sold off. A vociferous protest campaign, 'Hands off Hibs', was launched anxd it actually received backing from a number of Hearts players, such as John Robertson, and supporters. Mercer received death threats and the police had to guard his Edinburgh home. He eventually climbed down, claiming he had won the business argument but not the emotional one. Whatever the truth, it seriously damaged his standing among Hearts fans who began to distrust his motives and his understanding of the club's traditions. In *A Tale of Two Cities*, Dave McPherson, who was made club captain in 1989, gave his thoughts on Mercer and the Hibs takeover episode:

> There were occasional brainstorms, like his takeover bid for Hibs. That was always going to be a non-starter, but Wallace was genuinely mystified and even hurt at the reaction. A lot of people don't realise just how great the rivalry is, or the depth of feeling both sets of fans have for their teams. In some ways it's even worse than the rivalry between the Old Firm in Glasgow, but Wallace was oblivious to this. He was horrified at what he'd stirred up after he started receiving death threats from both sets of fans, a Hands off Hibs campaign started and there were rallies at the Usher Hall. It was bedlam, but I could see the thinking that lay behind it. Like everything else, it was strictly business, but his attempt to be the Godfather of Edinburgh football was an offer the fans could refuse. The punters took it personally, while he explained it to me as simply a matter of supply and demand and basic football economics.

Also in 1990, Mercer approached Alex Ferguson about the possibility of taking up the managerial reins at Tynecastle if he was forced out at Old Trafford. According to Mercer, Ferguson was offered a 'very attractive package' but, when Manchester United went on to beat Crystal Palace in the FA Cup final, Ferguson's job was safe once again. However, as Mercer now admits, the incident was an 'error of judgement' which destabilised the relationship between manager Alex MacDonald and chairman at Tynecastle.

The dismissal of popular manager MacDonald several weeks into the 1990–91 season may have been inevitable but it did little to reassure the critics. MacDonald had made some questionable signings, not least the costly Derek Ferguson and the ineffective Husref Musemic from Red Star Belgrade. There had been grumbles from the terraces after a mixed start to the season but few expected MacDonald to be axed with such haste. There was a suspicion that he did not court the media as would have been expected. But Mercer, who said he had offered to stand down as chairman before the board decision was taken, insisted that a new man was needed for a new era.

In response, MacDonald's thoughts turned to the players and fans whose respect he had won. He said, 'After hitting the post so often during the last few years, it would have been nice to have left the club having given the players and supporters a trophy to enjoy from my spell in charge.'

Former player Sandy Clark, who was by now a coach at Tynecastle, took over as caretaker manager and successfully guided the team to a stormy 3–0 win over Hibs and achieved a 1–1 draw away to Ukrainians Dnipro Dnipropetrovsk. But it was during that UEFA trip that details emerged of plans to bring in a new manager – the up-and-coming Bristol City boss and former Scotland striker Joe Jordan.

As with the bold recent transfers, Mercer appeared to be driven by ambition more than anything else. The chairman's vision of Hearts and the changing nature of Scottish football were clear in *Ten of Hearts*, a 1990 book which Mercer contributed to and featured in through a chapter entitled 'Into the Nineties'. During the decade, TV revenues and admission prices were increasing at a time when the cost of recruiting top players was inevitably accelerating and the size of the crowds was potentially falling. In this climate, Mercer correctly anticipated that 'the rich will get richer, and the poor will get poorer'. He may well have been aware of the planned changes to the European Cup, which would soon see it altered to the Champions League, and even the licensing system which has led to Tynecastle being declared 'not fit for purpose'. His projections and reflections in this respect are telling even now:

When this will all happen is very difficult to predict, but one thing is for certain – Hearts, and anyone else who wishes to be a part of this new international football scene, must start preparing now. This in some way was the motivation behind the recent bid to buy Hibernian plc. In hindsight, it might have been done differently, but there is no doubt that Edinburgh will need a top club playing in a top stadium if it wishes to be competitive at the highest level in the future.

Mercer's latter words must still be ringing in the ears of Hearts, given the recent controversy over the possible move to Murrayfield. But the comments were not simply a corporate response to potential business opportunities and pitfalls. As Mercer offered the forecast above, the inquiry into Britain's worst football disaster had just published its findings. The Taylor Report looked into the Hillsborough tragedy, where ninety-six fans were killed and hundreds injured in a massive crush at the Sheffield stadium just before the start of the FA Cup semi-final between Liverpool and Nottingham Forest in April 1989. Poor stadiums and outdated facilities were among the issues covered in its seventy-six recommendations on crowd safety and control at sports events. The response to the report would revolutionise football in Britain, notably through the instruction to provide all-seated grounds. The author, Lord Justice Taylor, himself suggested that this may require clubs to share or relocate stadiums.

Hearts had been on the lookout for available land adjoining Tynecastle before the report but none came on the market and, by this time, a proposal to take the club to a new site on the western outskirts of Edinburgh had been developed. Mercer outlined the scheme in *Ten of Hearts*:

> We are determined to see this through whatever the obstructions, and that is why the decision to move from Tynecastle has already been taken. We could have upgraded the ground to a perfectly acceptable standard, but we would forever be plagued with the problem of bad access. Therefore, to commit millions of pounds to refurbishing our present home without solving problems that can only get worse was not an acceptable option.

His comments must send a shudder down the spines of Hearts fans as well as those of the board members behind the redevelopment of Tynecastle and subsequent proposed move to Murrayfield. But, like the champion of the recent Murrayfield option, Chris Robinson, Mercer also took the opportunity to take a swing at our elected government representatives. He said:

> The cost of land in some of the areas on the city outskirts which would be suitable takes them outwith our reach. There is no way that we can finance a scheme where between £10 million and £20 million for a site is being asked. We simply cannot afford that. Politicians will have to make up their minds exactly what they want. We cannot in one instance be forced to provide such accommodation without the assistance of the community.

In any case, Mercer clearly believed that Joe Jordan was the man who could help Hearts to respond to these challenges. The former Manchester United and AC Milan star was appointed on a salary package, according to Mercer, of £140,000. It was thought to be the second-highest manager's salary in Scotland after what Graeme Souness was earning at Rangers. Despite the sympathy for MacDonald, there was confidence that at least he had been replaced by an ambitious young manager who had done well at Bristol City. But the players quickly saw a side to Jordan which did not bode well for the future. Dave McPherson described the reaction to Jordan's appointment in *A Tale of Two Cities*:

> When Joe Jordan took over from Alex MacDonald at the start of the 1990–91 season, it could have been the proverbial breath of fresh air, but instead it was more like a cold front. Going by the good relationship he had with the Scottish press when he was down south with Bristol City, he seemed to be a young go-ahead boss who recognised the value of good PR. Nothing could have been further from the truth. At times, even the players found it hard to get a word out of Joe, never mind the press gang, and it was definitely a problem for those who had to deal with him. When he took over he was almost the complete opposite of Alex. Doddy was a bubbly character, very up front, whereas Joe had a serious

personality. As a result I don't think many of the players liked him much.

McPherson added that he was a good coach but he expected perfection from the players. He could also be distant, and according to McPherson, he would have players sitting in his office and get on with doing other things before he would speak to them. On one occasion, he left five players behind on a pre-season trip and later fined them because they were late for the team bus after being caught in traffic.

Jordan had a poor start to his Hearts managerial career with a 3–0 loss to Celtic but the team picked themselves up and went on to record victories over Dundee United (1–0) and Dnipro (3–1) in the home leg of the UEFA tie. The latter was enough to progress to the second round where they would play Italian side Bologna.

The importance of European competition to the club's finances was illustrated when prices were doubled for the visit of the Italians and the crowd duly slipped to almost half that of the previous round. The team managed a 3–1 victory and looked favourites to qualify but then slumped to a hugely disappointing 3–0 defeat in Bologna. Life was not proving any easier in the Premier Division, with the club slipping to the foot of the table before flying out to Italy. League performances improved after the turn of the year and the team was given an added boost by winning the Tennent's Sixes for the second time but the season ended weakly with Hearts out of the Scottish Cup early and in fifth place in the table.

Once again, the board was left to count the cost of the team's underachievement. Despite an increase in gate receipts and a near 40% jump in other income to more than £1 million, the club recorded a loss of £1.4 million and bank debt stood at £3 million. Chairman Wallace Mercer said part of the reason for the downturn was the onset of economic recession but he also highlighted interest on borrowings, which surged to £426,000, and ever-increasing staff costs, up 30% to £1.7m. Worryingly, wages and staff costs rose to more than 70% of turnover. Compensation had been paid to Bristol City for Jordan's appointment and the abandoned Hibs takeover bid had incurred costs of £191,000. But the board pressed ahead with its search for a new all-seated home for Hearts to meet the requirements of the Taylor Report, identifying Millerhill on the south-east fringes of Edinburgh as a potential site. In yet another echo of the more recent debate about the sale of the old ground to house-builders Cala, Mercer said in the 1991 annual report that outline planning consent had been granted for a housing development at Tynecastle, with an expected windfall of up to £4 million from the site.

Hearts got off to a much better start in 1991–92, notching up a number of commendable league wins and reaching the quarter-final of the League Cup only to be knocked out by Rangers (1–0). Joe Jordan was attempting to build his own team and, as a result, new players arrived at Tynecastle as others headed for the exits. The strategy appeared to be working when the team sat top of the table at the end of 1991, the only disappointment being that rivals Hibs had won the League Cup by defeating Dunfermline 2–0. A string of league defeats in early 1992 and a Scottish Cup exit to Airdrie on penalties after two scrappy draws at Hampden brought some disappointment but the team still managed to finish second in the Premier Division, nine points behind Rangers.

However, despite the solid league campaign, some fans were already growing disenchanted with Jordan's reliance on a solid, organised team that seemed happy just to scrape wins by the odd goal. In turn, Jordan claimed he could have performed better if the board had provided the cash he needed to strengthen the team when it sat top of the league the Christmas before. The claim led to a public disagreement with Mercer amid suggestions Jordan had been promised a bigger transfer budget than had been forthcoming.

Perhaps because of the team's stuffy style of play, crowds slipped and were consistently below the 9,000 mark in the final quarter of the season but that did not seriously affect the improved financial position at the club. Turnover was up by more than £1 million to £3.5 million and the club recorded only a marginal loss. Yet interest payments remained high and wages once again leapt by more than 20%. The doubling of the existing £50,000 management fees that were payable to Pentland Securities Ltd, the company in which Mercer was the majority shareholder, was, according to the 1992 annual report, for 'the time and effort of Mr Mercer spent as chief executive acting for the club'. This received little attention at the time but it would provide his enemies with ammunition in the days ahead. The sale of club captain Dave McPherson back to Rangers for £1.3 million may have helped to boost the coffers but it too brought criticism from the fans.

Meanwhile, the board was also having little success identifying a site for a new stadium. Hearts were unable to obtain planning permission for a 20,000-seat stadium and leisure facility at Millerhill and, by 1992, had turned their attention to the area around Hermiston on the western outskirts of the city. Indeed, Mercer took the unusual step in the 1992 annual report of issuing a rally call to shareholders to back the campaign for a new home. He said:

> As the chairman of the company I call on each individual shareholder to write to the Region[al Council] as it is an absolute priority for this company to improve facilities. As our application at Hermiston is for stadium only and [the site is] well located for the road system we look forward to receiving approval.

At the same time, local authority figures were involved in discussions about a joint stadium for Hearts and Hibs at Ingliston. This would involve Hearts, Hibs and the council all sharing the costs. But Hearts were clearly attracted to the Hermiston site. The possibility of a shared stadium with Hibs at Straiton in Midlothian was also mooted but was unpopular with the fans and made little headway. So the debate over Hearts' future home was put on hold as the 1992–93 campaign got under way with the team in reasonable form.

A League Cup quarter-final exit to Celtic (2–1) was followed by another European adventure. Opponents Slavia Prague won the first leg 1–0 in the Czech Republic but Hearts went through after a thrilling 4–2 victory at Tynecastle two weeks later. The second round was always going to be tough after Standard Liege won the 1–0 in Edinburgh and so it was that Hearts went out of the competition when that scoreline was repeated in Belgium.

The team started well enough in the league, even challenging at the top of the table in the early weeks. But even when results were going their way, the Hearts fans seemed unimpressed. Most crowds were in four figures. The apathy turned to anger towards the end of 1992 after defeats by Aberdeen (6–2), as well as lowly Falkirk (2–1) and Airdrie (3–1), with fans demonstrating outside the ground. The team rallied in 1993 but there was yet another downturn after the 2–1 Scottish Cup semi-final defeat to Rangers in April. It culminated in a disastrous 6–0 rout by Jim Jefferies' Falkirk, on May Day. It was the worst defeat since the infamous 7–0 embarrassment by Hibs. And it provoked furious protests from the supporters, including threats of a boycott. Two days after that humiliation at Brockville, Jordan was dismissed. He claimed he had been forced out by senior players whom he referred to as the Tynecastle mafia. Wallace Mercer admitted the decision had caused him 'great heartache' but said he recognised the need for the team to 'adjust its policy and style of football'.

The experience scarred Jordan, as he reveals in his autobiography *Behind the Dream*. He admits that 'the bitterness [he] felt when [he] was fired still lingers', adding:

> I was locked into a professional relationship that was destined to do me and my career damage that in some ways would be irreparable. One moment you have a destiny, the next you do not, and that was always my nagging sense when I worked at Hearts . . . If you are wise, you bury such occasions among the debris of your experience; you shrug your shoulders and make the best of what is before you. It is more difficult when you are obliged to look back and can see, as if drawn on a map, where your journey went amiss.

Sandy Clark once again took control of team affairs but he could not reverse the decline and failed to win any of the last three games. In the end, the team finished the season in fifth place, enough to scrape into Europe once again. The Jordan experiment had failed to advance the team in Europe or at home and average league attendances had dropped below 10,000. The fall-off in spectator numbers was reflected in the club's accounts.

In his annual statement to shareholders, Mercer noted that turnover had fallen by £575,000, with £400,000 of that due to reduced television and other sponsorship income. It was 'of greater concern', however, that gate income was down by £165,000, he said. Once again, a loss of £101,000 before tax was recorded, although interest charges had been reduced and wages only showed a small rise. One factor on top of the pre-tax loss was the £65,000 spent on the failed Hermiston planning application, which led Mercer to backtrack on a previous assertion that 'the decision to move from Tynecastle has already been taken'. With the 1994 deadline for compliance with the Taylor Report looming, he told shareholders in July 1993 the news many fans had been hoping to hear:

> Your directors tried to show vision and ambition in pursuing a 'green field' alternative to Tynecastle and costs have been incurred in the last two years on the Millerhill and Hermiston proposals as the preference for long-term stadium development was identified as an out-of-town location. Lack of political support and commercial subsidy made the directors reconsider their policy in discussion with the supporters and shareholders association and a Tynecastle solution has evolved.

He said the plans for a 20,000-capacity stadium at the club's traditional home had been drawn up by a group of experts and was supported by planning consent and a Football Trust grant. The efforts of architect Jim Clydesdale were singled out for praise by the chairman. The fans would also be expected to help out by paying £500 into a so-called 500 Club. Those who did so would receive discounts on season tickets and merchandise in return for their investment.

Mercer expressed satisfaction with the financial results during 1992–93, particularly as it was a period of recession, and anticipated that they would further improve in the future. The football side of the business was also flourishing, he added, with seven international players in the first team squad. In addition, Craig Levein had experienced the honour of becoming the first Hearts player to be Scotland captain for thirty-five years (the last being Dave Mackay) and, during the 1–0 defeat by Berti Vogts' Germany at Ibrox, four Hearts players had been in the same international side for the first time in fifty-five years. But the man who had steered the Hearts roller coaster for the past twelve years would not be there to enjoy future successes. Mercer, who appeared to be spending increasing amounts of time abroad in the south of France, dropped a bombshell. He said:

> Commercially, the company has never been better constituted with some excellent contracts. In addition, the company has a solution should it wish to pursue it in regard to the Taylor Report at Tynecastle and an enthusiastic young manager who has produced significant results with our younger players. It is with considerable confidence and pride that I report these results not only currently but for the future of Heart of Midlothian in what has been the most difficult recession for a generation. After twelve challenging and invigorating years as chairman, I have decided, for family reasons, to spend more time abroad and, should a suitable offer be made which in my view reflects the value of the business and its potential (for Pentland Securities Holdings Limited which owns 75.1% of the company), then it would be considered seriously.

He had saved Hearts from part-time football at best and closure at worst. He guided the club through the miserable days of being a near-certainty for relegation from the Premier Division to allow the fans a tantalising whiff of glory in 1985–86 and in subsequent European campaigns. The team was packed with internationals, the finances had been stabilised and a modern commercial approach adopted. Sectarian bigots had generally been silenced and there was genuine hope for the future. Yet some of those who chanted

Mercer's name in acclaim had more recently been calling for his head. The loss of the Sandy Jardine and Alex MacDonald management duo and the appointment of the unpopular Joe Jordan were regarded by many as a mistake. The sale of John Robertson and release of several other key players were inexcusable to a portion of the support.

The accounts which accompanied Mercer's message that he was prepared to sell his stake in the club showed that bank borrowings had reached £3.8 million but, at the same time, the stadium and land were valued at £5.5 million and the directors' report 'conservatively put a value of £7 million on the senior members of the playing squad'.

Mercer and the board had shown the ambition to provide a bigger transfer budget than ever before as Rangers stretched away from the rest of Scottish football on their way to winning nine titles in a row. But some questioned his commitment to the club, regarding him as a 'Rangers man' due to his early associations with the Glasgow club. However, the final straw for most was the ill-fated attempt to close down Hibs and create an Edinburgh super team, with all the uncertainties that held for Hearts as well as for their great rivals. His declaration that a decision had been taken to move away from Tynecastle was also unpopular, as Chris Robinson has discovered more recently. But he regained respect when he made the announcement about remaining at Tynecastle and afterwards when he began work on the 5,900-capacity Wheatfield Stand. The day he walked out of Tynecastle, the frame of the new Wheatfield Stand was going up.

Mercer believes he achieved many of his objectives but also acknowledges making mistakes. He says:

> I would probably wish to be known not only as the club's longest serving chairman in its history but also for being part of making Hearts more socially acceptable by raising their public profile on social positions and issues of the day such as unemployment and religion. That all culminated in a substantial increase in gates both home and away with the spin-off benefit of a much more competitive

team with many internationalists which took Hearts to sadly missing the league by six minutes and losing the cup in a seven day period.

Mercer also acknowledges a series of disappointments over a two-year period or so towards the end of his spell in charge. There are three things in particular that he pinpoints:

The Hibs takeover which we could have concluded – we could have gone on with that but I pulled that because it showed to me that social engineering wasn't going to work; the failure of developing the business further with Joe Jordan as the manager, thinking that major appointment would take Hearts on to a different level; and the failure to unlock Hermiston as a way forward for the club – these three things together made me decide that, as owner of Hearts football club, I had taken the business as far as I could and, for the betterment of the club and my own peace of mind, I should hand over to a new group.

12

NEW OWNERS, NEW HEARTS

Sandy Clark's team had made an erratic start to season 1993–94, with the new side finding it even more difficult to score than Joe Jordan's stuffy line-ups had. There were memorable victories – the 2–1 win over Atletico Madrid in Edinburgh, although that was followed by an error-strewn 3–0 defeat in Spain, and against Hibs in the Scottish Cup when Wayne Foster tucked home a late, decisive goal. But Hearts went no further in the cup and league results were even worse than in the previous year. The team scored less than a goal a game and still faced the possibility of relegation on the final day of the season. They escaped that fate with a 1–0 win over Partick Thistle but it had been an unconvincing season and big-name newcomers such as Maurice Johnston and Justin Fashanu had failed to live up to expectations.

Rumours of a takeover by former Rangers manager Graeme Souness proved unfounded and it was the less colourful combination of an Edinburgh lawyer, Leslie Deans, and caterer, Chris Robinson, who stepped forward to buy-out Wallace Mercer in 1994. The purchase of just over 50% of the club, two-thirds of Mercer's holding with the remainder following some years down the line, was concluded by their company, New Hearts Ltd, in a £2.1 million deal.

However, the accounts issued shortly after their arrival showed a pre-tax loss of £862,000, which was attributed to the fact that no major transfers had brought cash in. Of even greater concern, bank borrowings topped £4 million in the summer of 1994. And

Robinson, who was appointed chairman, hinted at his displeasure when, in bland terms, he revealed that a review of the club's accounting systems had identified the need for new 'reporting procedures, systems and controls'. He added, 'These will enable the company to improve its financial management, which will be essential given the current trend of losses and the level of indebtedness.' He would later expand on that, describing the set-up as containing 'major weaknesses in financial management'. The criticisms aimed at the previous regime were the first salvos in a dispute which would later lead Mercer to successfully take court action to protect his title as honorary life president of the club with access to the directors' box and a car parking pass. It would also lead to a disagreement which Mercer says 'was related to the financial position of the company which they thought was in better shape than it was'. Robinson still maintains there were issues involving the finances at the time, although Mercer denies such claims.

In any case, Robinson promised to continue with the redevelopment of Tynecastle, although he described it as a 'last resort' which had gone ahead because, if it did not, reduced attendances in the post-Taylor-Report era could force the club out of business. Further, he announced that so-called 'club' shares (shares whose holders had only limited voting rights at meetings etc.) would be offered to the public in a bid to raise much-needed cash.

Sandy Clark had performed well when he was in charge of the youngsters at Tynecastle and some of them went on to forge successful careers but the first team results had been disappointing under his stewardship. One of the first decisions of the new board, then, was to sack Clark and appoint former Motherwell manager Tommy McLean. The decision still rankles with some Hearts fans and it may have contributed to the frosty reception given to the new boss. McLean may have done well with a cash-strapped Motherwell – guiding them to a Scottish Cup victory in 1991 and a third-place league finish while Hearts struggled during 1993–94 – but he had also been part of the 1965 Kilmarnock team which painfully snatched the league title from Hearts' grasp. Some believed there should be no forgiveness for such cruelty. Despite Clark's treatment when he had been given little time or money to build a competitive team, a significant number of fans were prepared to give the new majority shareholders and McLean the benefit of the doubt. But some of the players were not as generous, as Dave McPherson revealed in *A Tale of Two Cities*:

> Throughout the season various bits of news filtered back to the dressing-room. It was rumoured that [McLean] and the chairman weren't on speaking terms and you could tell that he wasn't happy at the club. As a result the players became increasingly disenchanted. I reckoned that, having enjoyed the relative security of his position at Fir Park, where he also had a seat on the board, he didn't really adjust to not having the same kind of clout and relationship with the directors. We all gave it our best shot, but on the park we were struggling and everyone knew something had to give.

McPherson was right – something did have to give. When senior players such as McPherson described McLean's attitude as one of 'doom and gloom' where he expected defeats and told the players as much, there was little surprise that change came in the form of the man in the dugout.

The 1994–95 season had certainly been disappointing, with McPherson describing it as the worst he had ever experienced in the game. There could hardly have been a worse start when team-mates Craig Levein and Graeme Hogg exchanged blows in a pre-season friendly against Raith Rovers. The competitive action was not much better, although McLean was hampered when he was forced to sell prize asset Alan McLaren to Rangers for a reported £1.25 million to help with the cost of building the new Wheatfield Stand. The players who came in failed to make significant progress in the league and, after yet another late battle against relegation, the team ended up in sixth place. The Scottish Cup had looked more hopeful as Hearts beat Rangers 4–2 on the way to the semi-final. But another soul-destroying defeat by bogey team Airdrie (1–0) ended the club's hopes for the season.

McLean's cause had not been helped by the injury to Stevie Frail and the sale of McLaren but he was given cash for new players such as Brian Hamilton and David Hagen. The share issue the new board had organised was a flop, with only 1,700 subscribers raising just £147,000 after expenses had been deducted. Clearly, the investment could do little to 'add strength and quality to the existing player pool' as had been hoped. Hearts attracted some criticism for the issue because the 'club' shares on offer gave only limited rights, essentially to vote for representative directors on the board but little else of substance.

The club did make a pre-tax profit of £436,000 through player sales but completion of the 3,700-seat Roseburn Stand at the school end in 1995 was yet another drain on resources. Although, by this time, supporters had contributed £582,000 through the 500 Club, debt levels were still rising, with borrowings now exceeding £5million.

It also emerged that McLean had offered his resignation during the season. It was clear the differences between the manager and the board were irreconcilable when he was sacked for 'unreasonable behaviour' in the summer break. Hearts had gone through four managers in as many years and the process of finding a replacement would now have to start all over again.

At least this time there appeared to be a ready-made replacement with a proven track record who would also prove popular with the fans. Jim Jefferies was a former Hearts player and captain and a boyhood supporter. He had taken Falkirk into the Premier Division twice and finished fifth, one place above Hearts the previous season. After a period of uncertainty, with Jefferies unable to make up his mind whether to move to Hearts or remain at Falkirk, he eventually decided to take the 'dream appointment' at Tynecastle along with assistant Billy Brown.

Jefferies immediately set about changing the formation and style of play to become more attacking. He also re-examined the bonus system, which he saw as rewarding 'losers', and sought to change the personnel, some of whom, he believed, 'should never have been allowed through the front door'. The low point was a 2–0 defeat by his old club in October. With the team bottom of the league, it was decided that even more radical surgery was needed. Jefferies' determination to foster a better team spirit and banish negative attitudes was also crucial. It was a strategy which would transform the club that season and reap even greater rewards in the years ahead. Jefferies described the mood he inherited in *All Heart*:

> I had been away from the club for thirteen years and I was quickly aware of a strange atmosphere around the place, almost a feeling that there was some form of mystical jinx at the place, with an undercurrent that things were just not going to happen here. There seemed to be an acceptance that we were destined not to do anything about it.

Also in 1995, the European Court of Justice had ruled in favour of an otherwise little-known Belgian player who had been blocked from transferring to a new club because of a prohibitively high transfer valuation. Jean-Marc Bosman's legal victory and the relaxation of the three-foreigner rule meant that football players, along with other European Union workers, should be allowed free movement between member states. Transfer fees would no longer be payable at the end of a footballer's contract and previous restrictions on players approaching other clubs to initiate a move were also lifted. The transfer system, as it had been known, was dead. Jefferies moved quickly to take advantage of this sea change, securing the signatures of former French international keeper Gilles Rousset and Italian hardman Pasquale Bruno, who had played for Fiorentina, Torino and Juventus. Other experienced players, including Neil Pointon and Stevie Fulton, were brought in and given their place in the team alongside youngsters such as Paul Ritchie, Gary Locke and Allan Johnston. As with Alex MacDonald, it was to prove a winning combination. Hearts went on to finish fourth in the league, on the same points as third-place Aberdeen, with memorable matches such as the 3–0 triumph at

Ibrox when Johnston scored a hat-trick. And the team also reached its first Scottish Cup final for ten years, although they were out-classed by Rangers 5–1 on the day and captain Locke picked up a serious knee ligament injury.

Huge advances had been made on the pitch under Jefferies but taking the club forward was proving costly. The opening of the Roseburn Stand, as well as the attacking football on display, had boosted average crowds by 20% to more than 12,000. Gate receipts rose by an even more impressive 45%. Yet a loss of £2 million was recorded. The Bosman ruling had allowed Jefferies to bring in some quality players but it also effectively reduced the value of those at the club. The capital cost of refurbishing the stadium was also proving a burden and the fans would have to contribute more for the Gorgie Road Stand to be built at an estimated cost of £2.5 million. Chris Robinson said a second 500 Club would be required to raise the cash. He issued a rallying call to shareholders in 1996, insisting that the club was moving towards a 'new and potentially profitable era' despite the debt levels. However, the completion of the third stand was central to that because it would contain corporate facilities, a new club shop and, of course, more seats for paying customers. According to Robinson, it would be possible to manage the debts when 'the new team and stadium deliver progress and results'.

The fans delivered their side of the bargain, snapping up 8,000 season tickets to fill the sparkling new stands. Jefferies, too, pur-sued the aim of putting together a winning team on the park with vigour. Midfielder Colin Cameron had already joined the club from Raith Rovers, while defender David Weir arrived from Falkirk and winger Neil McCann and, later, Jim Hamilton arrived from Dundee. Former AC Milan player Stefano Salvatori was then brought over from Italy, although the Hearts suffered their first loss under the Bosman rule when Allan Johnston moved to Rennes under freedom of contract.

Two cup competitions gave early encouragement to the support-ers. A tough Cup Winners' Cup draw against Yugoslav side Red

Star Belgrade kicked off the season and the team secured a commendable 0–0 draw in the away leg. A 1–1 scoreline in the second leg ensured Hearts went out on away goals but they had acquitted themselves well. Next it was the League Cup, which included a tense 1–0 win over Celtic in the quarter-finals despite having a depleted first-team squad because of four red cards three days before at Ibrox. The final paired Hearts once again with Rangers and, although they lost out by the odd goal in a 4–3 thriller, the spirit with which they fought their way back into the game after going 2–0 down inspired renewed belief that success was on the horizon. It did not come in the league, with a fourth-place finish, but the team had certainly consolidated under Jefferies.

Senior professionals moved on but valuable additions were made ahead of the new season. Midfielder Gary Mackay, who appeared a record 738 times for Hearts, joined Airdrie on a free transfer while veterans John Colquhoun moved to St Johnstone and defender Craig Levein retired due to injury. Pasquale Bruno was released by the manager. Another legend, John Robertson, decided to remain at Tynecastle and he held the club's then all-time league goal-scoring record of 208 – overtaking Jimmy Wardhaugh – when he scored a double in the win against Rangers on the final day of the season. Robertson went on to score another six goals for Hearts in 1997–98, taking his overall total to 310. He was now joined by fresh talent from the continent under the Bosman rule, notably French striker Stephane Adam and Austrian utility player Thomas Flogel.

There was no doubt that a feel-good factor had arrived at Tynecastle. Chris Robinson, who had taken up the post of chief executive while Leslie Deans became chairman, certainly thought so when he described 1996–97 as 'one of the most significant in the company's history'. The decision had been taken for Hearts to become the first Scottish club to obtain a full listing on the London Stock Exchange by issuing new £1.40 shares, despite the loss of control over ownership and shift in focus towards maximising returns for shareholders which that entailed.

The move was in keeping with the times. Football in England in particular was becoming increasingly fashionable. The Heysel and Hillsborough era appeared to be a thing of the past and the clubs were competing in Europe once again and attracting the world of business as never before. The arrival of big-spending BSkyB in England in 1992 and increased competition from terrestrial broadcasters resulted in a live and highlights rights package of more than £300 million that year. And the promise was of untold riches both north and south of the border when new contracts were negotiated with the satellite company around the time Jefferies was putting together his team. No doubt inspired by television's interest, other sponsors also rushed to sign up with football clubs. Likewise, there was a flood of clubs trading on the stock market after the successful flotation of Manchester United in 1991.

It was therefore a satisfied Robinson who reported that the Hearts' flotation had raised more than £5 million, although his shareholding along with Deans had been diluted to 45% of the club. The board said the money from the share issue would be put towards the new Gorgie Stand and the installation of a new playing surface with under-soil heating. Bank loans and the overdraft were reduced by £3 million, leaving net debt at £1.9 million. Turnover was up by a reassuring 13% but a pre-tax loss of £1.5 million was nevertheless recorded.

Robinson reported that season ticket sales were again healthy and the new strip was expected to sell 10,000 by the start of the following season, making it the most commercially successful strip in the club's history. He also highlighted income from broadcasting rights and sponsorship as growth areas which would help to realise the prediction to shareholders that he was 'confident that Scottish professional football is set to enjoy a new era of improved quality, entertainment and profitability following the completion by the major clubs of their stadia redevelopments'.

Robinson's optimism was shared by Jefferies, although he was more concerned with the future events on the park. In the 1997 annual report, the manager boldly said, 'I look forward to the day when we surely will take one step nearer to winning a trophy.'

With the new 3,300-capacity Gorgie Stand opened at the end of 1997, complete with club shop and corporate facilities, the challenge of building the new stadium appeared to have been met. Losses were being sustained but the overdraft had at least been reduced. Both the manager and the board were looking forward with confidence. The seeds for a speculate-to-accumulate policy were sown and the sense of progress held the lure of trophy success. But, as with any advance, it also raised the possibility of a dramatic fall from grace – or both. Season 1997–98 would prove pivotal in the history of Hearts.

13

FROM TRIUMPH TO TRAGEDY

It started with an inauspicious, if not entirely unpredictable, 3–1 defeat by Rangers at Ibrox. It would be the first of many disappointments against the Old Firm but results against other teams picked up and Hearts were challenging for the league by the turn of the year. They continued gathering points in 1998 but unfortunately their form dropped off towards the end of the season. Jim Jefferies later said he knew one or two quality players were needed to strengthen the squad and sustain the challenge. His request for transfer cash was turned down by the board but the temptation of spending freely to build a title-winning side would yet return to haunt the club. In any case, they had failed to beat the Glasgow two, who proved too strong in the end – Celtic won the title, preventing Rangers from making it ten league wins in a row. Hearts finished third, just five points behind Rangers.

But, if the high-scoring style of play favoured by Hearts resulted in too many leaked league goals, it appeared suited to the knock-out format of the Scottish Cup. Helped by a kind draw which paired them against lower league teams at Tynecastle, they eased past Clydebank (2–0), Albion Rovers (3–0) and Ayr United (4–1) before meeting Falkirk in the semi-final at Ibrox. The First Division side proved much tougher opposition but Hearts eventually over-came them 3–1 with two late goals, despite being outplayed for long spells by Falkirk.

Hearts had prepared thoroughly for the final – taking the team to a training base in England and even tempting fate by tantalising the players with details of the celebrations should a victory be secured. The scene was set for a classic showpiece match as Hearts lined up against Rangers at Celtic Park on 16 May 1998, while Hampden was still being redeveloped. Around 22,000 Hearts fans in the 49,000 crowd looked on in disbelief when Stevie Fulton was brought down for a questionable penalty a minute after the whistle had gone. In fact, some estimated the award had been given before 3 p.m. – revenge for the goal Rangers scored to take the lead in the 1976 final. Colin Cameron calmly banged home the spot kick and the Hearts supporters celebrated, barely able to believe that they could be ahead in this make-or-break game. Their optimism, however, was dulled by the fact there were 89 minutes still to go. The system adopted by Jim Jefferies – packing the midfield and hitting on the counter-attack, rather than the usual three up front – did little to calm the nerves as Rangers piled on the pressure. But the tactic worked to perfection when Rangers defender Lorenzo Amoruso failed to cut out a long ball. Stephane Adam nipped in behind the Italian and slotted the ball past Andy Goram in 53 minutes. Now the Hearts fans started to believe it could be their day. Rangers, desperate not to finish the season without any trophies, pushed forward and there was no real surprise when Ally McCoist scored with nine minutes to go. Five minutes later and with Hearts still on the back foot, Rangers looked to have been awarded a penalty but the referee gave a free kick on the edge of the box. Despite a number of heart-stopping goalmouth scrambles and match-saving stops from Gilles Rousset, Hearts held on until the final whistle – four minutes into injury time. Such was the bedlam at the Hearts end that many fans could not even hear the referee blow for time. So strongly entrenched was the fear that the team could never win a trophy, that some believed the Hearts bench had run on to the pitch prematurely and they would be ushered off as the final, nail-biting seconds were played out to an inevitable tragic end. In the event, it soon became clear that the cherished dream had become a reality. After a barren thirty-six years without any trophies to celebrate and forty-two years since the last Scottish Cup, the nearly-men of Scottish football would have their names etched on a piece of silverware, their feats logged in the record books.

The reaction at Celtic Park was certainly one of jubilation, particularly when skipper and Hearts fan Gary Locke – who had missed the game through injury – was called on to the pitch to lift the trophy jointly with match captain Fulton. And again, when John Robertson – who Jefferies had planned to bring on but left on the bench because he did not want to upset the team in those nerve-wracking final minutes – raised the cup, he held the Hearts crest on his jersey and quietly dedicated the medal in his hand to his late father. Yet, amongst the celebrations, there was an over-whelming sense of simple, inner relief – or perhaps it was uncer-tainty about exactly how to celebrate a trophy triumph. If that was the case in the unfamiliar surroundings of a Celtic Park still under construction, it was no longer the case as the supporters started to arrive back in Edinburgh.

Even on the outskirts of the city, people were lining the streets, flags and banners flew from sunroofs and car horns responded to the waves and cheers from the pavements. Most headed for Gorgie where the streets and bars thronged with Hearts fans finally able to celebrate in style. The players joined in too, climb-ing onto the roof of the team bus after it arrived back in Gorgie. If anything the scenes were even more remarkable the following day as the Hearts open-top bus began its journey at the City Chambers in the High Street, past the site of the old Heart of Midlothian Tolbooth, before winding its way down the Mound and inching along Princes Street towards Haymarket and then along Gorgie Road to Tynecastle. Edinburgh is a city familiar with observing historic occasions and it seemed this was in the minds of its citi-zens when an astonishing 200,000 packed the streets to witness this parade. The Hearts fans themselves, of course, turned out in previously unseen numbers. Hanging from windows, huddled on top of bus shelters, straddling walls and perched on phone boxes – anywhere that would provide the best vantage point. The party continued in the sunshine at Tynecastle or it did for those who made it that far – with players and their children juggling the famous old trophy as fans applauded.

The supporters, the team and the management duo, of course, had every reason to bask in the reflected glory of the cup through the summer months of 1998. Jim Jefferies said:

> It is a source of great pride and personal pleasure that I managed the first Hearts football team to a major honour for thirty-six years. Having supported Hearts as a youngster, I have fulfilled the dream of playing for the club, managing the club and now winning silverware.

And Leslie Deans still recalls the triumph as the proudest moment in his time at the club. He says:

> There was immense pride and pleasure in being the first chairman of Hearts football club in forty-two years to return with the Scottish Cup and it will stay in my memory as long as I live. It was a wonderful experience and one I have relived many times since, although the credit goes to Jim Jefferies and the guys on the park.

The 1997–98 annual report statement paid tribute to the achievement as well, while also taking encouragement from the 20,000 replica jerseys sold during the season past as well as the upturn in hospitality and banqueting. Meanwhile, gate receipts, with an average home attendance of some 15,000, showed a huge 40% increase to bring in more than £4 million. But there were niggling concerns. Staff costs were also up by a third, to £3.8 million, and other operating charges rose by more than £1 million. The club made a loss of £1.9 million and net debt had risen almost three-fold to £5.5 million. There were even concerns that winning the cup would actually cost the club through the £10,000 bonuses to players and effectively sharing season ticket revenue with away teams in every early round of the cup. The fans would have to reward the success by pumping more money into the club through merchandise sales and continuing to back the team in 1998–99.

Chris Robinson appeared to recognise the future challenges

when he said, 'In the current post-Bosman era there is considerable inflationary pressure on players' wages and, like all major professional football clubs, we shall see a significant increase in our wage costs.' However, he promised that the increase was 'carefully budgeted'. Indeed, the new Scottish Premier League had formed as a breakaway from the rest of the league and there was confidence it could cash in on sponsorship and marketing rights without undue interference from the smaller clubs. Robinson insisted that a series of deals had already been negotiated with BSkyB, other broadcasters and commercial companies which would guarantee the new league at least £70 million over four years. Hearts season ticket sales were already up by a third to 11,000. Robinson made his intention clear, saying, 'If we continue to invest in all aspects of the business and, in particular, in the strength of playing squad, the company can see significant added value, improved profitability and a secure trading platform for future growth.' The speculate-to-accumulate policy was gathering pace.

14

THE HEARTS FAMILY AT WAR

The desperation to secure silverware for the Tynecastle trophy room had bordered on obsession as the comments from a succession of fans, players and Hearts staff illustrated.

Dave McPherson, a player who achieved everything the Scottish game had to offer, concluded *A Tale of Two Cities* with his understated hopes for the future. He said:

> One ambition I've got left is to win a medal with Hearts. It's hard to explain just how much it means to the Hearts fans . . . Everybody's dream down Gorgie way is finally to take that journey in an open-topped bus through the streets of Edinburgh . . . I'm lucky enough to have a fair collection of medals and caps, but after so many years of second prizes, holding a trophy with maroon and white ribbons on it would top the lot.

McPherson was fortunate – he fulfilled his ambition, as did the others connected with the club in May 1998 – but there was a danger that the drive to win something with Hearts, fuelled by the failures of 1965 and 1986, as well as many other mishaps along the way, would push the club beyond its limits. It is difficult to fault Jim Jefferies and his players or, indeed, Leslie Deans, Chris Robinson and their directors for trying to achieve what every other Hearts fans wanted – sustained success. And, given that previous triumphs occurred over ten- to fifteen-year periods, that may have been a reasonable assumption. But the football environment towards the end of the twentieth century was very different to that at the turn of nineteenth or even that of the 1950s and 60s.

One way or another, the cup win seemed to act as a release to the pressure which had been building up inside Tynecastle. It was at this time that the first cracks in the relationship between Deans and Robinson appeared. Deans expressed concern about a possible salary increase for Robinson. The chief executive, who, in turn, raised the issue of fees claimed by Deans for attending a series of SPL meetings, even threatened to resign over the issue. In the end, the matter was resolved before it escalated further. A wage rise of around £18,000 was agreed for Robinson, while the chairman received £5,000 to cover his costs for going to the meetings.

In any case, the season started well in 1998–99 with a 2–1 victory over Rangers but was followed by a run of mixed results. The last year of the Cup Winners' Cup drew Hearts first against Estonian minnows FC Lantana and they won comfortably 6–0 on aggregate. The next round was to prove more eventful. The draw paired them with Spanish side Real Mallorca and, despite a 1–0 home defeat, Hearts were determined to extend their European run. The build-up to the game on the Spanish holiday island in October 1998 verged on the farcical. Robinson's claims that there was an uneven surface in one of the goal mouths and, therefore, they were too small in places led to an unseemly row with the club. Hearts made a formal complaint and the game was eventually played under protest. The complaint was later thrown out by UEFA, who deemed it inadmissible because it had not been put in writing before the game. There is some irony in the fact that the Spanish side's pitch was deemed suitable for European football – in fact Mallorca went on to appear as losing finalists in that season's Cup Winners' Cup final – when Hearts would fall foul of similar rules in the years ahead.

The hangover from Spain seemed to linger on during the domestic campaign and, remarkably, the team which challenged for the double the previous season found itself potentially struggling against relegation when it sank to the foot of the table after a hapless 2–0 defeat by Dundee in March 1999.

It later transpired that the slump had prompted the board to consider sacking Jim Jefferies, despite his recent cup success. But a deteriorating Tynecastle pitch and the loss of Scotland internationals Neil McCann to Rangers for £1.6 million and David Weir to Everton were more significant reasons for the cup dream turning sour. Proven players such as Steven Pressley and Gary McSwegan were brought in but they were joined by bargain-basement flops – Leigh Jenkinson and Mo Berthe among others – for which Jefferies, even given his much-reduced budget, must take responsibility.

The injury to key midfielder Colin Cameron had been a particular problem and his return to fitness, along with the signing of ex-Hibs player Darren Jackson for £300,000 from Celtic, eventually turned things around. However, the team still finished a disappointing sixth and out of the European places. The League Cup was even more of a let down, with the team dumped 3–0 by St Johnstone in the semi-finals after a dreadful performance at neutral Easter Road.

The cup success had also masked a growing rift between Chris Robinson and the fans. First, the club announced a new official club logo had been designed, with the traditional heart-shaped badge now surrounded by a circle and the letters HMFC removed from the four segments of the old heart and replaced by the words 'Heart of Midlothian' in the new outer circle. The traditional lettering was ditched in favour of a more modern typeface. The club magazine explained in the summer of 1997 that the new design was 'a fine marriage of the old and the new'. It added, 'A strengthened St Andrew's Cross and the tan ball in the middle reinstate elements from the original logo from the last century but still portray a fresh, crisp image.' The new badge was to be used on official paperwork and documents but, crucially, it would also appear on the team kit. Traditionalists were furious.

A heart-shaped badge had been sewn on to the very first club strip in 1875 and it appeared on several subsequent jerseys. It largely disappeared from strips for much of the twentieth century but a crest with a ball surrounded by a heart enclosed in a circle was used on club stationery, season tickets and other documents during the 1890s and beyond. In 1954, a badge similar to today's – a copy of the Heart of Midlothian that is set in the cobbles at the entrance to the old Tolbooth in the High Street – was painted over the players' tunnel. It also began to be worn on club blazers but not strips and was commonly used as the official crest in subsequent years. The heart-shaped crest even formed the basis of the 1954 League Cup winning medals awarded to the victorious players. However, it did not appear on the Hearts strip until 1977–78, where it has remained since. The heart shape, worn on the left side of the chest was unusual but highly appropriate. For these reasons and the fact that it first appeared in its modern form during the 1950s golden era, the badge was extremely popular with fans. The suggestion that it was to be changed, with what was regarded as inadequate consultation, provoked uproar among a section of the fans. The cause was taken up by the Federation of Hearts Supporters Clubs, which wrote to the club. But the response from Robinson only served to aggravate the situation when he famously described the old lettering as an 'Olde English typeface more appropriate to a tearoom in the Cotswalds (sic) than a Scottish football club'. In his letter, Robinson added:

> We believe that the current version is no longer appropriate. It is very poor reprographically and in many other ways ... The new badge has met with great approval from those who have had an opportunity to view [it]. I would venture that your statement is inaccurate in saying that the current badge is historic, given that it has changed from the original. We would also contend that the vast majority of Hearts supporters will welcome the change.

He was even more outspoken in an interview with the fanzine *No Idle Talk*, when he said the old badge had been 'prostituted over the years'. He then hit out at his critics, adding:

> You guys don't know the first thing about the history of the club badge ... I've watched this club since the 1950s and the badge you are getting your knickers in a twist about is a modern invention. It

was a modern invention which was designed to make the club more olde worldy. The original badge is on the floor in the hall of the club. We've actually gone back towards the real original badge. What you guys don't like is change.

Robinson was wrong if he hoped that the matter would quietly disappear. The club soon announced that changes would be made so that the crest on the strip and other merchandise would remain close to the fans' favourite. The only significant change to a second heart-shaped design – described as the 'new corporate identity' – would be new clean lettering. Robinson explained in another letter that the corporate identity would be used where reference was being made to the *company* name, Heart of Midlothian plc. He added that a new design would be protected by trademark, which was not possible with the traditional crest because it was so widely copied and abused by others. He insisted:

> There is no intention to use the full corporate identity throughout the range of merchandising, strips etc. . . . On all stationery, printed material, signage and other appropriate mediums the full corporate identity will appear. We are, therefore, able to redefine the image of the club whilst holding on to the best tradition.

The compromise appeased most, though not all, fans.

But relations with the chief executive were further strained over several other squabbles. He niggled some by changing the ground's traditional name from Tynecastle Park – made famous in the opening lines to the Hearts song – to Tynecastle Stadium. And there was anger at suggestions that the Willie Bauld restaurant could be renamed the Premier Suite, although the titles were eventually combined as a compromise.

Then, Robinson was accused of describing supporters at a Youth Cup semi-final as 'parasites' when a row about using season tickets for access to the match broke out. It is more likely he actually called them 'pathetic', although misplaced anger over the 'parasites' insult remains today. Robinson did little to appease his critics when, in November 1998, he launched into a tirade against the supporters' federation and its committee in the fanzine, *No Idle Talk*:

> I'll tell you what, the supporters federation would have been sitting on a tip here if I hadn't come forward, so hell mend them because they have short memories going back to what it was four years ago. If I listened to the federation, this club would never make any progress. My job is to make hard decisions which some supporters don't like ... I have meetings in this office regularly with various members of the committee. These guys are crawling in here looking for help and advice then they are going back to their members and saying let's vote no confidence. So what? On the one hand, they are crawling up us to make sure they get their tickets for Mallorca. It's two-faced stuff.

By 1998, he had received his first full year's salary as chief executive. The award of a package worth £95,000 may have been the going rate for his position but it annoyed some supporters. A 19% increase in remuneration in 1999 to £112,900 invited further criticism, particularly when the season had been so poor.

There was little surprise when the executive committee of the federation met in September 1999 to discuss recent issues involving Chris Robinson, Jim Jefferies and others. The committee gave its full backing to Jefferies but called on Robinson to resign as 'his position has now become untenable and an amicable working relationship with the manager is unlikely'. A vote of no confidence was passed and the board was informed.

Jim Jefferies recognised the difficulties experienced in 1998–99, blaming inconsistency, lack of confidence and the poor playing surface for the below-par performances. He said in the annual report:

> After the heady excitement of winning our first major trophy in 36 years, last year was a major disappointment. Having put together a squad of players which won the cup, the changing face of football affected Hearts. Players who had achieved success with the club decided for their own reasons to move on or take advantage of contractual positions in the post-Bosman era. Although we were

able to add new players to the squad, our plans for the season and building on cup success did not progress as I had hoped.

But the quarrels between Robinson and the fans were not the only troubles behind the scenes at Tynecastle. Jefferies, too, had been reported as unhappy that money had not been made available for new players when Hearts were challenging for the league. The manager was even linked with a possible move to Aberdeen. The speculation prompted Jefferies to commit himself to the club. He then attempted to clear the air in the December 1998 issue of the club magazine, when he said, 'All I did was express ambition and, as far as I am aware, there is no crime in that.' The fact that the manager also attracted headlines over an apparent row with cup-winning midfielder Stafano Salvatori and for leaving striker Jim Hamilton out of his plans suggested all was not well at Hearts.

Jefferies had motivated his triumphant 1998 team by promising them the status of Hearts legends if they brought some silverware back to Tynecastle. Yet he now questioned whether those very players and some others still had the same 'hunger and desire' to win after that cup success. In fact, the scorer of the decisive goal in that final, Stephane Adam, conceded that 'maybe the hunger for victory isn't as great after winning the cup'. However, some of those players were awarded new contracts to fend off other interested clubs. There is no doubt that there was an odd mixture of increased expectation and diminished desire – even among the fans. An editorial *No Idle Talk* summed up the feelings on the terraces in November 1998 when it pointed out that 'there were people at the cup final who said they didn't need to go back because a "lifelong ambition" had been realised and nothing could top it'. Robinson told the same fanzine, 'I think that a lot of people were waiting for a trophy for so long and now they've got it they are quite happy to play golf on a Saturday.' It was certainly true that some supporters seemed to lose interest, although they could not have been tempted much by the football on offer which even the most ardent fan would admit was not of the best quality.

But, by summer 1999, the headline figures suggested that financial stability was returning. At this stage, the debt and wage-inflation issues remained and were acknowledged by Robinson but the club had recorded a profit (of £220,000), the first since 1995. The improved performance was largely because of increased television and other sponsorship revenue in the new breakaway Scottish Premier League, although the sale of Neil McCann in particular helped to balance the books. As a consequence, turnover had reached an encouraging £7.7 million but the figures would look less encouraging in twelve months' time. Ironically, before then, there would be the promise of more, rather than less, cash.

Also in 1999, rumours first emerged of a possible takeover and a boardroom bust-up. Both stories contained some truth, although it was the Glasgow-based company Scottish Media Group (SMG) who moved on Hearts and not the cable company NTL, as had been first suggested.

After months of negotiations through a scheme that went by the odd name of Project Spencer, it was announced in September 1999 that SMG was to invest a massive £8 million in the club. Just over £3.5 million would be ploughed in through the purchase of 19.9% of the club's shares and £4.5 million would come in the form of 'convertible loan stock'. The latter was essentially a loan which could be converted into shares at a later date if SMG chose to take up that option. At the time, SMG said it was the company's 'current intention to convert'. The company revealed the thinking behind the deal in a face-to-face interview for this book:

> We are a plc and we have to take account of risk. While there was nothing immediately on the horizon, there was always the possibility that something might happen in the future which would make investing too deeply in one place as being unadvisable. The whole point of having equity and loan stock was to hedge that risk.

Chris Robinson, on the other hand, described conversion as 'just a matter of timing'. He admits in an interview for this book that the club made no provision for that failing to happen.

The club magazine described it as 'the biggest deal in the club's history, and Robinson was able to outline an ambitious series of spending plans. The £8 million, he said, would provide Jefferies with his first 'meaningful player budget', while it would also go towards a new youth academy and some stadium improvements – like all older grounds, Tynecastle required almost constant running repairs and there was always the pressing need to modernise. SMG was best known as the owner of *The Herald* newspaper and Scottish Television and Robinson hoped that Hearts would benefit from link-ups with the group's companies involved in cinema, outdoor advertising, e-commerce, merchandising and publishing. In corporate language, the idea was to 'build the Hearts brand' and, thereby, raise the club's profile.

SMG, for its part, was one of a number of broadcast organisations keen to secure a foothold in the football industry. BSkyB had launched a high-profile bid for Manchester United in 1998, media companies had invested in Liverpool and Leeds and similar tie-ups existed in France at Paris Saint-Germain, Bordeaux and Lyon and in Italy at AC Milan, as well as elsewhere. And, while no such deal had been struck in Scotland, SMG was well aware of the possibility that Celtic and Rangers could soon get their own satellite or cable TV deals or breakaway from the Scottish set-up altogether and therefore marginalise the mainstream broadcasters. The media group, in the words of those involved in the link-up, 'had to be at the negotiating table' when broadcasting rights were agreed. A memo to senior executives highlighted the two Edinburgh teams and Aberdeen as the most attractive possibilities apart from the Old Firm, with Hearts the preferred option as the club with the most potential outwith Celtic and Rangers.

The purchase of shares at £1.40 each when they were trading for around 94p by SMG was good business from Hearts' point of view, although the decision to spend the convertible loan was clearly a gamble. The value of shares in football clubs was subject to unpredictable fluctuations at this time and would very soon embark on a steady and seemingly irreversible descent.

But the deal had its critics, not least Leslie Deans. Deans had already been replaced by Chris Robinson as the official spokesman of the club – apparently, this was because of the release of conflicting information about the sale of Neil McCann – and it was clear there were tensions between the partners. But the relationship deteriorated further as Project Spencer negotiations continued. Deans resigned three days before the SMG announcement, citing concerns that the link-up would prove damaging in the long-term. He expressed anxiety that the media group may decide not to convert its £4.5 million loan stock into shares. Such a decision, he warned, could financially cripple the club by providing it with cash it had no means of repaying. In addition, he believed that 'no satisfactory answer' was given when he raised this possibility. Yet it was exactly that scenario which 'pushed Hearts to the brink of financial ruin', Deans says today. He takes full responsibility for events that happened during his tenure but insists that debts were manageable when he left. He describes his part in allowing the wage bill to start to spiral as 'minimal', claiming that any suggestion to the contrary would be a distortion. He insists the financial damage was done after he resigned. He was replaced as chairman by Doug Smith.

With so many off-field distractions it was little surprise that performances during 1999–2000 were mixed. New players arrived towards the end of 1999. Serbian defender Gordan Petric, who previously played for Dundee United and Rangers, was signed for £500,000 from AEK Athens on a bumper £8,000-a-week salary, while Jamaican international captain Fitzroy Simpson arrived from Portsmouth for a nominal fee. Later, Finnish international goalkeeper Antti Niemi was bought from Rangers for £400,000 and Slovakian skipper Robert Tomaschek was also added to the squad for a similar fee after moving from Slovan Bratislava. But central defender Paul Ritchie had made it clear he intended to move when his contract expired and was roundly booed by Hearts fans thereafter. Fellow international Gary Naysmith would soon follow him out of Tynecastle.

The changes in personnel seemed to improve Hearts' fortunes. A convincing 4–1 victory over St Johnstone opened the campaign but a solid run was followed by some disappointing results, particularly the 3–0 defeat by Hibs in December. There was some improvement after the turn of the year, including a rare victory at Parkhead (3–2) after being two goals down. The team also gained revenge for the earlier derby loss by beating Hibs 2–1 on the final day of the season to finish third and qualify for Europe, although there was no notable progress in the cups.

There had also been cause for genuine optimism with the announcement in February that Hearts were to join forces with Heriot-Watt University to build a new £5 million youth academy. The facility was to be built on the Riccarton campus, with the university providing the land and an additional £1.5 million. Hearts, with support from sportscotland, would contribute £3.5 million and the construction of the academy would be to their specification. It would include training pitches, a sports science and medicine centre and rehabilitation facilities for injured players. Hearts staff and university students would share the facility in a joint venture unique to Scotland. It was hoped the doors would open by 2001, although this completion date would overrun by almost three years after a contractor went into receivership.

But that could not disguise the financial troubles mounting at Tynecastle. Cash was needed for the youth academy and Jim Jefferies had been permitted a £1.2-million splurge in the transfer market, although Chris Robinson later added that a further £1 million had gone on signing-on fees and £300,000 in agents' commission. But by the end of the season, Jefferies was already telling the club magazine:

> It was well publicised about the investment, and we knew some of the money was to be kept for the academy also. It was highlighted that we would have a considerable part of the money for signings. Maybe there was not as much as people were told, but everyone looked to us to make signings . . . We must make space available because the resources aren't there. It is unfortunate and maybe we

thought there was more money, but that is the way it is and we will get on with it.

Chief executive Chris Robinson also admitted that it had been a 'roller-coaster season'. He acknowledged that the club had turned a corner and the big-spending days were over. The prospect of capitalising on the 1998 cup win and cashing in on the SMG investment had quickly disappeared. Losses were running close to £250,000 a month and the speculate-to-accumulate policy, while helping to secure that trophy success, had failed to pay financial dividends. Robinson admitted as much when he told the *Hearts* magazine in summer 2000:

> Over recent years the club has made heavy losses and no company – especially a listed plc – can continue to sustain losses and increase the level of borrowing. The 1998 season, with our cup win, clearly demonstrated that the speculate-to-accumulate theory does not hold water. There is no instant panacea to increase crowds and revenue at Hearts. Supporters can rightly argue that, to get the best players, you have to pay the best wages and/or high transfer fees. However, with a total sales turnover of £7–8 million, it should not be difficult to realise that big money signings are not a reality. At present, our total wage bill is not far short of our total income. So the board strategy is to increase income and bring wage costs into line ... We know that many supporters simply always want to see new faces and players bought. However, since the SMG investment we have brought a new core of players to the team. We can't keep adding and adding.

He later went further in an interview with the *Daily Record*:

> You grow in life and learn from your experience and mistakes and I've made plenty of mistakes at Hearts ... Perhaps at times I should have been stronger in not spending money on the team but had that happened I would have been hounded out ... I'm not for one minute sitting here refusing to accept responsibility. We did ride with the market and at times we have been over-ambitious.

Proposals included more direct marketing and merchandising but, importantly, it had been agreed that the aim was to reduce what an article in the club magazine called 'the current spiralling wage bill'. Robinson dressed it up as a progressive attempt to adopt the French system of maintaining a relatively small squad of up to twenty-one senior professionals, augmented by youngsters coming through the ranks. The chief executive said such a system would help to avoid dealing with 'greedy' agents and would, therefore, minimise costs. Of course, it also meant getting rid of players. In the club magazine, Robinson spoke of how 'the final piece of the jigsaw' was, ironically, to make Tynecastle bigger and better, with a 22,000 capacity and improved corporate facilities to boost income levels.

From the high of the cup final win and the hope of the SMG investment, Hearts fans were forced to face a new reality – too much had been spent on players and their wages. Now it was time for cutbacks.

15

FOOTBALL FINANCES IN THE NEW MILLENNIUM

The 2000 annual report and accounts did not make pleasant reading.

Chairman Doug Smith wasted no time in admitting in his statement to shareholders that 'we have clearly not yet seen the move to the next level which was hoped for by the SMG investment'. The target turnover of £10 million, with a near-capacity average crowd, had not been achieved. Indeed, not only had the club failed to move to the next level, a year after the cash injection, it now seemed to be heading backwards. Record pre-tax losses of £3.7 million had been endured during 1999–2000, with staff costs soaring 40% to £5.6 million. Meanwhile, gate receipts from a reduced average attendance of 14,200 and other income both fell. Worryingly, the wage bill was now almost 80% of turnover. Or, as Smith said, 'The losses announced reflect increased costs of investing in the playing squad not being matched by increased revenue levels ... The contrast between the on-field results and the financial losses is stark and at an unacceptable level.' In addition, net debt was up to £6.8 million.

The club had suffered some bad luck but had also overspent. The full impact of the Bosman ruling was starting to take effect, with Hearts increasing their wage bill while, at the same time, losing out on transfer fees from players sold on to other clubs. Jefferies, in turn, had explained in his 1998 book *All Heart* how he dreamed that 'the day will come when I will be handed a lump sum of money, for me to spend just as I wished to bring in the players I thought could take the club up another step of the progress ladder'. Yet that seemingly spendthrift attitude was married to a prescient sense of reality when he added:

> There is every likelihood that, in the early stages of this new era, clubs will pay out big money in wages for four or five players but then find they cannot afford to go on like this. Whether we like it or not, football is business and clubs have to live within their means.

There was uncertainty about the effect of the so-called Bosman-2 ruling, which abolished domestic transfer fees for players over the age of twenty-four, although made provision for compensation for younger players. Publicity over the possibility of Rangers and Celtic joining a European league also placed a question mark over the future of Scottish football. More money had been lost when kit supplier Olympic went into liquidation. But revenues from television and corporate hospitality were seen as healthy and the club had even turned down an £800,000 offer for Paul Ritchie from Rangers on the basis that it undervalued the player. Unfortunately, the offer was not raised and no other clubs came in for Ritchie until his contract had almost expired and Bolton offered £50,000.

Chris Robinson repeated his strategy for extracting Hearts from the financial mire – cut the club's costs, particularly the wage bill. He described it as ending the 'spiral of escalation in the cost of our playing squad to ensure that there is no long-term damage to the club'. But the chief executive did not endear himself to supporters when he accepted a £30,000 increase in his own package of salary, pension and other benefits to £142,900.

It was against this backdrop that details of a takeover bid emerged. This time, former chairman Leslie Deans and a consortium of backers were said to be behind a move to invest £4.5 million into the club, with one of the conditions being that Robinson resigned. The bid, which was to involve half the cash up front, received the backing of the Federation of Hearts Supporters Clubs which, once again, moved to declare a motion of no confidence in the chief executive. The federation also collected a 7,000-signature petition expressing dissatisfaction with the board of directors and chief executive. The Deans offer was rejected on the basis that it was not in the best interests of Hearts, apparently because the offer of 95p per share was not considered sufficient. But the episode further alienated Robinson from Deans, who insisted the bid was serious, and the supporters, who were desperate to see an injection of new money.

Robinson hit back aggressively through the club's website, although conceded he had made mistakes running Hearts. He accused Deans of promising the manager a transfer budget the club could not afford as well as leaking confidential information to the media relating to the Neil McCann transfer and discussions about sacking Jim Jefferies. Robinson said:

> The 1997–98 season culminated in a splendid day at Celtic Park when we won the Scottish Cup. Everything in the garden was rosy – it was fair to say we all basked in that glory for a week or two. But that's when it all started to go wrong.

He also claimed Deans and his allies had been trying to increase their stake in Hearts only to be 'trumped by the SMG deal', details of which had been kept from Deans during negotiations. Robinson accused Deans of jeopardising the SMG investment by not signing up to the deal. Deans later said the board had failed to act in the best interests of the club by turning down the offer.

The boardroom revelations from the close season suggested 2000–01 would be yet another campaign fought in unsettled times and so it proved. On the park, Hearts produced a memorable, if short-lived, European experience. Icelandic unknowns Vestmannaeyjar were disposed of 5–0 on aggregate to set up a tie with German side Stuttgart. Hearts left Germany with a narrow 1–0 defeat and the second leg at Tynecastle will surely go down as one of Tynecastle's special European nights, for the atmosphere if not the result. The team was eventually beaten 3–2, and exited the

UEFA Cup on the away goals rule, but it had been a nail-biting finish and a thrilling occasion.

Injuries to key players, such as Stephane Adam, had not helped the league campaign but the team was performing reasonably well, at least until they came up against Hibs at Easter Road in October. The players looked out of sorts from the early stages of the game, despite leading 1–0 for most of the first half. But the second-half was little short of a nightmare, with Hibs 6–2 winners by the final whistle. The fans who made their way out of the ground, thankful only that the opposition had not managed a fateful seven goals, raged that someone would have to take responsibility for such an embarrassing defeat. Jim Jefferies at least spoke for the supporters when he told the club magazine, 'It is the worst I have ever felt. There is no point in saying it is only three points, it is much more than that.' But the fans were not placated, particularly after a gutless 3–0 defeat by St Johnstone at Tynecastle the following week. They may have shuffled out of Easter Road to escape the misery but they were determined to remain at Tynecastle until after the final whistle to stage a noisy red-card protest about the decline of the club.

News had also filtered out that the club was due to announce more huge losses and the anger was mostly aimed at the board, although some blamed Jefferies for his recent signings. Steven Pressley and Antti Niemi would go on to earn their place in the unofficial Hearts hall of fame but the other newcomers failed to reach the heights of those they had been brought in to replace.

Hearts did recover their fighting spirit, which was on display in the 5–2 extra-time defeat by Celtic in the League Cup quarter-final and then a 3–0 dismantling of Aberdeen at Tynecastle a week later. But it seemed inevitable that someone would pay the price for the slippage in fortunes which culminated in the Hibs debacle. So it was that, several days after the Aberdeen game, an announcement was made that Jefferies and the board decided, by 'mutual agreement', that he should leave the club, while assistant Billy Brown was sacked.

Once again, there was an outcry from the supporters and this time their fury was mostly directed at one man – Chris Robinson. The front-page splash of the *Edinburgh Evening News* was simply headlined, 'Time to go Chris'. The back-page lead declared, 'Wrong man has gone'. High-profile supporters and fans' organisations lined up to call for Robinson's resignation over the loss of the popular and successful Hearts manager amid claims he could not work alongside the chief executive. Hundreds of supporters were even reported to have staged a demonstration outside Tynecastle on hearing the news, forcing the directors to leave the ground in the back of a police van.

The full details of discussions between the management duo and the board never emerged but the chairman Doug Smith brushed aside the criticisms in an effort to focus attention on the potential successor. He thanked Jefferies and Brown for their commitment to the club but said the new man should be a 'coach', concerned only with team matters rather than a manager who would also be expected to conduct contract negotiations among other administrative matters. The reason was clear – the board wanted more control over the purse strings. Smith added that the new coach must also be able to 'maximise the resources' available. He said, 'Recent football history shows that football teams cannot buy success by trying to pay unaffordable prices and costs for players. That can have a short-term impact, but is damaging in the long-term and we have long-term aspirations for Hearts.'

As Robinson said, it all appeared to go wrong after the cup was brought back from Glasgow two years earlier. Jefferies had sought to build on his winning team and challenge for further honours. He must have imagined his prayers had been answered when SMG decided to invest £8 million into the club, with a 'meaningful player budget'. The money made available was, no doubt, influenced by the massive crowds who welcomed the triumphant team back to Edinburgh. But it was quickly spent on players who could not always match up to the likes of Neil McCann, David Weir, Paul Ritchie and Gary Naysmith. And, with the expected upsurge in attendances failing to materialise, revenue dropped and the team had nowhere to go but downwards.

To make matters worse, the Bosman ruling, which allowed Jefferies to build a squad in the first place, had resulted in a soaring wage bill which could not quickly be brought under control unless players were moved on. Stephane Adam alone was said to be on up to £8,000 a week. The board was clearly concerned that Jefferies was not the man to take Hearts forward, as was evidenced by the discussion about his dismissal the year before. It seemed as though Jefferies was being blamed for the recent demise, even though the board must have signed off any transfers he made. And Jefferies would rightly argue that the transfer cash recouped on players he had brought to the club more than compensated for the money he had spent. There was certainly much speculation that tension existed between Jefferies and Robinson. Leslie Deans later described the relationship as 'hellish – they just spoke [to each other] when they had to'.

A number of external factors had not helped Hearts' cause but essentially they had been victims of their own good fortune and ambition. In business jargon, it was now time to 'downsize'. Coach Peter Houston took charge while the search for a new coach got under way. He started with a 2–1 victory over St Mirren but, when that was followed by a 6–1 trouncing by Celtic at Parkhead, it was clear he was out of the running.

16

A RETURN TO TYNECASTLE

On 1 December 2000, it was announced that former Hearts central defender Craig Levein had been appointed the new Hearts coach, with Peter Houston as his assistant, despite strong competition from John Robertson and others.

Levein had admittedly done well at Third Division Cowdenbeath, taking them from the depths of Scottish football to top of their league, but there were concerns that he lacked the experience for a SPL side. At thirty-six, Levein may have been the youngest boss in the top league but he took charge with single-minded authority, promising to ditch the big earners, bring through the youngsters and pick up bargain buys in an effort to cut costs. Players such as Darren Jackson and Fitzroy Simpson were immediately told they were free to move on and they were soon to be followed by Gordan Petric and Gary Locke. Young players such as Austin McCann and Andy Webster were brought in. Canadian international Kevin McKenna was signed from German side Cottbus and Steven Boyack arrived from Dundee.

The coach was given a baptism of fire with a game against Rangers but the narrow 1–0 defeat offered some hope. Another 1–0 loss, this time to Aberdeen at Pittodrie in January, led Levein to accuse his own players of 'theft' for picking up their wages after such a lacklustre display. It seemed to have the desired effect and performances improved. The team remained in touch in the league but missed out on a UEFA Cup place on the final day of the season. Hearts beat Dundee 2–0 but Kilmarnock defeated an under-strength Celtic side to secure fourth place in the table, prompting Stephane Adam to accuse the Glasgow team of cheating by resting players before the Scottish Cup final the next week.

But the behind-the-scenes troubles refused to disappear. In the same edition of the club magazine that trumpeted Levein's appointment, major shareholder SMG was forced to intervene in the row of the stewardship of Hearts. In a vote of confidence in Chris Robinson, SMG chief executive Andrew Flanagan declared that he did not believe the company's £8 million investment had been mishandled or the club had been mismanaged. He added:

> Hearts have, for many years, invested in players beyond the club's day-to-day means. This strategy depended on periodically selling players – a high risk plan but one which initially resulted in success . . . The risks of buying success and reaping the rewards relied on supporters coming out in ever-increasing numbers to watch a new, exciting, cosmopolitan Hearts. It didn't happen . . .
>
> The speculate-to-accumulate business model at Hearts has been well and truly tested and, despite the protestations of those who want to undermine the management team at Hearts, there's nothing to be gained from throwing blame around. Didn't the players try hard enough? Did Jim Jefferies make the right buying decisions? Did Chris Robinson give him the support he needed? What happened to the 100,000 who welcomed the team back after the Scottish Cup win? It doesn't matter. What matters now is the future. Clearly, we have to balance the books. The cost of players has to be brought into line with what the club earns. And yes, this will mean cutbacks in the playing pool, but in conjunction with the wishes and judgement of the new coach.

But, if he hoped the intervention would draw a line under Hearts' difficulties, Flanagan was to be disappointed when yet another controversy surfaced just two weeks later.

In the spring of that year Robinson had come to an uncomfortable conclusion – Tynecastle Stadium would have to be sold. The realisation arrived in the form of a hefty package from UEFA. It contained a lengthy discussion document detailing proposals for a new licensing scheme. The draft regulations sought to improve standards of football administration and safety in the European cup competitions. One of the key areas under consideration was the size and suitability of the pitch and larger 'playing arena', which included trackside areas. While Tynecastle met and exceeded the required pitch width, the 98-metre playing surface was seven metres short of the preferred length and two metres shy of the absolute minimum length. It was later suggested by Hearts that there would be some leeway until 2010 but, one way or another, there was a degree of uncertainty about Tynecastle's suitability for European football in the years ahead.

On 20 December 2000, Robinson broke the news to shareholders at the AGM. He added that plans had been drawn up to quit the club's spiritual home at Tynecastle and relocate to a 30,000-capacity stadium on the western outskirts of Edinburgh within five years, a notion which most thought had disappeared with Wallace Mercer. Robinson promised it would be more than a stadium, it would be a 'multipurpose arena', possibly even with a retractable roof. The idea seemed far-fetched but it actually gained some support among the gathered shareholders – and it deflected attention away from those calling for Robinson's head. But there was more to the chief executive's 'Towards 2005' presentation than a diversionary tactic.

A crucial question remained – how could such a vision possibly be funded? The 2001 accounts recorded yet more record pre-tax losses – this time of £3.8 million. Staff costs had leapt to £7.2 million, although that included £1.1 million compensation for the termination of contracts for Jim Jefferies and Gordan Petric among others, on a turnover of just £7.9 million. In other words 90% of income had been spent on staffing costs. Average league crowds were down to below 13,000 and income was up but not sufficiently to balance the books. And, of course, Hearts had sold Gary Naysmith to Everton for £1.8 million and made a reported record £500,000 from the Stuttgart tie. With regard to the latter, Robinson pointed out it had been the 'highest earning match in the club's history' and made more than the whole of the 1998 cup run. Sadly, it did little to dent the net debt which, by now, had reached £10.2 million.

It was little surprise, then, that Robinson received such a hostile reception when he presented the results to shareholders later in 2001. At the meeting, the chief executive faced repeated shouts and insults from around 650 shareholders as he was accused of failing the club. Leslie Deans demanded that Robinson follow First Minister Henry McLeish's recent decision and resign. He was given backing from the floor but the chief executive insisted he had no intention of stepping down and told his former partner to 'put up or shut up'. A show of hands also failed to support the re-appointment of chairman Doug Smith but that resolution was carried by block proxy votes.

The issue of SMG's £4.5 million convertible loan stock was also becoming of wider concern and was raised at the meeting, although no clear explanation was given as to what would happen if the media group did not take up its share option. Similarly, questions about a £14,000 pay rise for finance director Stewart Fraser were deflected by the top table.

The heated discussions certainly provoked a reaction. One of those who entered the debate was former chairman Wallace Mercer who had, until that point, maintained a diplomatic silence. But the AGM prompted Mercer to declare to *The Scotsman* on 15 November 2001, 'We have a civil war at Hearts.' He went on to issue a warning:

> It's not my place to take sides, but it's there for all to see. We already knew about the division between Robinson and [Leslie] Deans, but it's become personalised against the chairman, Douglas Smith, as well. This kind of animosity can only damage the club. On the one hand you have around 25% of the shareholders who are completely disaffected. And on the other you have the chief executive supported by SMG. For 13 years I went through the mill as chairman of Hearts and people are still free to criticise my stewardship. But I would suggest there was never an AGM as torrid as this week.

Mercer questioned how SMG, as power brokers at the club, would react to the 'torrid outpouring of emotion' at the meeting. He added that the board should seriously consider Deans' offer of investment and any other. He expressed concern at what he described as a 'cavalier attitude towards the presentation of debt'.

But the problem of losses and debts was not confined to Hearts. The PricewaterhouseCoopers (PwC) Financial Review of Scottish Football for 2000–01 highlighted some worrying trends. With the total wage bill reaching a new high of £101 million among the SPL clubs that year, losses were pushed to a record £48 million, while net debt more than doubled from £55 million to £132 million. Greenock Morton had gone into administration and, in the SPL, Motherwell were heading in the same direction. The PwC report found doubts over the finances of Hearts, Dundee and Dunfermline. It said, 'During the season the number of clubs in a technically insolvent position, i.e. total creditors greater than total assets, increased from two to four, with Dundee and Hearts joining Dunfermline and Motherwell in this unenviable position.' The review said the blame for the downturn was simple – wage costs, fuelled by the Bosman ruling, and a lack of the same kind of television revenues enjoyed by other countries to balance the books.

Back at Hearts, the club insisted that the stadium relocation proposal was simply one of several options up for discussion. The main stand could still be renovated but this would be tricky and could cost up to £10 million. With the issue under 'consultation', it did not provoke the storm of protest which would erupt some years down the line but it did re-emerge at the start of season 2001–02. It was at this point that Hearts raised the stakes when they told the SFA they wanted to be considered as part of Scotland's bid for Euro 2008. The proposal was for Hearts to provide a new 30,000-seat stadium, possibly at a site on the western outskirts of the city at Braehead Quarry.

Almost immediately, concerns were raised about the possibility of gaining planning permission on green belt land and the issue faded from the minds of most fans. But the plan was pursued behind the scenes with the formation of a stadium steering group involving the City of Edinburgh Council and other experts in September. The club's architects advised that redevelopment of the Tynecastle site, including the acquisition of nearby land and construction work, would add up to almost £39 million, whereas provision of a new stadium at an out-of-town location would cost around £20 million. With soaring Edinburgh land values, even a new main stand would cost £12 million and additional car parking space around £10 million, Hearts claimed. The steering group was later told in February 2002 that new health and safety regulations would create planning difficulties in expanding the McLeod Street stand. It was later confirmed that the stadium could, however, be developed on its current 'footprint'.

The stadium issue was not the only controversy simmering below the surface in the run-up to the start of season 2001–02. First, it was reported that there were plans to drop the club's full historic name, Heart of Midlothian Football Club, and replace it with Hearts FC. The club denied this was the case, although it did plan to use the shorter name in some official capacities. But even that irked supporters already angered by rows over the design of the crest and stadium name change. Despite criticism, Hearts FC is still in common use today – for instance, on the web site and for other official functions – and some supporters believe it should be dropped in favour of the full title or the abbreviation HMFC.

Then, rumours emerged of a fresh takeover bid. Leslie Deans was again involved with a consortium of his associates that included businessman Robert McGrail. This time, they approached the board in the summer with the promise of a massive £8 million cash injection into the club, with half up front followed by sums of £3 million and £1 million in later years. The offer involved creating new shares, which would be purchased for 75p each, but again, the bid was rejected, with Hearts chairman Doug Smith claiming on the club website that, once more, Deans' offer 'significantly undervalues Heart of Midlothian plc' and was not in the best interests of shareholders. In response, Deans hit out at the board later for 'misleading' the fans about the details of the proposal.

Amid this furore, the season kicked off. Despite the loss or imminent departure of so many players, there was some hope that Hearts could improve on the previous season and at least qualify for Europe. The season started as it would end, with a defeat (2–1) by newly promoted Livingston. The loss of Colin Cameron to Wolves for £1.8 million and long-term injury to Robert Tomaschek did little to lift the gloom. However, Craig Levein did move to strengthen his defence with the capture of experienced left back Stephane Mahe from Celtic and Republic of Ireland international Alan Maybury from Leeds.

The team continued to slip down the table and suffered a humiliating League Cup exit to First Division Ross County (5–4 on penalties after a 0–0 draw) in September 2001. The arrival of Jamaican forward Ricardo Fuller, on loan from Tivoli Gardens, marked a turning point in Hearts' season as he began to find the back of the net. Two goals from the striker gave Hearts some revenge over Ross County, with a 2–1 victory in the Scottish Cup, although later in January Hearts crashed out of the tournament to another First Division side from the Highlands. The 3–1 defeat by Inverness Caledonian Thistle was the first Scottish Cup loss at Tynecastle since the Forfar fiasco twenty years before.

For the second year, the SPL was split into the top and bottom six teams for the final five games. Once again Hearts made it into the top group but they finished a disappointing fifth after a final-day loss to Livingston (3–2). A commemorative evening for the 1997–98 cup-winning team had been organised by the supporters' federation the week before the season ended. And the nostalgic mood continued when three of those players, Thomas Flogel, Stephane Adam and Stevie Fulton, joined others such as Ricardo Fuller in making their farewell appearance at Tynecastle in the Livingston match.

Continued efforts were being made to cut the wage bill and experienced servants on high salaries were the obvious targets.

But further financial uncertainty had been caused by a row over broadcasting rights which had threatened to explode towards the end of 2001–02.

The £45 million satellite television deal which had been in place for four years was due to expire in the close season. With a downturn in the media and advertising industries, particularly since the terrorist attacks on New York and Washington on 11 September 2001, there was a question mark over the value of any renewed deal. Further damage had been done to the bargaining power of the SPL clubs by Rangers and Celtic openly and eagerly discussing the ludicrous prospect of joining the English league system or, more plausibly, a new European league. It was a notion which led Aberdeen chief executive Keith Wyness to describe them as acting like 'two old girls in Sauchiehall Street, lifting their skirts to every league that walks by'. The Old Firm did eventually play down any such possibility and joined with the other ten SPL clubs in formulating plans for a SPL subscription-only television channel which, it was hoped, would bring in up to £30 million a year. But, after months of negotiations, Celtic and Rangers questioned its viability and pulled out of the initiative. Amid accusations that the big two were simply hoping to keep their options open should any better offer come along, the ten other top-flight clubs decided to resign from the SPL and freeze out the Old Firm. To a certain extent, the ploy worked. With the possibility of being left out of any new league the ten may establish, Rangers and Celtic re-opened negotiations and made concessions over a number of issues, such as voting structures and the split of broadcasting cash. But the damage had been done from the nine-month dispute. SPL TV failed to get off the ground and the two-year £18 million deal with the BBC was considerably less than would have been expected from BSkyB if an earlier agreement had been reached. Needles to say, Scottish football's reputation had reached a new low.

Chris Robinson was one of the most outspoken critics of the Old Firm over the row and he earned some rare praise from Hearts supporters for his determined stance. He had good reason to be concerned about the sport's dwindling revenues. Not only was television cash a fraction of the past few years but the team had also failed to make progress in the cups or take part in the lucrative European competitions. No doubt as a result of the poor fare on offer, average attendances were down to little more than 12,000. There was no surprise, then, that turnover in 2001–02 was down by a quarter to just £6.1 million at the same time as yet another huge pre-tax loss of £2.7 million was recorded. Staff costs had dropped by more than 20% to £5.7 million but that remained perilously close to overall turnover at 94%. Net debt meanwhile stood at a worrying £14.8 million.

Robinson took the opportunity to point the finger of blame at the Old Firm. In his statement to shareholders, he said:

> Unfortunately, as events unfolded with the Scottish Premier League, even achieving small increases in television and media revenues has not been possible. The reasons for this are complex and largely market driven but we should not overlook the actions of members of the league in destabilising the value of our broadcast rights through their stated desires to migrate to more lucrative pastures.

Whatever the reasons, the board had failed to achieve its own targets of turning the company from loss-making into profit by keeping wage costs below 60% of income and increasing revenue.

Leslie Deans was clearly concerned because he was planning to up his takeover bid for the club by summer 2002. This time the former chairman, along with backers including the south-of-England-based Scot, Ken Burnett, raised the price to £10 million, with half up front and the remainder over two years. The money would buy new shares at 50p each and, once again, Robinson would be expected to step down as part of the bargain. Deans claimed the offer was rejected because the board wanted up to £1 a share when the price was 54p. Angered by later accusations that the money he offered did not exist, Deans also claimed Robinson had offered to sell his own stake rather than create new shares.

Deans refused because he wanted the cash to go directly to the club rather than into the pocket of another investor.

If the previous season began disappointingly, the start to 2002–03 could hardly have been more explosive. The tame 1–1 draw with Dundee on opening day may not have promised much but eight days later Hearts fans were certainly in for a treat. There was some trepidation before the first derby on 11 August after the previous season's indifferent form but new signing Mark de Vries, making his home debut, ensured it was an afternoon to remember. The big Dutchman scored four in a stunning 5–1 victory which more than compensated for the earlier 6–2 defeat by their city rivals. It would not be the first derby sensation of the season but there were setbacks to endure first.

The sale of goalkeeper Antti Niemi, arguably the club's last major asset, provoked a storm of criticism from fans, although the £2 million transfer fee was desperately needed to improve the finances. New players Phil Stamp from Middlesbrough and Frenchman Jean-Louis Valois were brought in and, despite the loss of Niemi, league results remained steady, at least until a young Hearts side was humbled 6–1 by Motherwell at Fir Park in December. In the meantime, the team had also suffered a scare in the League Cup, going down 1–0 to Third Division Stirling Albion after two minutes before fighting back to win 3–2. The next round at least provided an opportunity for more revenge against Ross County, with a 3–0 victory at Tynecastle. Hearts then seized the opportunity to take part in their first semi-final under Craig Levein with a 1–0 quarter-final defeat of Aberdeen at Pittodrie.

But the most dramatic game of the season was reserved for the New Year derby at Tynecastle. Hibs looked to have gained revenge for their 5–1 defeat when they went 4–2 up with goals in the 89th and 92nd minutes but somehow Hearts raced back upfield with substitute Graham Weir scoring twice in 42 seconds – a turn of events which prompted Hearts fans to break into a chorus of 'We only won four-four'. The team continued its good league form, including a late 2–1 win over Celtic in April, finishing third and qualifying for Europe. However, they were beaten 1–0 by Rangers in the League Cup semi-final after a weak performance and crashed out of the Scottish Cup following a crushing 4–0 defeat by an on-form Falkirk side.

Off the field, there were the familiar issues surrounding cost-cutting – six young players were released in April – and the search for a new stadium site continued. Braehead Quarry had dropped out of the reckoning, while the Ingliston area was given some consideration. But a new worry had also emerged, with Hearts expressing concern about a group with links to the far-right turning up for games at Tynecastle, particularly when Celtic were playing. Earlier in the season, Union flags and Irish tricolours had been taken from both Hearts and Celtic fans who used them as provocative symbols representing the Protestant–Catholic divide in Scotland and Ireland. The club and large numbers of supporters, who rightly believed that religious differences had nothing to do with Hearts, applauded the action. But it was difficult not to feel that the culture of negativity which had developed at Tynecastle had, in some way, allowed a noisy and divisive minority to develop a presence by exploiting that anger.

The six-monthly figures produced by the club at this time gave some cause for optimism at Hearts. Gate receipts had held up during the season, with average crowds up to 13,300, even though season ticket sales were down. The sale of Antti Niemi had obviously helped the finances and a pre-tax profit of £746,000 was recorded up to 31 January 2003, although that would become an annual loss of £1.1 million by July. But the real bombshell would be dropped when the full-year accounts were published in November 2003.

OVERVIEW

Hearts limped into football's modern age in a state of disarray. As the commercial era dawned, the club was struggling against repeated relegation, attendances had plunged and the deteriorating financial situation was becoming critical. The very existence of Hearts was even brought into question.

Hearts were not the only ones in difficulty. Crowds and, therefore, revenues were falling to dangerous levels at crumbling grounds around the country, leaving a vacuum for the new generation of football hooligans to fill. Even Rangers, with their lowest average crowds of just over 16,000 in 1981–82, and Celtic, with attendances of little more than 18,000 two years later, were not exempt. In fact, some Old Firm home games were reported to have attracted fewer than 5,000 fans, although there is some doubt over the accuracy of records from this period as detailed records of crowd numbers were not kept at this time.

The fault line did at least allow others to challenge for honours. However, it was the New Firm of Aberdeen and Dundee United that made the breakthrough in the late 1970s and achieved most success in the 80s, rather than the capital city teams. Aberdeen had been in and out of the race for honours since the war but it was not until the appointment of Alex Ferguson from St Mirren, in 1978, that their fortunes began to really take off. The club also had the foresight to develop Britain's first all-seated stadium, years before the Taylor Report forced others to do likewise. Like Aberdeen, Dundee United also appointed one of the all-time greats of Scottish football management, with Jim McLean arriving at the club in 1971. United went on to develop a hugely successful youth policy under McLean's expert tutelage.

In any case, the top clubs responded to the uncertainty of the period by seizing control of the sport's purse strings. First they formed an elite ten when the Premier Division was established in 1975. Then, the 1980s marked the beginning of major competition sponsorship. The first Bell's League Cup was in 1979–80, to be replaced by the Skol Cup five years later. The Fine Fare League was launched in 1985, to be followed by the B&Q League three years later. Shirt sponsorship took off at this time as well, with Hearts attracting the car dealership Alexanders in 1982–83. The financial markets also recognised football's potential as Spurs became the first club to list on the stock exchange in 1983 – a move subsequently followed by numerous clubs, including Hearts.

Also, in 1981 a special general meeting of the Scottish Football League (SFL) was called and it was agreed that the system of providing away teams with half of the match-day receipts (after expenses) would be abolished, in favour of allowing home sides to retain everything from league matches. Effectively, gate sharing had acted like a progressive system of taxation, allowing the underprivileged to boost their status thanks to the bounty of the more affluent. Similarly, in 1981 the distribution of £1 million pools cash and other income gathered centrally by the SFL was altered so that payments were based at least partially on the division a club played in as well as the number of points gained in a season. It was befitting of the era that these changes would transform Scottish football's social order to benefit the rich, at the expense of the poor.

It was apt also that, in the world beyond football, Margaret Thatcher had assumed power at Westminster with a promise to shake off Britain's industrial and social past. The might of the worker and the place of the local community within society – both key features of football's development during the preceding century – were to be swept aside. The new order would be driven by the individual and powered by enterprise, even if that led to increased polarisation of wealth and poverty.

So, clubs in the early 1980s faced an uncertain future. Football's many troubles were evident yet there was some hope that the sport could be rescued by a new generation of money men. It was into this environment that Wallace Mercer stepped when he gained control of Hearts in 1981. His investment of £350,000 not only rescued the club but also transformed the system by which it was owned. Gone were the cliques of shareholder-directors, accused in the past of neglecting the long-term interests of the club. In came Mercer, a thirty-four-year-old entrepreneur and Edinburgh property developer – the very epitome of the Thatcher era.

Despite some early setbacks, including two seasons in the First Division and admittedly 'flying it by the seat of my pants', as he described his initial time at the club, Mercer must be credited with the appointment of the management team of Alex MacDonald and Sandy Jardine, who steered the side from its lowest ebb to within a whisker of a league and cup double. Off the field, commercial activities were revolutionised and the club found itself on a firm financial footing towards the end of the decade. It had been helped by the tragic events at Heysel in 1985, which gave Scottish clubs greater prominence in European competitions and allowed them to compete in the transfer market on a more competitive basis. Rangers, in particular, capitalised with the capture of several big-name English players, such as the international captain Terry Butcher in 1986. The flip side was that transfer money which previously had almost all remained in Scotland in the past, now began to drain away, first to England and soon overseas.

But other events would work against Hearts' continued progress. The very success, or near success, of the team in 1985–86 coincided with Rangers finishing a lowly fifth in the league with less than a point a game for the first time in their history. That, in turn, led to the appointment of Graeme Souness at Ibrox and the start of the Rangers revolution, which was spurred on by David Murray's purchase of the club in 1988. Arguably, the tantalising brush with victory, after a similar experience in 1965, instilled a near-obsession with trophy success at Tynecastle. Yet this occurred at a time when Rangers stretched the ambitions of the chasing pack to breaking point.

Meanwhile, the series of disasters which had befallen English football, culminating in the 1989 Hillsborough tragedy and the Taylor Report a year later, would also have serious consequences north of the border. The key recommendation to improve crowd safety and control at sports events was the need to replace terracing with all-seated stands by 1994–95.

The post-Taylor era may have proved a financial burden for clubs but it at least began to offer greater commercial rewards at the same time, particularly south of the border. With English clubs back in Europe by 1990, the image of the sport gradually improved. Television companies recognised football's potential and a massive £300 million deal was struck by the new FA Premier League in 1992 for the rights to broadcast live games and highlights. In Scotland, the SPL agreed a £45 million deal for four years following its inception in 1998, although other commercial deals with the new league boosted this figure even further.

Wallace Mercer may have predicted this trend but he was not in a position to reap the rewards after selling his controlling interest in Hearts to Chris Robinson and Leslie Deans in 1994. He had succeeded in balancing the books at the same time as the team was able to challenge for the league and Scottish Cup and compete regularly in Europe. But the previously sure touch seemed shakier in the late 1980s, the first sign of which was the unpopular sale of John Robertson. Then there was the dismissal of Sandy Jardine and Alex MacDonald, followed by the appointment of Joe Jordan. During the early 90s, there were the ill-fated Hibs takeover and stadium relocation plans. But, despite being hindered by the onset of an economic recession, Mercer did produce what he called a 'Tynecastle solution' and began the redevelopment work which would transform the Gorgie ground into one of the best in the country. Borrowing had increased as the club faced the challenge of beginning construction of a modern stadium at the same time as the team chased a resurgent Rangers. But the club was still in a relatively healthy condition and, as Mercer stresses, could trade its way out of debt. Nevertheless, in his own words, he had taken the club as far as he could, allowing Robinson and Leslie Deans to step forward and buy a controlling interest in the club. On reflection, Mercer now describes his decision to sell to them as 'the greatest regret in [his] life' because of how the club performed financially in more recent times.

The appointment of Tommy McLean did little to improve on-field matters at Hearts but his replacement by cup-winning manager Jim Jefferies and subsequently Craig Levein, who achieved an impressive level of consistency albeit in a weak league, must be seen as sound choices by the board. In addition, Jefferies was provided with a budget that allowed him to build a successful team and Tynecastle was completed to a high standard at a cost of £12 million. Hearts' own figures show the stock market flotation provided £5 million towards this, while Football Trust grants totalled £2 million and £1.5 million were raised through the two 500 Clubs.

However, in the late 1990s, the tide began to turn. First, there were the financial penalties of winning the cup in 1998 – players' bonuses and the sharing of gate revenues with visiting teams in the early rounds, for instance. The decision had been taken to specu-late to accumulate, a policy spurred on by the subsequent SMG investment. Lucrative new contracts were awarded to some of the victorious players and new signings were made. Unfortunately, key players still left and neither those that remained nor the new-comers could match the feats of the 1997–98 team. Jim Jefferies, a dyed-in-the-wool Hearts supporter, had used the lure of becoming a club 'legend' to inspire the team to silverware success but the motivation appeared to diminish thereafter. The fans seemed to suffer from a similar malaise – with crowds down by around 1,000 per match – believing either that a lifetime ambition had been realised or that there was little point in turning up as it would not be repeated. In any case, the vast majority of the 200,000 who took to the streets to watch the cup victory parade decided not to pay their cash at the Tynecastle turnstiles. However, it is worth pointing out that the throngs on Princes Street and elsewhere clearly did not have to stump up a sizeable admission fee to join in the celebrations. One way or another, the hoped-for increase in attendances did not happen.

There were other factors working against Hearts. The Bosman rule, which had initially worked so convincingly in Hearts' favour as they put together a winning side, was starting to prove costly. When it was clear the wage bill must be reduced, players on long contracts were difficult to offload. But, not only was Bosman caus-ing surging wage inflation, it also reduced the chances of earning cash by transferring players.

Tommy Walker, who would go on to become Hearts' most successful manager, takes to the field as a player in 1937

Huge crowds watch as Hearts beat Third Lanark 2–1 in the 1959 League Cup final

The King of Hearts, Willie Bauld, shows his determination

Jimmy Wardhaugh was a goal-scoring hero
after the end of the Second World War

Hearts legend Donald Ford became a
respected accountant after his playing career
ended. Along with Gary Mackay, he was a
vocal supporter of the Save our Hearts
campaign to keep the club at Tynecastle

Dejected Hearts players leave the Hampden pitch after
losing 3–0 to Aberdeen in the 1986 Scottish Cup final

Tearful fans are broken-hearted after Hearts
'lost' the league title in 1986 at Dens Park

Chairman of Hearts Wallace Mercer pictured
in 1988. Mercer gained a controlling interest
in the club in 1981 and left in 1994

1956 Scottish Cup heroes Bobby Kirk, Freddie Glidden and John
Cumming are reunited with the trophy after the 1998 triumph

The ecstasy – John Robertson after
scoring the winner against Celtic in 1996

The agony – Robbo is incensed at being
booked by Hugh Dallas during a league
game against Rangers in 1997

Jim Hamilton and Stephane Adam celebrate winning
the 1998 Scottish Cup after beating Rangers 2–1

Chief Executive Chris Robinson crowns
Chairman Leslie Deans with a hard hat
following the flotation announcement in 1997

Craig Levein, Hearts' manager from
2000 to 2004, vents his frustration
from the dugout

Hearts fans show Chris Robinson and the board the red card over the plans to move from Tynecastle to Murrayfield towards the end of Season 2003–04

Dennis Wyness and Mark de Vries celebrate during the famous 2–1 defeat of FC Basel in 2004 as the stunned Swiss players look on

Hearts players in pre-match training at Murrayfield prior to one
of the three UEFA cup games that were played there in 2004

Chris Robinson at the EGM in January
2005 which saw shareholders vote to
scrap the deal to sell Tynecastle

Chairman George Foulkes looks pleased at
the reception his *Stadium Working Group
Report* received in December 2004

The major shareholder at Hearts, Vladimir Romanov, holds a Hearts scarf aloft as a new era at Tynecastle with financial backing from the Lithuanian banker is ushered in

Manager George Burley with some of the promising new signings at the start of Season 2005–06

With the projected income rise failing to materialise, the downturn in the media and advertising industries – reinforced by the 9/11 terrorist attacks and later the war in Iraq – was little short of disastrous for Hearts, with clubs around Europe suffering a similar fate. The clumsy attempts by Celtic and Rangers to leave the Scottish league set-up for Europe or England appeared to hinder negotiations with the broadcasters even further and a much-reduced TV deal was eventually agreed.

But mistakes had been made and some decisions were open to question. The £250,000 start-up cost of listing on the stock exchange may have been justified by the healthy initial return but the ongoing annual cost of around £50,000 in regulatory and administrative expenses is surely an expensive luxury. The low volume of trades suggests the exercise is now largely meaningless in any case. The SMG deal, while attracting large sums of cash at favourable rates, ultimately burdened the club with a huge chunk of additional debt which it had no means of repaying.

The speculate-to-accumulate strategy had clearly not worked – the gambles were taken but the rewards were not forthcoming. In addition, attempts to reduce the wage bill were not as ruthless as might have been expected. From a high of £7.2 million in 2001, it was reduced to £5 million, including European bonuses, by July 2004 – a drop of 30%. But, if the exceptional costs of £1.1 million are taken from the 2001 figure, the fall was just 18%. Meanwhile the turnover-to-staff-costs ratio went down from a runaway peak of 94% to a more respectable to 70%, although still short of the 60% target. The result was four annual losses of £2 million or more between 2000 and 2004, with debt soaring from £6.8 million to £19.6 million during the same period.

With Chris Robinson at the helm as these events unfolded at Tynecastle, it was clear he would come in for some criticism. But his deteriorating relationship with others connected with Hearts ensured that the objections were expressed with increasing ferocity. His estrangement from Leslie Deans created a dogged adversary, while ordinary fans also turned against him in ever-larger numbers.

There were some who had always been irritated by his sometimes abrasive manner but his approval ratings took a further dent when he meddled with the club's traditions. The departure of cup-winning manager Jim Jefferies caused further anger. Then Robinson – the man reputed to have had a poster on his office wall which said, 'The turtle only makes progress when he sticks his neck out' – made yet more enemies when he first announced plans to move from Tynecastle amid a deteriorating financial position. The proposals which followed would transform the anger into fury.

PART 4

TWO TURBULENT SEASONS

17

SWITCH TO STRAITON OR MOVE TO MURRAYFIELD?

Initially, as Scottish football's attention turned to the national team, there was little to suggest that the pre-season break would provide any drama. On 27 May 2003, Tynecastle Stadium played host to the first of two Scotland matches, an insipid and dispiriting 1–1 friendly draw with New Zealand. Sadly, it now seems that this uninspiring match will be the last international ever played at the ground because UEFA's new licensing laws would deem the pitch too small to stage full international fixtures. There was some consolation that two Hearts players featured in the team, captain Steven Pressley and his central defensive partner, Andy Webster. The friendly was simply a dress rehearsal for the big game against Germany, Scotland's rivals in the Euro 2004 qualifying group, less than a fortnight later at Hampden. That game also finished 1–1 but the team at least put in a heartening performance, with Pressley and Webster again solid at the heart of the defence. The week after winning his third cap, twenty-one-year-old Webster put pen to paper and committed himself to Hearts until the summer of 2007. It was encouraging news for the club which had so recently qualified for the next season's UEFA Cup.

Days later, the prospect of football matters remaining the primary focus of season 2003–04 faded. On 16 June, with the new season just four weeks away, Hearts and city rivals Hibs confirmed they had agreed in principle to build a 25,000-seat stadium on the outskirts of

Edinburgh at Straiton under a form of private finance initiative at a cost of up to £15 million for the facility and £5 million for new roads. Both clubs referred obliquely to the financial advantages of shared running costs and new revenue streams. They also had combined debts of some £30 million and must have recognised the possibility of cashing in on soaring property prices in the capital. Initial reports suggested the sale of both grounds could bring in up to £50 million.

Both clubs talked of the benefits of playing in a state-of-the-art, showpiece stadium yet both had recently spent a combined £26 million developing Tynecastle and Easter Road into two of the best grounds in the country. It also did not escape attention that the proposed 40-acre site at Straiton was in Midlothian and not within the boundaries of Edinburgh City Council's control. The embarrassing possibility was obvious – the city, which had already lost top-class sporting events that included athletics, speedway, greyhound racing, basketball and American football, could be left with no professional football clubs. It was a fact which had not escaped the notice of those at Tynecastle and the move was a deliberate ploy to provoke a reaction from the local authority. The situation allowed Hearts chief executive Chris Robinson to have a dig at the Edinburgh council. He told the *Edinburgh Evening News*:

> We have looked systematically at sites in conjunction with Edinburgh City Council. One by one these have been ruled out. The site at Straiton is the site which best meets our needs. The clubs will be just as competitive as ever on the pitch while co-operating off it. Edinburgh needs two vibrant clubs.

The plan was met with widespread criticism. A proposed move to the same site a decade before had failed to get off the ground and this time Hibs supporters quickly took up the baton and expressed their opposition. First they staged a mass meeting of around 1,000 fans and then they set up a pressure group, FARMER (Fans Against ReMoval from Easter Road). Supporters in the west of the city greeted the plans with more muted disdain while still warning that it could threaten the future of the club. But Hearts' reasons – a larger debt burden and the prospect of UEFA restrictions on their current stadium – were greater. It also soon became apparent that Hibs owner Sir Tom Farmer had an interest in the site and it would be given to the clubs for free, although he strenuously denied there was any hidden agenda attached to this offer.

Some Hearts supporters took perverse pleasure in the prospect of being rescued from a financial hole through the gift of a large chunk of land from their greatest rivals. Hibs fans, on the other hand, feared ground-sharing may be the first step towards a merger of the clubs, first proposed by former Hearts chairman Wallace Mercer in 1990. They also argued that their club had the option of selling the old car park land behind the East Stand for an estimated £10 million.

Others also questioned the wisdom of the proposal. Local residents opposed to developments on green belt land launched a campaign to thwart the plan and the government's leading transport adviser, Professor David Begg, warned that the traffic problems around the site by the city bypass would be a 'potential nightmare'. Edinburgh city's sports and leisure leader Ricky Henderson, a Tynecastle season ticket holder, said it would 'rip the heart out of' Gorgie and Leith. The capital's council leader, Donald Anderson, also wasted no time entering the debate when, less than two weeks after the story broke, he suggested that Hearts and Hibs should consider 'more ambitious proposals' than the Straiton option. His vision was of a multipurpose sports complex as a replacement for the ageing Meadowbank Stadium at the east end of the city centre. As well as football, there would be facilities for rugby, athletics, basketball and ice hockey. It later emerged that this new facility could be in the west of the city, close to Tynecastle. On 28 June, he told the *Edinburgh Evening News*:

> It's possible that a replacement could be part of the same site as a shared football stadium and we could be talking about a major regional sporting hub for the whole of the east coast of Scotland. It has the potential to be a very prestigious development, not just for Edinburgh but for the whole of the country. There's an argument

that, if you're going to lose some of the green belt, then you should aim for something more ambitious than a stadium solely for football. Anything of that scale is obviously going to cost many millions of pounds and would need the support of the [Scottish] Executive. However, I plan to discuss this idea at ministerial level.

The olive branch from the council, which also insisted it had obligations to protect the green belt and parkland, was met with a cool response. Both clubs expressed concern at the prospect of sharing a stadium with other sports, insisting that a football-only facility was their preference. Hearts chief executive Chris Robinson explained that 'football and athletics don't mix particularly well' and the club had to look after the needs of its own fans. But the more the clubs argued the merits of the move, the more the opposition of the fans grew. Then, as the pre-season friendlies kicked off on 16 July, a further option emerged.

The Scottish Rugby Union (SRU), itself heavily in debt, had previously had discussions about the possibility of Falkirk Football Club playing at the 67,500-capacity Murrayfield Stadium. The First Division club was seeking promotion to the SPL but its ground at Brockville did not meet the 10,000 all-seated standard set down by the top division. The Falkirk deal had subsequently broken down after the club's application to the SPL was rejected. But the situation the First Division club found itself in was not unlike that faced by Hearts seeking to play in European competitions.

The SRU confirmed that talks had since taken place with Hearts, although not Hibs. However, it recognised the problems of the football clubs playing in a largely empty stadium and cited the example of Espanyol, in Barcelona. In 1994, the club sold Sarria, its British-style stadium, wiped out £45 million debt and moved to the city's Olympic Stadium, which is similar in size to Murrayfield. As Espanyol found, the use of huge sponsors' flags and careful sectioning of fans could help to produce a better atmosphere. 'There are ways and means', it was promised and Edinburgh's football clubs should seriously consider the proposal. The clubs, however, appeared to do little to encourage the rugby authorities. Hearts coach Craig Levein highlighted the 'atmosphere issue', while Hibs were even more dismissive. John Borthwick, the secretary of the Federation of Hearts Supporters Clubs, reflected the views of many fans when he described it a 'red herring' which was deflecting attention away from the possibility of keeping the club at Tynecastle.

Doubt was later cast on the success of the experience at Espanyol – their crowds fell, a promised new stadium failed to appear and debt began mounting once again. An analysis of the club's situation and comparison to Hearts appeared in *The Times* on 24 April 2004:

By the time 2005 comes, Celtic and Rangers fans will probably hear their cries echoing around the home of Scottish rugby, when it will be lucky to be a third-full for such encounters. That is how Barcelona feel when they travel across town to face Espanyol at the Montjuic Stadium, home of the 1992 Olympic Games: even Ronaldinho and Co can't do any better than half-fill a venue that is simply not suited for football. There are giant banners to screen off, and cover up, the acres of empty seating. Just as Hearts intend to do at Murrayfield. But while you can fool some of the people some of the time, you cannot do it 20 times a season. Montjuic is the millstone around Espanyol's neck – and Hearts fans fear Murrayfield could be theirs . . .

This season, crowds at the Montjuic have dipped to 19,000. The stadium is the least-used in La Liga. Not the lowest crowds, simply lowest occupancy rate of seats – at 37%, Espanyol are the only club unable to even half-fill their ground. The empty seats in the 55,000 arena have damaged the club's reputation.

Chris Robinson has admitted for this book that, like Straiton, the Murrayfield connection was designed to put some pressure on the local authority. He says, 'We felt that, if we pushed hard, the council would see that Hearts needed a solution and something might give elsewhere – if we couldn't get Sighthill, it would be Murrayfield or bust.'

The focus on Murrayfield quickly faded, with supporters venting anger at the Straiton proposal instead. Hibs declared that their 'first priority' was to remain at Easter Road, while the federation representing around 3,000 fans from Hearts supporters clubs became more emphatic in its opposition. After consulting members, Borthwick now insisted that it was 'a short-term fix leading to a long-term disaster'. No one wanted to go – crowds could slump. It was simple – Hearts should remain in their atmospheric and appropriately sized 18,000-seater Tynecastle home. For once, Hibs and Hearts fans were in agreement.

18

SEASON 2003–04 KICKS OFF

Given the new-found consensus, it was fitting that the new season kicked off between Hearts and Hibs with the inaugural Festival Cup match on 2 August. The competition itself – timed to coincide with the start of Edinburgh's international arts and fringe festivals – may not have convinced supporters of its merits: as thousands of seats remained empty; but at least the Hearts fans who turned up had the satisfaction of a 1–0 victory, courtesy of a first derby goal from Scotland international Andy Webster. The first SPL game, a 2–0 victory over Aberdeen a week later, set the standard for what was to become a formidable home record. It was followed by comfortable victories at Tynecastle against Dundee United (3–0) and Dunfermline (1–0) later in the month, although sandwiched between those results was an injury-time defeat to Hibs at Easter Road. The 1–0 scoreline provided the Easter Road men some revenge for the Festival Cup defeat.

Speculation about the future of the club and where it might play its football had at least subsided after the start of the season. August ended with Hearts moving into third place in the league and the major off-the-field controversy had become the row between Craig Levein and the SFA. The SFA had imposed a £1,000 fine on Levein following sarcastic comments he made about referee Dougie McDonald in a match against Kilmarnock the previous season and the Hearts coach was refusing to pay up because he felt he had been treated unfairly. Levein then failed to turn up at a SFA committee meeting in August and his fine was increased to £4,000. There was the additional possibility of a four-month touchline ban and even the threat of a ban from playing in European competitions.

It was amid this dispute that Hearts began to give more explicit and public backing to the possibility of selling Tynecastle and leasing Murrayfield. Chris Robinson told a consultation meeting of some 300 fans that 'Murrayfield has to be considered. It's within walking distance of Tynecastle and is a state-of-the-art stadium'. He also repeated the SRU suggestions that large banners could be used to screen off empty seating areas and 'create the illusion of a smaller stadium – it's a possibility but an imperfect solution'. The chief executive added that the preferred option remained a shared stadium on a greenfield site but insisted that Hearts would go it alone if necessary.

During September, attention turned further from discussions about the club's future as supporters looked forward to the season's participation in the UEFA Cup. One of Hearts' most convincing performances under Levein came at Rugby Park with a 2–0 defeat of Kilmarnock, the main challengers for Europe the previous season. However, the promising home form suffered a setback when Rangers won 4–0 at Tynecastle, although the denial of two Hearts penalty claims helped to turn the game in the visitors' favour. The UEFA Cup first-round match against Bosnian team Zeljeznicar, from Sarajevo, took place at Tynecastle on 24 September. Despite, their dominance, Hearts could only finish with a 2–0 victory and were no doubt concerned that their opponents appeared capable of passing the ball well.

The month ended with a dreary 1–1 draw against Motherwell at a drenched Fir Park, while October began with an exciting 2–2 tie against Dundee in Edinburgh. The seriousness of the Murrayfield proposal was highlighted the following weekend when, on 10 October, Hearts met the same opponents in a closed-door match at the rugby stadium. This 'road test' to judge the suitability of the venue ended 0–0.

Hearts' trip to Sarajevo in the UEFA Cup return leg on 15 October was expected to be difficult. The result in the first leg had been far from convincing and the facilities in Bosnia had been damaged badly in the recent Balkans war. Dutch striker Mark de Vries was reported to have been subjected to racist abuse in Sarajevo from the Zeljeznicar fans, who were known as the 'Maniacs', but the game otherwise passed off without any further unsavoury incident. The 300 Hearts fans in the crowd watched as Zeljeznicar piled on early pressure but the players fought their way back into the game and earned a 0–0 draw which took them through to the next round of the competition. The return home brought news that Hearts had drawn the glamorous French side, FC Girondins de Bordeaux, in the second round of the UEFA Cup. Levein described them as a 'massive team', adding that it was 'an incredible draw for us'.

Unfortunately, the team's first outing after returning from Sarajevo resulted in a 5–0 thrashing by Celtic at Parkhead, although that was followed by wins against Partick Thistle (4–1) in the league and Falkirk (2–1) in the League Cup. Also, on their arrival back from the UEFA Cup trip, Hearts became embroiled in a row with the SPL over the scheduling of a match against Aberdeen on Remembrance Sunday. The date is regarded as virtually sacrosanct by the Tynecastle club because it has been set aside for a service since 1922, when the Haymarket War Memorial to the Hearts players and members killed in the First World War was built. The club pleaded with the SPL to alter the date, although all they would do was put the kick-off time back to 4 p.m. to allow the team to attend the services before heading north. The supporters' federation complained that the decision showed 'a complete lack of respect'. Still, the issue of where the club was destined to play its football in the future remained remarkably low-key.

Then, at the end of October, Hibs announced that they were to stay at Easter Road, an alternative business plan having been drawn up to ensure the club could break even in its traditional home. In return, crowds – already down by around 10% – were urged to turn up in numbers to ensure commercial success. Hearts chief executive Chris Robinson was unfazed – Hearts would press ahead with their plans regardless of Hibs' decision and now Murrayfield was emerging as the most likely option. Few realised how quickly events would move.

19

A TASTE OF BORDEAUX – THE VICTORY HANGOVER

At the beginning of November 2003, the focus was firmly on the much anticipated tie against Bordeaux and the team left for France after a battling 3–1 success against Livingston at Tynecastle. The attention at the end of the month would be on a very different issue. A travelling contingent of some 3,100 fans followed the team across the Channel, most hoping for a decent draw or narrow loss – few could have expected to return with a famous victory. But Craig Levein reshuffled his team to pack the midfield and an inspired performance from young goalkeeper Craig Gordon helped the team record a 1–0 victory – surely, at that time, the best result ever achieved by a Hearts team away from home in a competitive European tie. The Bordeaux management curiously criticised the Hearts players for celebrating at the final whistle, including throwing their jerseys into the crowd, but the fans toasted the victory in the Connemara pub and other bars around the Place de Tourny and Place Gambetta then packed the Bordeaux club shop the following day for mementos of their trip. The memorable success seemed to lift the club and wins over Aberdeen (1–0) and Hibs after two own goals (2–0) were the perfect build-up for the return leg on 27 November. But, while fans saw the memorable derby victory as the ideal countdown to the Bordeaux game, in truth, as the hours passed, the club was heading towards a very different deadline.

SMG – the Glasgow-based media group which invested £8 million in the club in 1999 – had been given a deadline of 11 October 2003 to decide whether to convert £4.5 million of that investment into shares. However, the Hearts share price had slumped to just 17p – a massive drop from £1.40 a share when the media company struck the original deal with Hearts. The original expectation in 1999 had been that SMG would convert. But, with the collapse in the share price, there was never any realistic possibility of that happening. Nevertheless, in order to allow more discussions to take place, the deadline was extended to 24 November – the day after that Hibs game and just three days before the crucial European tie. As the build-up to the game against the French team became more fevered, the financial consequences of failure must have become all the more apparent to those behind the scenes. Perhaps with that in mind, on the day of the Bordeaux match, the club's bank, the Bank of Scotland, agreed to increase a 'multi-option facility' – which could be used as an overdraft or for guarantees – from £3.5 million to £5.75 million. It was also agreed that the matter would be reviewed by the bank on 31 July 2004.

Before the match, the Edinburgh club was presented with plaques and souvenirs from Bordeaux's police in honour of the 'fabulous' behaviour of Hearts supporters who had followed their team to the French city, describing them as the best fans ever to have visited the area. A crowd of 17,587, the biggest crowd of the season, packed into the stands hoping for yet another famous victory. Sadly, the players failed to respond and Hearts were beaten 2–0 by a revived French team. After the euphoria of the first leg, the result was a major let-down but it was to be followed the next day by an even bigger bombshell.

Half an hour before the stock exchange closed and as the next day's papers and the Sundays were finalising their news schedules, the club announced that it was to sell Tynecastle, apparently within eight months. Results for the year ended 31 July 2003 showed that, while pre-tax losses for the year were down to £1.1 million from £2.7 million the previous year, overall net debt had gone up from £14.8 million to £17.6 million. Despite the fact that supporters had believed the SMG cash would cover Hearts' share of a new youth academy, almost £1.8 million of the debt was 'a development credit facility' to fund construction of the centre. Staff costs were down but only by 10% to £5.1 million, still a troubling 85% of turnover. Both the chairman, Doug Smith, and the chief executive, Chris Robinson, blamed a reduction in media income in the annual report. The £2 million sale of goalkeeper Antti Niemi to Southampton prevented the figures being much worse. Robinson's statement avoided emphasising the unsustainable debt situation, referring first to the UEFA regulations and new health and safety rules which would hinder development of the Tynecastle site. The intentions, however, were clear when he announced:

> As part of the strategy to move from loss to profit, we have had to consider the commercial viability of our stadium. Despite significant investment in the late 1990s to comply with the Lord Justice Taylor Report, we now have a stadium that cannot meet the needs of the company going forward. The UEFA licensing and competition rules in relation to pitch size are operational from season 2004. The Scottish Football Association has recently stated that we cannot rely on it achieving derogation from the regulations. Financial analysis of our business, particularly in relation to commercial and revenue-generating facilities, highlights that, as currently configured, our stadium in Gorgie cannot match the income generation required for a club such as Hearts. The land values and the situation with regard to recent legislation is (*sic*) such that it would be impossible from a planning perspective and prohibitive from a cost perspective to replace our existing McLeod Street Stand. It would not, in any event, provide a solution to the deficiency in the playing arena dimensions.
>
> As has been widely stated by the company, we are examining options in respect of a replacement for Tynecastle Stadium. This will allow us to realise the value of land at Tynecastle assuming we obtain appropriate planning permission for development and give the added benefit of substantial debt reduction that will assist the company in its strategy through lower ongoing financing charges.

The statement went on to pledge a detailed analysis of the options and consultation with all interested parties because 'the decision on stadium relocation will be the most important we can take, as it is our most valuable asset and we must ensure that we get it right'. It also sought to play up the potential benefits of the soon-to-be-completed youth academy at Heriot-Watt University, despite the fact that the construction company had gone into receivership earlier in the year. But the final passage in Robinson's statement, almost incidentally, added that SMG would not be exercising its option to convert £4.5 million of that total into shares. That money must be paid back, with interest. The first instalment of interest, £767,000, was 'deferred for payment until the earlier of 31 July 2004 or the realisation of the value of land at Tynecastle'. But where would Hearts find the cash to pay SMG?

The notes to the accounts added that the bank was providing only conditional support to the club and backed plans to cash in on Tynecastle, explaining:

> The company is currently examining options in respect of the sale of Tynecastle Stadium, the repayment of related borrowings and relocation to a replacement stadium by 31 July 2004. Under this strategy, the company has support from its lenders in providing the necessary working capital until 31 July 2004 ... The directors expect that the stadium position will be concluded satisfactorily by 31 July 2004 ...

Essentially, the bank had decided enough was enough. The club had been told that, if it wanted to increase its borrowings, it would first have to produce a business plan that would convince the bank that its cash was safe. The board produced a business plan – a single option according to the bank – to sell Tynecastle. The Bank of Scotland not surprisingly supported the sole option it was presented with.

Supporters, unaware of the passing of the SMG loan deadline and the negotiations with the bank, were stunned. The comedown from the high of the first leg of the Bordeaux tie could hardly have been more swift and startling. Most simply did not know how to react – the ground they had been attending for years or even decades was to be sold, razed to the ground and flats would spring up in its place within a matter of months. To compound the misery, the club had no long-term plan for a new home. A debate, of course, had been taking place about the future of the club but few believed the proposals under discussion would imminently become a reality, particularly because of the obvious flaws associated with each option.

Coach Craig Levein was reported to have estimated that success against Bordeaux would have earned the club an additional £500,000 but the actual cost of failing to qualify for the third round had never been quantified. Now the club was being forced to sell its spiritual home and its very existence was being threatened by moving into a stadium unsuitable for football. The potential for disaster was obvious – crowds and possibly corporate hospitality would fall as few chose to watch football in such uninspiring surroundings. On the pitch, the team would lose the advantage of playing home games in the tight and often intimidating Tynecastle atmosphere. Revenues would continue to fall as less committed supporters stayed away and the playing budgets were cut further. A vicious circle of decline was possible, if not probable. Again, *The Times'* analysis of Espanyol's plight was to articulate the initial fears of many fans:

> Stop me if you've heard this one before. A big city club with a century of tradition which can trace its roots back to the dawn of the professional game decides to uproot and sell its spiritual home. The reason? Massive debt. The solution? A huge modern stadium – admittedly, not a football one – is available to rent. The story does not have a happy ending. No one likes the new ground. It's big, draughty and swallows up the modest crowds. Eventually, people begin to fall out of love with the club and stop coming. The debt, that was once cleared off, begins to grow again and the promised gleaming, new home of their own is nowhere to be seen. Heart of Midlothian fans can stop worrying. This has not been a bad dream yet. This is the story of Espanyol, one of Spain's proudest clubs, but one fighting to survive in La Liga after a series of badly thought-out decisions over where it played its football.

20

'TYNECASTLE STADIUM: NOT FIT FOR PURPOSE'

Almost immediately, opposition to the stadium sale began to organise. The newly formed Heart of Midlothian Supporters Trust had held its first AGM at Tynecastle the week before the Bordeaux game at the same venue. Now the board members gathered in Melville's, a bar in Edinburgh's west end, for a very different meeting. It was agreed that a 'Keep our Hearts in Gorgie' campaign should be launched as soon as possible and office-holders were appointed on the spot.

Meanwhile, Chris Robinson was the first key figure to make a meaningful public contribution during the turbulent month of December. The chief executive weighed in first when he told *The Scotsman* on 6 December that he was disappointed that SMG had chosen not to convert its loan into shares. In an admirable admission, he said the SMG deal 'hasn't worked'. He added:

> The partnership never really worked. It was made at a time when media companies down south were investing in football clubs and no club like Hearts would turn down £8 million at the time it was offered. Not long after the investment by SMG, the markets for both organisations collapsed.

For its part, SMG admitted likewise, saying the link-up had been disappointing for both parties. A spokesman later acknowledged that, with a representative on the Hearts board, the company also took its share of responsibility for Hearts' difficulties. He said,

'Anybody who was part of the decision-making process has to share responsibility for a speculate-to-accumulate policy which didn't work in the end.'

Former chairman Leslie Deans was quick to enter the debate in an attempt to rally the opposition, not least because he had seen investments into the club rejected. Two days after Robinson's interview, he told the same newspaper, 'My message is [that] the fans are mobilising. There is going to be change at Tynecastle.'

Deans' intervention was an attempt to prove his version of events relating to the latest takeover bid, which involved the injection of £10 million on condition that Robinson be removed as chief executive. Angered by Robinson's claims that he did not have the cash to back up the bid in 2002, Deans decided to reveal precise details of the deal, which involved buying a block of new shares at 50p each. At the same time, he accused Robinson of treating the fans like 'mugs' for not acknowledging the significance of the debt problem. Homing in on the financial crisis at the club, Deans claimed the ground was being sold because the club had no other means of paying back the SMG loan. He asked how Hearts would attract future investment with no significant assets and was the first to clearly warn that the Murrayfield move could lead to the club disappearing without trace. He told the *Edinburgh Evening News* on 12 December:

> For Scotland's third biggest club not to own its own stadium would be desperately sad. You don't dispose of the family silver like this because you can only do it once. To sell Tynecastle would be to give up our birthright – it would be like selling the club's soul.

The chief executive responded with accusations that his former colleague was dealing in 'smoke and mirrors' and 'airy-fairy ideas'. He continued to insist the main problems were UEFA regulations in relation to the pitch size for European cup competitions, health and safety rules which would prevent effective redevelopment of the main stand, and the lack of car parking space. The pitch problem, he claimed, simply could not be solved by any means while the latter two issues had to be addressed to generate sufficient commercial income. The day after Deans' outburst, Robinson was reported in the same paper to make the remarkable claim that:

> If someone was to invest £10 million or £100 million in Hearts, it doesn't alter the need to move away from Tynecastle . . . The pitch size is too small and we are unable to rebuild the main stand. The reason we are unable to do so is we would have to acquire a huge amount of land behind it at an enormous land cost . . . We are only looking for a metre either end of the pitch but it simply can't be made longer.

Robinson also produced a report, 'Tynecastle Stadium: Not Fit For Purpose', outlining the thinking behind the board's controversial strategy. It expanded on the issues of pitch size, explaining:

> Any examination of the structure of Tynecastle, taking into account the position of the corner towers will show that it is simply not possible to create even this minimum pitch size. To achieve the minimum playing arena, which is based on safety implications, would require us to remove the first eight concrete plinths at the Gorgie and Roseburn Stands. We would also require to virtually reconstruct the stadium due to the four corner towers.

And just weeks before the stadium report, details of new health and safety rules relating to Control of Major Accident Hazards (COMAH) were confirmed. These regulations, which were introduced by legislation in 2001, restricted developments in a zone around industrial plants. In this case, the club said it was constrained by the existence of the nearby North British Distillery and Macfarlan Smith chemical works as the new laws would take into account the fact that large crowds of people gathered in a small area on match days and could, therefore, be in danger in the event of a major industrial accident. The Health and Safety Executive, the club argued, would oppose any expansion of the existing site although it could not object to development on the existing 'footprint' of the McLeod Street Stand. In claiming that, because of this, the stand needed to be replaced, the report said:

The McLeod Street Stand is rapidly approaching a position where its safety certificate is under threat. Structural engineers are concerned about the integrity due to corrosion of the internal steel beams. The stand itself does not conform with the 'Green Guide' in terms of exit widths and evacuation times. The roof of the stand, which is asbestos, has become very brittle and breaks and fragments on the rare occasions that balls land on the roof. Netting has been placed underneath this to protect spectators. The main seating deck is timber and therefore a higher risk for fire.

Like the annual report, the document made only a passing reference to the club's huge debt, accepting that 'the move to occupy nearby Murrayfield can also be carried out against a background of significant debt reduction'.

But publication of the stadium report failed to convince most fans and, in fact, led to increased resentment amid accusations of 'spin' by the board. Also, there was mounting anger that much-needed money from Leslie Deans had been turned down by a board which was failing to make a convincing case to its 'customers'. The high-profile squabble was, therefore, also to provide an opportunity for the new supporters' trust to enter into the debate publicly.

The Heart of Midlothian Supporters Trust had been formed earlier that year with a mission statement which declared that, 'regardless of who the custodians of HMFC may be, the supporters are the lifeblood and [the] only constant'. Its original aims were to ensure more supporter involvement in running the club, to support the development of the team and to benefit the community that was served by Hearts. The central role it would assume in the coming weeks and months could not have been anticipated. But the day after Robinson had hit back at Deans' claims, the 300-strong trust announced the recently agreed plans to launch the Keep our Hearts in Gorgie campaign. Then, on 15 December, trust leaders turned up at Tynecastle for a showdown with the Hearts chairman, chief executive and finance director. They urged a delay in the plans but it was clear events were moving quickly. Trust minutes show that Robinson outlined the 'Not Fit For Purpose' arguments before revealing that he was already looking at possible new stadium sites, including one he was going to see the following day. The minutes also recorded Robinson agreeing that 'there could be the option of building a half-sized Murrayfield in the back pitches of the main stadium'.

As Deans had predicted, the fans were mobilising. The trust then took part in a summit with other supporters' groups – the Federation of Hearts Supporters Clubs and the Heart of Midlothian Shareholders Association – and was buoyed by the revelation that Hearts shareholder and businessman Robert McGrail had offered to buy Tynecastle from Hearts for £10 million and lease it back to the club. The suggestion, which cast doubt on the board's claim that there was no alternative but to move to Murrayfield, was apparently 'brushed aside' by the club but warmly welcomed by fans alarmed at the speed of developments.

But, unknown to fans, a series of other meetings had been taking place. In addition to his sale-and-leaseback proposal, Robert McGrail had approached SMG to discuss the possibility of buying its debt and shareholding, the latter of which was then worth around £440,000. On top of his own cash, he had the backing of a major bank and was deadly serious in his intentions. He has revealed for this book that the talks led to an agreement in principle to purchase both the debt and the shares. But the deal would only get the go-ahead from his backers if it also included buying out the Bank of Scotland debt. The businessman would have passed the discount on the debt on to Hearts, leading to a reduction of up to £4 million in the club's overall debt position, he says. At the same time, he put in place a new business plan and was prepared to act as chief executive for two years without payment. Robert McGrail explains:

> This was very much a win-win proposal for Hearts. The bank I approached to partly finance this deal loved the simplicity of the plan and agreed the figures stacked up and was happy with the personal guarantees I was prepared to offer in addition to the security of the land value at Tynecastle. They were also happy with the

business plan I had developed for the club going forward which would have seen revenues increase by at least £1.5 million without breaking sweat which, combined with savings on wages in the new reality of Scottish football, would have put Hearts on a sound financial footing. Hearts' problems could have been solved back in January 2004 if the board had sanctioned this proposal.

He adds that 'SMG were very co-operative and, contrary to what many think, were interested in the greater good for Hearts'. But the Hearts board did not give the bank the authority to discuss the offer further, he says. The deal collapsed before it had a chance to succeed but it did at least put pressure on the board to consider other options. McGrail says, '[Hearts] might be at Murrayfield now if it wasn't for the pressure being exerted behind the scenes.'

Robert McGrail was not the only one trying to force the agenda. His brother, Peter, had met with the campaigners and was also concerned about the implications of selling up. Peter McGrail, a business strategist, who was also a neighbour of Chris Robinson and had commercial links with Hearts through the publication of the club's annual report, wrote to the chief executive on New Year's Eve, the day after his meeting with the fans' groups. He said:

> The massive debt, leading to what I view as the virtually untenable proposition that we move to Murrayfield, has spurred me into action in order to find a better solution. Now that I have done some background work in the last two weeks, I believe there could be another way forward that must be fully investigated before we accept the Murrayfield option as inevitable.

And the fledgling campaign appeared to be achieving some success with a flurry of letters to newspapers contradicting the arguments of the Hearts board. First, SMG appeared to point the finger at Hearts in a letter to *The Scotsman*, insisting all its attempts to 'build the Hearts brand proved too difficult for the club to implement'. It added that the £8 million investment should have been spent on players, developing a youth policy and stadium improvements but, instead, it only went on players and club running costs. The next development was when UEFA confirmed that Hearts could remain at Tynecastle but play their European games elsewhere. Finally, a further letter to *The Scotsman* from the city council stated that it was 'entirely satisfied' about the safety of the old McLeod Street Stand.

But the off-the-field uproar appeared to have taken its toll on the players during December. Two days after the original announcement there was little surprise when the team went down 2–1 to Dundee United at Tannadice – a combination of the criticism directed at the club over the stadium announcement and a hangover from the UEFA Cup exit seeming to damage the confidence of players and supporters alike. Further defeats away from home followed, first to financially-stricken Dundee (1–0) after extra time in the League Cup – a continuing cup run could have brought much needed semi-final income to Hearts – then to Dunfermline (2–1) in the league. The season's worst losing run was halted by the fortunate 2–1 defeat of Kilmarnock at Tynecastle but that was followed by a further 2–1 loss at the hands of Rangers at Ibrox. A disappointing 0–0 draw with Motherwell between Christmas and New Year completed a miserable December for the team and forced Craig Levein to concede that it was difficult to ignore the fact that 'monumental' decisions were being taken off the pitch and it was proving difficult for everyone at the club.

21

THE FANS MOBILISE

Hearts moved into 2004 amid frantic activity at the club itself. However, there was surprisingly little visible opposition among the fans as a whole. It was a situation that led Hearts' all-time-appearance record-holder Gary Mackay – a stern opponent of the board's strategy – to bemoan the 'apathy' shown by the supporters to date. At matches, groups of fans had begun to express their concerns through songs critical of the board and a handful of banners appeared in the crowd and outside the ground around New Year but suggestions of organised protest initially failed to get off the ground.

The scheduling of games by the SPL meant that the team did not have its traditional New Year derby against its city rivals but that did, at least, allow for a noticeable improvement in performances. Despite the recent run of indifferent results, a creditable 2–1 win over Dundee at Dens Park was the first away victory for two months and consolidated Hearts' third-place league position at the beginning of January. Campaigners, meanwhile, were looking to a run of three home games as an opportunity to organise opposition to the board's plans. Then, on 9 January, the day before the first of those home games, a further alternative to the Murrayfield strategy emerged.

Peter McGrail had been working on his own plan – as suggested in the earlier letter to Chris Robinson – without the knowledge of his brother, to avoid accusations of conflict of interest. It was based on providing Hearts with a new, state-of-the-art stadium as part of a wider regeneration of the Gorgie area. A press conference was held to publish the discussion document, 'Murrayfield: There May Still Be An Alternative for Heart of Midlothian Football Club'. Journalists were told that a ground-share with the SRU would be 'cataclysmic' and a viable alternative existed. That involved the club, council and a private property developer joining forces to redevelop the area around the current stadium, school and roads depot. He added that football 'has gone through a ridiculous delusional period for 10–15 years whereby it has treated what is a cornerstone of local and national life as some sort of superficial leisure product that can be bought and sold like a McDonald's hamburger'.

The discussion paper, named in parody of the club's own stadium report, said:

> They, like so many other clubs, were doing their work in an envi-
> ronment in which it was nigh impossible to avoid the inflated
> player wages, fees and bonuses. The carrot of greater reward from
> TV coverage and further success led to an imbalance that has cre-
> ated severe debt and a position where in reality they no longer
> have full control of the club. The pressure from their creditors is
> now forcing the club to capitulate and take a course of action that is
> highly likely to lead to anything other than a slow, painful death for
> Hearts as a major football club . . . Unfortunately, I think the fight is
> over but only for Chris Robinson and some of his colleagues. It is
> time for the current regime to stand down.

The supporters' organisations had also been active. A survey of fans at the cup tie against Berwick Rangers at Tynecastle on 10 January, which Hearts won 2–0, found massive opposition to the board's plans. A total of 96.5% of those polled opposed mov-ing to Murrayfield the following season. Almost 4,800 fans from the 8,400 crowd took part, with only 146 in favour of playing at the rugby stadium and twenty-seven 'don't knows'. Derek Watson, secretary of the supporters' trust and one of the survey organisers, described the result as 'overwhelming'. He urged the board to consider the call for a year's delay to examine all the options, warning, 'This is being rushed into and it could be the death knell for the club.'

The poll and the growing pressure on Chris Robinson in particular was followed by a perceptible softening of the club's attitudes, with chairman Doug Smith entering into negotiations with Robert McGrail over his leaseback offer. But the ninety-eighth annual general meeting (AGM), two days later, was still expected to be a stormy affair. Former chairman Wallace Mercer even suggested it could be the most significant in living memory.

More than 800 shareholders crammed into the Gorgie Suite at Tynecastle with dozens left standing when the seats were filled. However, the revolt failed to materialise. Robert McGrail was given the opportunity to address shareholders but, while he attempted to adopt a conciliatory tone, he had clearly been given little time to prepare. As a result, the audience was offered little concrete reassurance of his intentions. Robinson, on the other hand, had prepared a detailed slide presentation, which lasted more than an hour. The presentation was entitled 'The Big Issue' and, therefore, ironically shared the name of the magazine for homeless people. It gave a detailed assessment of the club's finances and included many of the arguments rehearsed in the 'Not Fit For Purpose' report. It argued that remaining at Tynecastle would result in continued losses and, because of this, there could be 'no future'. Murrayfield, on the other hand, was a world-class stadium with modern facilities and it was close to the club's current Gorgie home. The chief executive also produced financial projections for both Tynecastle and Murrayfield. He estimated that the club would make a loss in 2004–05 of £2.5 million on a turnover of £5.8 million at the former and a profit of £75,000 on a turnover of £7.5 million at the latter. He said, even after paying rent, Murrayfield would reduce costs by £875,000. Wages would have to be reduced by £850,000 in both cases. In addition, a £12 million offer had already been made for Tynecastle, although that had been rejected because the board could expect to earn up to £22 million for the sale and, thereby, eliminate the club's debt within two to three years, Robinson claimed. He concluded his presentation, saying, 'We are left with little or no option – stay at Tynecastle [and] remain loss-making with dire consequences or bite the bullet and plan for the opportunity that Murrayfield can deliver. What we cannot do is nothing.'

The presentation was interrupted by a number of outbursts from the floor, including angry calls for Robinson's resignation, but it also received a ripple of applause from the gathered share-holders. Questions from the floor focused on the financial crisis at the club and accusations of mismanagement were levelled at the board. The financial projections comparing Tynecastle and Murrayfield were also questioned, although the board would not give further details about how the figures were calculated. The long-term prospects for the club also came under scrutiny, with one shareholder failing to receive a satisfactory answer when he asked what contingency plan was in place should the Murrayfield move prove damaging. Another pointed out that Robinson had previously questioned the viability of using the rugby stadium, which suffers flooding and has poor catering facilities, when he was arguing strongly for a move to Straiton. The chief executive admitted he had been 'talking up the merits' of Straiton and claimed it was his job to do so. He also conceded that the lack of atmosphere at Murrayfield could pose problems for the football club but repeated previous suggestions that empty areas could be screened out. In a further admission, Robinson said redevelop-ment of the stadium since 1994 should never have gone ahead because the club was suffering from compromises made then.

A handful of those present spoke in favour of the strategy, pointing out that supporters should back the club rather than the stadium in which they play. However, dozens of shareholders, including former player Gary Mackay, drifted out of the meeting before it ended after a marathon four-and-a-half-hour debate. One departing shareholder, Peter Thompson, said, 'I was surprised that there wasn't more opposition – unfortunately, I think he's won some of the shareholders over. But I'm convinced the fight will go on.'

The legacy of the meeting was an announcement that an extraordinary general meeting (EGM) would be held, probably within three months, to approve the sale of Tynecastle. As all motions at the AGM were passed with a block vote of more than 51% backing the board's position, the controversial move once again appeared inevitable.

However, later that week, the supporters' trust upped the stakes by demanding the resignation of both the chief executive and chairman and calling on SMG to sell its shares to fans. The volume of protest was turned up for the next match, the televised game against Celtic on 18 January. The players concentrated on their own efforts, despite the distractions, and were unfortunate to lose 1–0. That narrow defeat was followed by a less than convincing 2–0 victory over struggling Partick Thistle the following week and, again, the game was played amid noisy protests from the stands. Inevitably, the on-field action was soon displaced by club politics.

Then there was a breaking of ranks among the fans' organisations. The supporters' trust and the Federation of Hearts Supporters Clubs had remained unified since the controversy broke, with the Hearts Shareholders Association involved in discussions but refusing to take a formal position, preferring to leave that to individual members. But the position of the Fans' Forum, an open organisation set up three years before as a link between the club and its supporters, had been unclear until it issued a press release towards the end of January. The statement, which was said to reflect the views of those at the previous meeting in November, said remaining at Tynecastle was the preferred option but confusingly then added that 'Murrayfield offers by far the best opportunity for the long-term financial viability of the club'. It went on to offer 'continued support for the board's strategy', albeit conditional on the fact that it explored the option of remaining at Tynecastle. The other fans' organisations criticised the forum for contributing 'nothing to the debate' and issuing statements based on 'out-of-date information' and, once again, the scene was set for an explosive public meeting at an Edinburgh hotel. This time it was organised by fans and involved all the key players.

When around 250 people jammed into the Orwell Lodge hotel, Chris Robinson and his principal adversaries once again found themselves in a packed meeting hall for the 'Big Debate'. As had happened at the AGM, dozens were forced to stand at the back of the hall. Statements were read out by the supporters' groups, the club's federation, the supporters' trust and the Fans' Forum.

Shareholders' representative Charles McLaughlin opened the meeting when he said, 'Leaving Tynecastle is the most important decision we have ever faced in our 130-year history so we must ensure it is the correct decision.' The federation and trust then reiterated their opposition to the Murrayfield move and lack of confidence in the board, while forum chairman Ali Hibberd was angrily heckled as he sought to defend the statement released a week earlier. The top table of Chris Robinson, Robert McGrail, Leslie Deans and Gary Mackay then delivered their own speeches before questions were taken from the floor. But already the mood of the meeting was extremely volatile, with Robinson subjected to fierce criticism and verbal attacks.

The chief executive argued that Hearts had been in 'financial dire straits' for years because of the cumulative effect of year-on-year losses, which would not be supported by the bank or other creditors. The alternative to leaving Tynecastle, he claimed, would be to virtually replace the first team with young players. He was also dismissive of Robert McGrail's sale-and-leaseback proposal, claiming that it would do little to solve problems with the stadium and money would continue to disappear into a 'black hole'. He said, 'I want to stay at Tynecastle but I don't see any viable options to do that.' However, he warned that such a decision may lead to the club going into administration, with the administrator then being forced to sell the ground. He added later, 'For the last ten years, while I have been at Tynecastle, the club has not built debt up for any other reason than ambition and desire to have better, more skilled players.'

Robert McGrail acknowledged that Robinson's reaction to his sale-and-leaseback deal meant it was now very unlikely to go ahead. The club later explained that the £10 million sale would not have made commercial sense because, while Hearts could reduce their debts by that amount, they would then be forced to pay an annual rent in excess of current interest payments to the bank. However, Robert McGrail challenged Robinson to 'name [his] price' for his stake in the club. He suggested a share issue or debenture scheme could also be launched to alleviate the financial problems and help to rebuild the McLeod Street Stand. He said:

Chris has had three years not to find a solution – we have had a matter of weeks so give us a bit more time. This is a very, very important decision for Hearts so give us a year to look at all the proposals. The board who have taken us to the precipice want to go over the precipice and beyond – that's what I find bizarre. It's time to change and that doesn't mean break our hearts and take the club to Murrayfield – all that it requires is a change of hearts.

Former chairman Leslie Deans called on SMG to abstain from any vote about the future of the stadium because the company faced a possible conflict of interest being both creditors and major shareholders. He said Hearts would have to cut costs if necessary and live within their means. The alternative, he said, was to put the club at the mercy of the SRU who, it had been speculated, may even move from Murrayfield at some point in the future. Prophetically, he also spoke of the expansion of the European Union and the fact that this would open up a market for Eastern European players who would regard Scottish wages as 'a king's ransom'. Although it was three months before he met future Lithuanian investor Vladimir Romanov, he added, 'We would all happily go with that if it meant we could survive and flourish.'

Gary Mackay, who became involved in a heated off-microphone discussion with Robinson and eventually walked away from the top table, warned, 'There can be no hindsight in a year's time because there will be no football club in a year's time if we move.'

Fans questioned the projected season ticket sales at Murrayfield, which had been judged to be the same as they would have been at Tynecastle, pointing out that many supporters would refuse to buy them. Trust secretary Derek Watson also asked Robinson if he would sell his shares to the fans. The chief executive simply answered, 'No.' After the meeting, the chief executive told the *Edinburgh Evening News*, 'It's a no-win situation for me. If I don't come to these nights, I'm accused of hiding. If I do, I get a hiding. It was a volatile meeting and I knew it would be.'

22

FAN POWER AND PASSION

The gloomy mood of Scottish football darkened further at the beginning of February when Livingston followed fellow SPL clubs, Dundee and Motherwell, into administration. Dunfermline Athletic admitted that they, too, faced the threat of a similar fate, while Hibs were also known to be suffering financial difficulties. It was at this time that a senior figure at Hearts acknowledged that those in charge of the club must take responsibility for the financial crisis. The admission, which many critics had sought, came during a meeting between finance director Stewart Fraser and a group of 'disenchanted fans'. An account of the meeting recalled that Fraser was asked why Hearts had found themselves in financial difficulties. The finance director explained:

> [The fans] said the directors were obviously responsible and ultimately they are but you would also have to say that about every SPL club in Scotland . . . If you go back to the 'speculate-to-accumulate' plan, it did not work and now we are trying to turn the club around.

The more publicly defiant stance of the Hearts board, however, was given a boost the same day when it was revealed that SMG would not abstain at an EGM. The media group also took the opportunity to maintain that there was no conflict of interest in its chief executive, Andrew Flanagan, also holding the post of non-executive director of the SRU, the rugby authority that was in negotiations with Hearts about the Murrayfield relocation. Corporate affairs director Callum Spreng insisted Flanagan would 'discharge his duties in a wholly proper manner'. Four days later, the relevance of the latter statement, in particular, became apparent. An announcement to the London Stock Exchange confirmed that Hearts had reached agreement, in principle, with the SRU over ground-sharing at Murrayfield from the start of season 2004–05. In addition, Tynecastle was to be valued to 'begin a process of selecting a preferred bidder for the ground'.

But the announcement and the earlier disappointment of a 3–0 Scottish Cup exit at the hands of Celtic seemed only to galvanise the fans further as the failure to reach the last eight was also loaded with financial implications. Plans were already being made for a rally of fans as a show of strength but an even more radical campaign of action was drawn up during a meeting of activists at this time, much of which was never implemented because of fears that it would be too divisive. These controversial tactics by the supporters' trust, which had doubled its membership to around 600 in the previous two months, included a mini boycott – described as 'a withdrawal of attendance' – for fifteen minutes at the beginning of a forthcoming game. Also, the formation of HBOS in 2001 following the merger between the Bank of Scotland and the Halifax led to claims that, with interests divided between Edinburgh and West Yorkshire, the bank's patience with clients from the world of Scottish football was running out. HBOS strenuously denied this, insisting its commitment had not wavered.

However, with those suspicions in mind, a campaign against the club's bankers, including threats to withdraw accounts, was also agreed but it was never carried out. Significantly, though, those present supported the formation of a new unified Save our Hearts group, along with the federation, to adopt a more high-profile stance than the Keep our Hearts in Gorgie campaign which had failed to attract mass support. Other supporters' organisations – the shareholders' body and the Fans' Forum – would be invited to attend, although the bedrock of the new group would be the federation and the trust. Trust chairman Martin Laidlaw issued a call to arms:

It's time to get off our backsides and do something. The situation we are facing is so serious that we can't sit back. We have to demonstrate our power and our unity. The fans have the power to do something about this and they have to realise that.

That meeting also resolved to turn up the pressure on SMG who were privately thought to be 'receptive to a bid' for their 19.9% shareholding. The day after Hearts' announcement to the stock exchange, details of just such a bid began to emerge. Those behind it were described in press reports as a consortium of wealthy businessmen. In fact, it involved the supporters' trust and federation along with three wealthy backers. They offered £2 million for SMG's shares – then worth around £540,000 at the market price – along with the £4.5 million loan debt and £767,000 interest, which would soon rise to £868,000. If they succeeded in taking control of the club, there was the added sweetener of £300,000 from the television windfall expected if Hearts reached the second round of the UEFA Cup.

The group would seek to keep Hearts in Gorgie and replace the current chief executive and reconstitute the board on gaining a power base. The consortium, which was understood to include Leslie Deans and Robert McGrail and a third anonymous backer, would effectively control the club and be in a position to force through its own policies. The initial talks with SMG finance director George Watt were described by one negotiator as 'very positive' but, within hours, the prospect of a deal disappeared and it emerged that the media company was seeking closer to £3.2 million.

The manoeuvring was followed by a charm offensive from the Hearts board. Two days after the team defeated Aberdeen 1–0 at the beginning of February, it was announced that the club was launching a consultation exercise to 'examine all aspects of the proposed move'. Four working parties would be set up to explore key issues connected with the relocation to Murrayfield. The head of Forth 2 radio station and Tynecastle announcer, Scott Wilson, would lead a group looking at ways to 'enhance the entire Hearts match-day experience in order to make it the best of its kind in

Scotland'. Edinburgh councillor and former Lord Provost Eric Milligan was to head 'a stadium-branding and signage group, looking at ways in which the home of Scottish rugby can be transformed into the home of Hearts FC' – in other words, how Hearts banners, screens and signs could give Murrayfield the appearance of the club's home ground. Jim Rigby, a management consultant who oversaw the redevelopment of Tynecastle, was to explore match pricing options, including season ticket deals and admission charges on the gate. Hearts sales and marketing manager Kenny Wittman was charged with consulting commercial clients on how to improve corporate income at Murrayfield. Hearts said the consultation exercise was designed to ensure the switch to Murrayfield was 'a roaring success' and high-profile supporter Milligan outlined his personal reasons for becoming involved in the scheme. Milligan, the councillor for the Stenhouse ward which includes Murrayfield, told the club website:

> I am a season ticket holder. I am a lifelong Hearts supporter brought up in Gorgie and I carry around with me all that emotional attachment that connects me to Tynecastle Park. If Hearts are shortly to play their last game there, I will be there with my maroon tissues. I instinctively understand and appreciate the fears that many Hearts supporters have – that to transfer Hearts' address is to tear them away from a big bit of their heritage. Not a step to be taken lightly. But I am a realist and I pride myself on always being pragmatic . . . It isn't enough to stand and shout abuse – I want to help heal this rift.

Alongside these efforts to court the fans, Hearts were also trying to apply pressure on the city council in the long-running struggle to get their backing for a new stadium site. In a half-time interview during the tough 1–1 draw with Hibs on 15 February, Chris Robinson said Hearts had identified a site but 'we just can't get our hands on it at the moment'. He told the BBC, 'As I have found, for the last three years, getting the site is the hardest part. We have a site we think could work but we just can't get our hands on it at the moment.' Somewhat surprisingly, he added that the current stadium could be dismantled, stored and then re-erected if necessary.

A carefully-worded article in the club's online *Hearts News* revealed more about the behind-the-scenes battle with the local authority. It said Robinson would not be drawn on the location of the possible site but added:

> *Hearts News* has ... learnt ... from planning sources around the project that the Tynecastle club has identified a site at Sighthill on the west of the city which they would share with City of Edinburgh Council and would incorporate Edinburgh Rugby in the long-term. Privately, it is understood that the chief executive, with support from the board of directors at Hearts, is keen to press the local authority on this matter. It is believed that the interview, broadcast to many people around Scotland, was designed to alert the council of Hearts' eagerness to be involved in such a project, following on from detailed discussions.

However, if the consultation exercise and lure of a Murrayfield alternative were intended to rally Hearts fans behind the board's strategy, the ploy backfired badly. First, the consultation was rubbished for being launched after the decision to sell Tynecastle and move away had been taken. Then, with tempers running high following the derby game at Easter Rood – which saw Hibs fans throw a rugby ball on to the pitch and sing mocking songs about moving to Murrayfield – the team bus was surrounded by angry fans as it returned to Gorgie an hour after the game. The events which followed were strenuously denied by some but backed by others. The *Edinburgh Evening News* said around sixty Hearts fans 'ambushed' and then attacked the team bus, forcing it to stop as it attempted to drive along Gorgie Road. The newspaper claimed that those involved shouted abuse and threw coins at the bus in the belief that Robinson was on board. It added that the police had actually warned Robinson not to travel with the players and coaching staff over fears for his safety. The report said that, some hours later, his house was pelted with eggs and posters with the slogan 'Robinson Must Go' were put up in the area. Those involved in the demonstration admitted they had staged the protest to keep Hearts in Gorgie but insisted it had been peaceful. They claimed the dozens of police officers who dealt with the incident and took the details of around thirty fans had overreacted. There were no arrests but the main supporters' organisations nevertheless publicly stated that they would 'never condone any kind of violence' and criticised the events as 'totally unacceptable.' Hearts described those responsible as 'thugs'.

It was clear that Eric Milligan's plea to lower the temperature and cut out the personal abuse had fallen on deaf ears. Milligan himself was harangued by fans outside the stadium and later at his councillor's surgery, where campaigners handed him a 1,000-signature petition as police looked on. Scott Wilson was also subjected to severe criticism on Kickback, the club's web chat room, for giving credibility to the board's unpopular proposals. Some even threatened to boycott his radio station. In the face of this pressure and just days after taking up the post, Wilson resigned from the focus group. He stressed he was not taking sides in the debate but admitted he had been angered by the comments of some fans. Wilson said he feared the impartiality of his radio station could be brought into question. Hearts responded by closing the Kickback forum, which Wilson had used to make his resignation announcement. The club claimed, 'This follows consultation with security advisors and the police regarding the misuse of Kickback in terms of intimidation and recent incidents of concern to the club.' Lothian and Borders Police later denied officers had advised the club to shut the internet facility over security concerns. Hearts, in turn, failed to respond to that denial and Kickback remained suspended although fans would later resurrect it under the same name. The move appeared to be another public relations blunder, however, as fans accused the club of censorship because the site was commonly used to exchange strong anti-Murrayfield views.

Indeed, the campaign against the move away from Gorgie stepped up a gear in the days that followed. First, fans opposed to the move gathered at a boisterous Fans' Forum meeting at Tynecastle on 19 February. More than 100 supporters turned up for the forum meeting, many determined to express their resistance to the Murrayfield move. In doing so, it was hoped they could force the forum into a U-turn on its previous support for the plan. Two votes were taken at the meeting. One found that the overwhelming majority would either not buy season tickets for Murrayfield or not go at all. The other unanimously expressed a lack of confidence in the chief executive and board, calling for their resignation. As agreed at the meeting, a letter from the forum was then sent to Chris Robinson. It outlined that, as an organisation which simply reflected the views of those who turned up at meetings, it had reversed its previous stance on Murrayfield. The letter from secretary Jim Wylie said:

> Throughout the meeting it was obvious that many present were vociferous in their opposition to moving the club to Murrayfield. While this view was dominant, there was also recognition by some that, unless finances were somehow drastically improved, the club could soon be faced with administration which most present wished to avoid. During the course of the meeting a large number of speakers were critical of the proposed move. A show of hands was twice taken towards the end. On the first approximately twice as many fans ... said they would not buy season tickets for Murrayfield. Admittedly there was no way of knowing how many on either side are currently season ticket holders. On the second show of hands there was clearly overwhelming support that those present at the meeting had no confidence in the current board and they felt that as chief executive you were to blame for this situation and should resign.

In fact, it became apparent during the meeting that Robinson could be due to leave Tynecastle sooner rather than later. Forum chairman Ali Hibberd predicted that he would not be at the club at the start of the following season.

The meeting also backed up the website story that Hearts' preferred site for a new stadium was Sighthill and they could be there within three years. Hibberd later added that, after earlier discussions with other interested parties on stadium requirements in Edinburgh, Hearts had been close to becoming involved in a shared facility at Sighthill but the plans foundered 'for political reasons'. Robinson has since acknowledged that the talks 'dissolved' after Hearts began looking at, first, Straiton and, then, Murrayfield.

In another frank dialogue at the Forum meeting, head coach Craig Levein, who had previously said little during the row other than praising the facilities at Murrayfield, also revealed his true feelings about the proposal. He explained that he would rather stay at Tynecastle than move to Murrayfield, which he realised would have its problems. He said it had been 'almost impossible' to keep the players focused on playing football over the past six months, adding that he could not publicly criticise the rugby stadium and then expect to motivate the team to play there in the event of a move. In despair at criticism from the floor for not offering more vocal opposition to the board he even suggested that 'if the fans want [him] to go, [he would] go'. Levein also expressed his frustration at not knowing his budget for the following year because of the ongoing uncertainty. He said he had cut £3 million from his budget over three years, including at least £850,000 for the coming season and between £500,000 and £1 million the year after.

Murrayfield critic Peter McGrail gave a public presentation of his vision for a new Tynecastle stadium in Gorgie the next day. The businessman, who had been working with a team of specialist consultants for several months to beef up his earlier discussion paper, declared boldly that he had found a viable option to the Murrayfield move. The key, he said, was that the Gorgie–Dalry area was growing in popularity as a residential area, with property prices also on the rise, but the area lacked facilities. As previously indicated, his scheme involved setting up a Gorgie Development Company with other partners, notably the city council and a private developer. He said the whole site around the current Tynecastle stadium and high school would be redeveloped as part of a major regeneration scheme. For planning reasons, the stadium would move to the site of the current council roads depot and the school would occupy the area where the ground now stands. Private housing on the site would help to lever cash into the scheme and other revenue-generating outlets would be approached to join the partnership. Hearts would still have to sell their ground to the development company – which would be used to reduce the club's debt – but would have a secure, long-term lease at a 20,000-capacity, multi-sports complex in return. Funding was in place, Peter McGrail assured, and the development would be completed by 2008. There was even a suggestion that Edinburgh Rugby may opt to ground-share in the new stadium. The strategy was backed by the Hearts supporters' trust and federation, as well as former player Gary Mackay, who led a rousing if drawn-out rendition of the Hearts song at the end of the presentation.

The club was not surprisingly dismissive of the plan, pointing out flaws such as the fact it required demolishing listed buildings and removing tenants from flats in McLeod Street, although these hurdles had been recognised by Peter McGrail. A club spokesman said, 'It would be extremely misleading to suggest this is a viable option. It simply is not.'

Peter McGrail had also written to each director reminding them of their legal responsibilities in relation to assurances that the company was able to justify its status as a going concern. The letters would lead to an approach by a third party, claiming to represent two key individuals at the club, who were said to be uncomfortable with recent developments. The prospect of change was perhaps not as unlikely as it appeared.

The campaigners suffered a minor setback when they were forced to postpone a march and rally before the Dundee United game at Tynecastle on 21 February. The police objected over issues surrounding their own manpower levels and potential traffic congestion. But they were determined to keep the momentum going, not least because the home match was followed by a run of three away games. With this in mind, a second survey was hastily arranged, this time to measure how many would be prepared to buy a season ticket at the rugby ground.

The issue of season ticket sales was seen as crucial way to undermine the financial case for moving to Murrayfield. Chris Robinson had admitted he was basing his projected profit-and-loss figures for both Murrayfield and Tynecastle on there being the same level of sales as for season 2003–04 – around 8,400. Yet central to the arguments of opponents of the policy was the belief that far fewer would buy season tickets in a stadium with a huge capacity, where the thousands of empty seats would eliminate the need to reserve a particular seat. Any significant reduction in season ticket sales would rob the club of guaranteed advance income and also discredit the financial case for moving.

The results, released after successive victories against Dundee United (3–1) and a first away league win at Livingston (3–2), must have made depressing reading for the board. A total of 3,774 fans from the 10,200 crowd took part in the poll, with 65% insisting they would not buy a season ticket for Murrayfield. Those current season ticket holders who would definitely renew at the rugby stadium added up to just 22%, a figure that would amount to just 1,700 guaranteed sales. A total of 14% of season ticket holders were undecided what they would do.

The reaction of supporters' trust secretary Derek Watson was emphatic:

> This result blows any projections and business plan we have been told about out of the water. On looking at this result I believe the HMFC board must change direction or admit they will be taking Hearts to extinction at Murrayfield.

In a bizarre reaction which was ridiculed in the press, Hearts actually welcomed the results. The official website claimed:

> At this stage of the debate, these results are encouraging for the club and are better than we might have expected. We're pleasantly

surprised. They suggest that already a very significant number of season ticket holders are committed to buying season tickets for Murrayfield next season.

Hearts finished the month with a dreary 0–0 draw against Dunfermline at East End Park but that at least maintained their position nine points clear in third place. It was not only the team that was proving difficult to beat – the club, too, appeared more resolved than ever to drive through its unpopular policies. The bullish reaction may have been encouraged in part by some unusually large trades in Hearts' shares on the stock market. In the quarter before February, broadly the period covering the stadium controversy and rumours of a buy-out, there had been just several thousand pounds of trades each month. The share price, which started at £1.40 when the company was floated in 1997, remained a static 17.5p during the period. Yet, in February, the level of trading soared, with transactions reaching a value of almost £230,000. By the end of the month, the share price had jumped to 29.5p. That level of activity dropped off only slightly in March, with the value of trades around £190,000. At the beginning of March the share price peaked at 38.5p, the highest level in recent times. But, while the supporters had made their intention of buying shares well known, the board was boosted by the discovery that significant blocks of shares were being bought by a London-based businessman. On 25 February, a stock exchange announcement identified the mystery buyer as Calum Lancastle, who acquired 250,000 ordinary shares of 10p each, nine days previously, to take his total stake in the club up to more than 450,000 shares or 3.6% of the company.

The campaigners made contact with Lancastle in an effort to establish his position and in the hope of persuading him to support their fight but the businessman was non-committal. However, the supporters' groups had no reason to believe the recent flurry of share acquisitions had been from 'friendly' sources. Their position, therefore, had not been weakened by the trades.

23

SAVE OUR HEARTS

Discussions had been ongoing for several weeks about the possibility of forming a more united front to bring the fans together. Initially, it was thought that it could take the form of a simple committee with representatives from the various supporters' organisations. But the importance of shifting the balance of power at the club became ever more apparent. The board, backed by a majority of institutional shareholders, had refused to change its position and the early buy-out bids had been unsuccessful. A more representative and potent campaign group was required. Not only did the fans need to form a united front, they also needed more cash to pursue their ambitions – and they needed it quickly. An EGM to agree the sale of Tynecastle was expected within the next six weeks. It was with this in mind that, on 4 March, Save our Hearts was officially launched by the combined efforts of the supporters' trust and federation, backed by high-profile ex-players Gary Mackay and Donald Ford, a former star centre forward.

Ford, who scored 188 goals for Hearts in the 1960s and 70s, and Mackay, who made a record 738 appearances for the club, issued an almost identical warning to fans – this is your last chance to save Hearts. Ford, an accountant, said, 'I don't think we should underestimate that this might be the very last chance that Hearts supporters have to save the club.' Mackay, in turn, urged fans to look themselves in the mirror and ask if they had done all they could to save the club they loved. Trust chairman Martin Laidlaw was in no mood to underestimate the gravity of the situation. He declared:

The next month is the most important period in the glorious history of our club. The present board has taken us to the brink and, despite all attempts to persuade them otherwise, they continue to ignore the supporters and head blinkered into oblivion. Our club is in danger of dying and now the only solution that remains for us is through buying enough shares to oppose the move to Murrayfield at the EGM. This is about saving our great club and we are calling on all Hearts fans throughout the world to back this campaign.

The fund-raising scheme, it was explained, would involve fans offering to invest sums of £100 or more. The money would be held in a bank account until enough had been raised to buy significant blocks of shares. The shares would continue to be owned by the trust but would be 'allocated' back to the fans, according to how much they contributed. Fans could cash in their investment at any time and would receive their money back if insufficient funds were raised to seize control of the club. The fund-raising launch coincided with a campaign to deluge the club chairman, Doug Smith, with letters urging him to suspend the EGM, replace Chris Robinson as chief executive and investigate Peter McGrail's redevelopment plans.

The campaign began well. The next game was away from home but it was the televised fixture against Kilmarnock, which ended 1–1, and fans used the opportunity to sing noisy protest songs, the Ayrshire side's equalising goal three minutes from the end increasing their anger. In the week that followed, the Save our Hearts campaign raised an impressive £100,000. Of that, £49,200 came at just one meeting of activists – which was described as a 'sensational start' by organisers.

Also that week, it was announced in its full-year results for 2003 that SMG had decided to write down its £8 million investment in Hearts to zero. The company said it had taken the decision because of 'uncertainty' over the club's future and stressed it did not consider its investment to be worthless. But Save our Hearts leaders claimed the move illustrated a lack of confidence in the club's board and its strategy.

The fund-raising campaign hoped for a further boost at the planned rally before the next home match, against Rangers on 13 March. The original plan, which had been to march from Roseburn to Tynecastle via Haymarket, was changed after discussions with the police and council. A rally with guest speakers would now gather at Saughton Park and march to the ground along Gorgie Road, congregating once more outside the McLeod Street Stand. The event was seen as an opportunity to project a united front but also to win popular backing for the fund-raising campaign after the media launch just over a week ago. Despite the fact that permission had only been granted three days before the protest, campaigners hastily arranged publicity and hoped for a good turnout at such short notice. Although the federation represented some 3,000 supporters (and membership of the trust had now jumped to around 800), anything other than a significant show of strength would seriously undermine their mandate to speak on behalf of the fans. As it turned out, the numbers met the expectations of organisers, with the police quoted as estimating that around 5,000 people took part while other reports suggested it may have been a little short of that figure. The demonstration was peaceful and well organised. Marchers carried banners criticising the Murrayfield move, the Hearts chief executive and the club board but they were politely applauded by shoppers and even Rangers fans who lined the route of the parade. The rally behind the old stand heard repeated calls for Chris Robinson's resignation with supporters' trust chairman Martin Laidlaw declaring, 'This day will be remembered for ever as the day when Hearts fans started to take back their club.' The rally ended with a hoarse Gary Mackay again leading the singing of the Hearts song. Having vented their frustration, the crowd inside the stadium directed less anger at the board and concentrated on an entertaining 1–1 draw and an overdue point against one half of the Old Firm – or, perhaps, the fans had decided to relax because they knew Robinson was on holiday.

The hints about the possibility of Hearts occupying or sharing a site at Sighthill also began to make more sense at this time. First, on 11 March, the city council unveiled its vision for a range of sports facilities across Edinburgh. The £110 million strategy, which it was hoped would tie in with Edinburgh and Glasgow's bid for the 2014 Commonwealth games, included replacing Meadowbank Stadium with a new facility in the west side of the city – at Sighthill. With help from a sportscotland pot of cash, which included government money from Scotland's failed Euro 2008 bid, the 10,000-capacity facility would stage major athletics, rugby, basketball, judo and badminton events. The capacity would be made up of 6,000 permanent seats and 4,000 temporary ones but there would also be indoor facilities with seating for 1,500. A feasibility study was carried out to establish if a football stadium could be included in the blueprint but a view was taken at the time that an SPL-type stadium would not satisfy planning policy requirements. And of, course, a 10,000-seat stadium would not meet Hearts' needs – it appeared that any pleas from the football club had fallen on deaf ears. Robinson was said to be 'not best pleased'.

By now, the chief executive was no longer dropping hints. Less than two weeks after the council announcement, at yet another meeting with fans representatives and, this time, some of the club's advisers, Robinson was more forthright than previously when he told those present about the process which identified three options for developing the area's sports facilities. He said:

One was at Jack Kane Centre, one was Saughtonhall and the other was Sighthill. It is this last option that the council has elected to support . . . I sat on that committee and it is in the minutes of that committee. I said that I believe that Sighthill was the best place for Hearts. It offers very good transport links, accessibility, parking and good public transport. To me there are not too many better alternatives.

Robinson added that he had suggested rugby and athletics share a smaller stadium at Saughton, a site Hearts could develop if it were not for planning difficulties which would constrain their needs. His view, given nine months earlier at the onset of the Straiton row, that 'football and athletics don't mix', would seem to have been more than a throwaway comment – it was, instead, a barbed message to the council. It was clear his preferred option was Sighthill, although he also revealed that another option existed. Later that week, it was reported to be land at Hermiston Gait belonging to Rangers owner David Murray, as was the case in 1992. Again Robinson appeared to be frustrated at the possibility of council planners standing in the way of his ambitions, adding, 'The challenge again is planning.'

These vague possibilities, however, failed to appease the bulk of the Hearts support. Match-day poster demonstrations had been taking place since January but were now becoming more commonplace and involving larger numbers of supporters inside the ground. In fact, a demonstration was to take place at every home game after the 3–1 victory over Dundee at Tynecastle on 27 March, with posters proclaiming, 'This Board Is Killing Our Hearts' and 'Robinson Out Now'.

It was no surprise, then, when Hearts fans organised a picket of the SPL meeting due to vote on whether Hearts could ground-share at Murrayfield in 2004–05. A busload of around forty fans made the trip through to Glasgow for the meeting at Hampden on 30 March but left disappointed after the move was sanctioned by the SPL board – subject to Hearts and the SRU agreeing a legally binding contract. Similar proposals were accepted for other clubs if they proved necessary. The SPL said it had voted in favour of the proposals because it had been reassured that there would be no fixture clashes between the parties involved in ground-sharing. Robinson must have been satisfied with the outcome but he left by the National Stadium's underground exit to avoid the waiting media and any protesters.

He was, however, spotted returning to Tynecastle after the meeting and surrounded by a group of supporters before being backed into a doorway. Press reports described how one fan then attacked the chief executive, punching him on the head and body and causing some minor bruising. Other fans were said to have pulled the men apart and Robinson escaped into the sanctuary of Tynecastle. The police were contacted but Robinson later revealed he had not been concerned enough to let his wife and daughter know about the incident. He was to tell the *Sunday Herald*:

> I won't be de-motivated by some idiot who decides he wants to have a go at me ... Yeah, maybe I'm lucky that I can shut these things out, but I don't think it's such a serious threat. I've never been spat on, and there's a lot of stuff that's been spun. It's never as bad as it seems. There have been posters, yes, but they've never threatened my health apart from last week, and I've never had death threats.

The fact that he felt the need to mention he had not received death threats highlighted the severe pressure he was under. And, while the organised fans' organisations condemned the attack, sections of the support were less sympathetic towards the chief executive. For instance, while most of those on the main internet chat forums joined in the condemnation of the attack, others underlined the anger he had aroused and suggested there was little surprise that one fan's fury appeared to have boiled over. A few remained downright hostile towards the chief executive. But the overriding issue appeared to be whether the attack would harm the protest and fund-raising campaign.

24

'FOR FOULKES' SAKE ... STAY IN GORGIE'

The fans' concerns about the campaign were unfounded. In its first month, the Save our Hearts campaign had raised £250,000 and celebrities were lining up to back the cause. Former stars such as Donald Ford, Freddie Glidden, Alan Anderson, Walter Kidd, Gary Mackay and Gary Locke gave their support along with Gary Naysmith, Gilles Rousset, David Weir and John Robertson from the 1998 cup-winning squad. Weir said, 'I feel remaining at Tynecastle is imperative to HMFC's identity and future success.' Goal-scoring legend Robertson, then manager of Inverness Caledonian Thistle, declared, 'All my memories are of Tynecastle. I feel strongly Hearts should stay there. It is vital that all the supporters get together on this.' Former striker Sandy Clark added simply that 'Tynecastle must be saved'. Others who joined the campaign included film and television actor Ken Stott and politicians David McLetchie, the Scottish Tory leader, and Lib Dem MSP Mike Pringle.

The momentum seemed to be shifting in the campaigners' favour and there had even been suggestions that divisions were opening up in the Tynecastle boardroom. Chairman Doug Smith had prompted such speculation when, several weeks before, he told *The Scotsman* that he had reservations about leaving Tynecastle. He said:

What I appreciate, as we found at the AGM, is we have a 51–49 majority for that move. Now, for such a momentous decision, do you want to go to Murrayfield based on that narrow a majority? . . .

I am spending a lot of time talking to people and if we go forward with Murrayfield then the issue will have to be decided at an EGM. When that happens, then I think it must be something which the vast majority of the shareholders and the fans embrace. Right now, I don't think we're at that stage.

Smith also referred to 'a very good' letter in *The Scotsman* from Brighton and Hove Albion FC which warned about how 'leaving a stadium which has been your home for a long time can rip the heart out of club'. That letter, from twenty Scottish-based fans, outlined how Brighton had struggled since selling the Goldstone Ground, their home for ninety-five years, against the wishes of the fans. When their old stadium was sold for retail development in 1996, the club had moved into Gillingham's Priestfield Stadium and then returned to Brighton but to a temporary home at the Withdean athletics stadium. The letter added:

> Since 1996, the club has had to fight exceptionally hard and against the odds for survival. As well as financial problems off the pitch, on the pitch the team has had to struggle against the atmosphere of a sports ground not designed for a football club, the capacity of which does not fit the club's size . . . We have no wish to see any other club suffer as we have done, and we call on all supporters of Hearts, and all of the people of Edinburgh, to fight Chris Robinson's proposal to sell Tynecastle and move the club to Murrayfield. The potential damage to the club and the city is incalculable, and Brighton's experience shows that once a club loses its home without a suitable replacement in place, the road back is a long and difficult one.

It is remarkable that a chance letter from a group of supporters of an English Division Two side, showing unselfish concern for fellow football fans, could help to set in motion a chain of events which would soon halt the unpopular move to Murrayfield in its tracks and, therefore, alter the destiny of Heart of Midlothian FC.

Rumours were rife on 5 April that a major decision would be made at the Hearts board meeting that evening. There had been private discussions about the future of the board members, with suggestions that an EGM may be called to force a vote of no confidence. Peter McGrail had even contacted Freddie Fletcher and his company, Mercer Consulting, had said that, during the 1990s, the former Rangers director and Newcastle United chief executive was willing to run Hearts on a temporary basis. The idea was that he would attempt to stabilise the finances and find a new chief executive.

Informed sources were convinced – chairman Doug Smith was increasingly uneasy about the way events were unfolding and would hand in his resignation as a result. The predictions proved accurate. Smith resigned at the board meeting and it was announced the following day. The self-confessed Newcastle United fan, who had served on the board since 1997, said he still believed the move to Murrayfield was in the best interests of the club but, in his resignation statement, he added:

> The success of the move will ultimately hinge on the board's ability to build broad support among Hearts fans, and I am disappointed that we have not yet been able to achieve this. Accordingly, I think it is in the best interests of the company if I make way for a new chairman who will bring a fresh approach to the issue and offers the prospect of building a solid consensus for the stadium and financial challenges we face.

If Smith's resignation did not come as a complete shock, the choice of replacement chairman was certainly a surprise. Former minister of state for Scotland and high-profile Hearts supporter George Foulkes was handed the unenviable task of finding a suitable way forward for the club at arguably the most important moment in its history. At the same time, the Ayrshire MP was expected to bring together factions which had never been further apart. He may have represented the seat of Carrick, Cumnock and Doon Valley but the experienced politician had also attended Edinburgh University. Crucially, he was also a former Edinburgh city councillor and later formed part of the Labour group on Lothian Regional Council in the 1970s. He also contested the

Edinburgh West constituency in 1970 and Edinburgh Pentlands four years later – both confirmed Hearts territory.

Foulkes credited Murrayfield Tory councillor Jim Gilchrist for drawing the club's attention to his availability. The board drew up a shortlist of candidates in association with the club's financial advisers and Foulkes' name was at the top. In fact, his potential as a link with the fans was regarded as his outstanding quality, according to Chris Robinson. Even some of Hearts' staunchest critics were forced to concede, possibly for the first time since the stadium controversy broke, that they had perhaps pulled off a tactical masterstroke. Here was a Hearts fan of more than twenty years, with two sons who were season ticket holders, who is reported to have flown straight out to a 1993 UEFA Cup tie against Atletico Madrid after a court appearance on charges of being drunk and disorderly. Those who were left in any doubt were reminded he was even a member of the supporters' trust (membership number eighty-two), an admirer of the passion and commitment of the Save our Hearts campaign and an advocate of fan involvement in decision making. Also, he was due to retire from the House of Commons and so could devote time to the task ahead. He would take no pay for his position as chairman.

Those credentials were immediately reinforced when, at the press conference to formally announce his appointment on 6 April, he declared that Hearts may still have to move but the rush to Murrayfield was 'premature'. He would seek to negotiate a year's delay in any relocation while all the options were explored. He would hold the necessary talks with the bank, including Bank of Scotland Governor George Mitchell (who was also a director of HBOS at the time), SMG and other interested parties and, at the same time, set up a working party to examine the future stadium options. Urged by e-mails from supporters the moment his appointment was made public, he had identified that, more than anything else, Hearts needed a 'Plan B' – an alternative to 'Murrayfield or bust'. A letter from the Hearts-supporting Lord Chancellor, Lord Falconer of Thoroton, went further – he expressed the hope that Foulkes would do everything in his power to keep the club at Tynecastle. Foulkes told the press conference:

> I am here to steer the club through difficult times, to offer some strong leadership and I think everyone realises that this is a very important time as far as the future of Hearts is concerned. The next few years will decide how we are to exist in the years to come ... I have no other objective than attempting to ensure the long-term survival of this club.

Chris Robinson welcomed the appointment of the 'well-kent' Hearts supporter but some of the new chairman's comments must have been difficult for the chief executive to bear. First, he paid tribute to the supporters' trust, the very campaigners who had been so critical of Robinson. Then he asserted that delaying the move to Murrayfield for a season would not necessarily result in additional costs, when the chief executive claimed it would lead to losses of £2.5 million. It also reflected badly on the Hearts chief that he had not followed the more palatable and, apparently, viable course pursued by Foulkes.

The MP's appointment was initially met with indifference. The bulk of the fans had grown accustomed to authority figures who paid little heed to their concerns. They expected more of the same. Foulkes had actually put on record his support for Hearts remaining in Gorgie during the debate over building a new stadium at Millerhill in the early 1990s. But he also revealed that he would accept a move from Gorgie if necessary. In the December 1991 edition of the fanzine *Still, Mustn't Grumble*, he said, 'Hearts need a new ground badly ... I would prefer it to be rebuilt at Gorgie Road but if that was not possible, I would go along with a move.' Less than a year later, the same fanzine predicted the possibility of a move to Murrayfield. The fans would have been wise to take notice. But many supporters did point to Foulkes' comments in the *Scottish Daily Mail* on 21 January 2004, when he said something similar:

> I have been very impressed with the set-up at Kilmarnock, with the new hotel right next to the stadium, and hoped a similar development

might happen at Tynecastle. But if that is not possible, for whatever reason, then I would reluctantly go along with the move to Murrayfield . . . If you're a supporter, as I am, you will go wherever the team plays. One of the things which made me more sympathetic towards moving to Murrayfield was something Craig Levein said . . . Craig made the point that the working conditions for the players would be ideal.

Others simply pointed to Foulkes' notoriously murky profession as a good reason to withhold their trust. Foulkes, however, was as good as his word. He quickly met with the fans' organisations and the leading opponents of the Murrayfield move, although he once missed a meeting with the shareholders association after being ordered to attend an event in Brussels by Prime Minister Tony Blair.

In the meantime, a round of talks took place with the bank, SMG and other creditors. Throughout this, Foulkes was keen to stress that he was an independent force and he would not operate as Chris Robinson's 'mouthpiece on the board'. With it looking increasingly likely that Foulkes would secure another year at Tynecastle, the latter point certainly appeared to be true. The heat had quickly been taken out of a crisis which was reaching boiling point. Even if Robinson had been uncomfortable with some of Foulkes' public remarks, he must have welcomed the new mood of relative calm around Tynecastle. It is a tribute to Foulkes the political tactician and communicator that the release of yet more depressing financial figures published on 29 April did not cause more uproar. The half-year figures up until 31 January 2004 showed that the club had once again posted a pre-tax loss, of £557,000, although operating losses were down and income was up because of cost-cutting measures and participation in the UEFA Cup. Most worryingly, overall debt rose to a massive £18.6 million.

The noticeable change in the mood of fans was even reflected in their demonstrations. The confrontational posters held up during previous games were replaced by at least one with the barbed but humorous plea, 'For Foulkes' Sake Robinson Let's Stay in Gorgie'. The upbeat mood was maintained with a social event, a Mayday

Jamboree, which was to be held on 1 May. Similarly, a second march and rally, which was being planned for the last day of the season, was to be as much a celebration of the team's achievements and the sixth anniversary of the cup win as it was to be a major protest. But, if the momentum driving Hearts towards Murrayfield had stalled during the past month, so too had results on the park. The team recorded four draws and one loss in April. From a positive point of view, the month began and ended with hard-fought draws against Celtic – 2–2 at Parkhead and 1–1 at Tynecastle – both of which could and perhaps should have resulted in three points for Hearts. Single points were again picked up away and at home in the disappointing 1–1 draws against Motherwell and Livingston respectively. Yet sandwiched in the middle was a sorry 1–0 defeat at Firhill to bottom-placed, relegation-bound Partick Thistle.

Despite that, there was little doubt that the outlook for Hearts had improved both on and off the park. There was to be no imminent move away from Tynecastle and the team was heading for a successive season in Europe. But the palpable loss of urgency was to coincide with a levelling-out of fortunes for the fund-raising campaign.

As the season drew to a close, the effort of all those involved in the campaign to fight the sale of Tynecastle and leap into the unknown remained as impressive as at any stage in recent months. In fact, one of the leading critics of the plan, business strategist Peter McGrail, had taken it upon himself to write to all of the club's 3,947 shareholders to canvass their opinions on the board's handling of recent events. There was some surprise that the results were so emphatic among a group generally considered more moderate than the mainstream fans, with 95% of those who replied expressing a lack of confidence in the board to run the company successfully. A similar number believed it was unacceptable to lease Murrayfield without another stadium strategy in place. Only slightly fewer said that they would not vote for Chris Robinson if he was up for re-election, with many expressing concern that he was acting out of 'self-interest'. The other directors were also given a vote of no confidence, although they fared better than Robinson. The survey, which attracted 1,357 responses, pre-dated Foulkes' appointment so he was considered exempt from the criticism.

Then, there was the potential embarrassment of a Sunday newspaper outlining Robinson's other business interests. Hearts supporters were quick to demand the chief executive's 'full attention' amid what they described as the club's biggest ever crisis.

But the one thing every fan craved – success on the park – was to detract from those embarrassments. In some ways, the timing could hardly have been better. Just hours before 1,200 fans were due to gather for the fund-raising Mayday Jamboree on 1 May, the team fought out a 2–0 win against Dundee United at Tannadice and secured themselves European football for a second successive season. United had improved on their early season performances and had gone unbeaten at home since November so the Hearts players, who left the pitch to rousing applause from the big away support, deserved full credit for the victory. The fans would have been even more jubilant had they realised the other major development of the weekend – the day before the Tannadice victory, potential investor Vladimir Romanov had made his first visit to Tynecastle to discuss the possibility of a buy-out. He was impressed by what he saw at the stadium and the youth academy, even buying a print of Tynecastle from the club shop.

The following Monday, George Foulkes announced that Hearts' domestic matches during season 2004–05 would be played at Tynecastle, although the UEFA Cup ties would take place at Murrayfield to conform to the new licensing rules. The board had unanimously agreed to the delay following the chairman's discussions with creditors, although Foulkes did insist it would be the club's last year at Tynecastle – a position he was later to retract.

The next day, the news leaked out that the property developer and Aberdeen FC major shareholder, Stewart Milne, had made a £24 million bid for the Tynecastle site. The figure was higher than even those close to events had predicted and double the sum the club had previously rejected. The story was never substantiated and the fans' groups cast doubt on its reliability but it further dented the efforts of Save our Hearts as fans began to consider the merits of selling up.

Then, on 8 May, Hearts secured third place in the league, which would ensure they avoided the qualifying round in next season's UEFA Cup, after beating their main league rivals, Dunfermline, 2–1 at Tynecastle. Once again, it was a battling performance, after going down 1–0, which kept Hearts as the best of the rest after the Old Firm, a position they had occupied since October the previous year. The follow-up to that success could hardly have been more encouraging, with Hearts coming away from Ibrox with their first three points there since 1996 after a 1–0 victory on 12 May. But a combination of what could loosely be described as a new feel-good factor and typical end-of-season apathy seemed to have dazed the once-animated fans. Save our Hearts announced that it had broken the £500,000 milestone but there had been some private concern about the relatively low number of contributors, at around 1,000. The number of fans prepared to contribute funds appeared to have levelled out and, with the close season approaching, there were no immediate signs of improvement.

The rally and march on the final day of the season again attracted big numbers. Queues formed at Saughton Park to sign the petition against moving to Murrayfield, Save our Hearts T-shirts sold out and the stall allowing fans to throw rotten tomatoes at an image of Chris Robinson did a brisk trade. But the mood of deep frustration and barely concealed rage evident at the same event two months earlier had been replaced by one of more relaxed determination. The pipe band played the same tunes, the banners were dusted down and hoisted up and the protestors again made the short journey along Gorgie Road. Fewer, however, seemed to re-assemble behind the old stand, some grumbling that they had heard the speeches before. Others just wanted to get to the bar first. There would, after all, be one last chance to protest with the disparaging balloon release during the match. For the first time, the protest itself was something to enjoy. The reward of previous demonstrations had been the decision to delay any move for at least a year. But that concession had, ironically, also reduced the need to protest. The latter part of Robinson's recent observation that 'once people get into protest mode, they can enjoy that feeling of protest' may have been true, but the campaigners would certainly reject any suggestion that they were simply going through the motions. However, in the same way that demonstrators drifted away at the end of the march, so sections of the support headed for the exits before the end of season 2003–04. While the team had maintained its desire right up until the final whistle, the mood of the fans had subdued. The events of season 2004–05 would provide an answer to Robinson's big question. 'Who knows what the campaigners will do? The Save our Hearts campaign is highly organised, although I'm not sure what they're saving us from,' he asked.

25

THE ROW RUMBLES ON

The summer of 2004 should have been a countdown to Tynecastle's final days as a football stadium, at least under the sale plans outlined by the club at the end of the previous year. The club declared then that 'the directors expect that the stadium position will be concluded satisfactorily by 31 July 2004'. But the controversy was far from over. In fact, the topsy-turvy events of June, July and August suggested matters were even less predictable than before.

Chris Robinson had declared that he was unclear about the intentions of Save our Hearts but he must also have been bewildered by the increasingly public interventions of his own chairman. George Foulkes had already stalled the move to Murrayfield for a year but, days after the end of season 2003–04, he was already hinting that options were being explored to remain at Tynecastle for 'a longer period'. By contrast, the club's official line was that 2004–05 would definitely be the last at the Gorgie ground.

But Robinson at least had cause for satisfaction when the long-awaited youth academy finally opened its doors at the end of May, with the final price tag of more than £6 million shared among Heriot-Watt University, Hearts and sportscotland. Hearts' 'football department' was to be based at the centre, which enjoyed a range of state-of-the-art sports and medical facilities. Some fans were later disappointed when they realised that Hearts had a twenty-five-year lease on the academy rather than a share in its ownership but there was broad agreement that it was an impressive facility nevertheless.

SMG was known to be prepared to sell its stake in the club if a buyer could meet its valuation of its shares and debt and prove an ability to come up with the cash. But the campaigners suffered a setback at the beginning of June when the company rejected a second buy-out bid by Save our Hearts, with business backing, again for around £2 million. The campaigners expressed disappointment that they had failed to buy the media group's 19.9% shareholding and wipe out the £4.5 million loan debt it was due from the club. It is worth noting that the shares at the time were valued at around £800,000 and both that holding and the debt had already been written down to zero in SMG's accounts. Save our Hearts described it as a 'serious and substantial' offer and acknowledged that the buy-out was a key tactic in their attempts to sway the balance of power at Tynecastle. They insisted the fight would go on and a further bid could be made to Hearts' biggest institutional shareholder.

Their task was complicated by the fact that Vladimir Romanov was also keen to acquire the SMG shares and loan stock and the media company wanted to find out how much he would be prepared to pay. Discussions took place but no acceptable offer was made, according to the media company. It was feared that then caused Romanov's interest to cool, although he would soon focus his attention once again on the Tynecastle club.

The momentum swung back towards the critics of the Murrayfield move in the middle of the month when the Stadium Working Group (SWG) promised by Foulkes was set up under the chairmanship of the peer, Lord Macaulay of Bragar, a retired QC and a season ticket holder at Tynecastle. There was optimism that those nominated to sit on the group were committed to the long-term future of Hearts but also represented a wide enough range of interests – fans' and shareholders' organisations, architects, surveyors and other businessmen – to carry out the remit thoroughly and professionally. The club, through Robinson and finance director Stewart Fraser, would act as adviser, along with senior representatives from the Edinburgh and Midlothian local authorities. The group would examine all the high-profile sites previously considered for a new stadium – including Sighthill, Saughton and Hermiston – but it would also consider the merits of remaining at Tynecastle and moving to Murrayfield. In addition, it would examine Peter McGrail's Gorgie redevelopment plan, described by Foulkes as 'an excellent and constructive proposal'.

Foulkes paid tribute to Lord Macaulay. He said:

> As a committed Hearts fan, he understands the huge significance of the challenge our club faces in the search for a permanent home and how important it is that we find a solution which unites the Hearts support once again.

The life peer responded with an equally committed message. He promised to carry out his task with independence and openness and to report back to the Hearts board before the end of the year. Tellingly, he added that he was concerned about the future of Hearts and he wanted to 'see them continue in existence' but he also warned that they must not be allowed to follow Third Lanark's sorry example and go bust.

But, while Lord Macaulay was resolutely diplomatic and non-committal in his comments, Foulkes displayed remarkable foresight when he highlighted Sighthill as an attractive long-term option. He told the club website:

> They will get excellent co-operation from the City of Edinburgh Council. I know that because I have spoken to the chief executive, and I know that they are very keen to help us find a new home. There might be two or three options, but a preferred option would be ideal. I think Sighthill is certainly an option that we could co-operate with the council with. I don't know exactly what they were saying before, but some people see that as a substantial step forward.

The veteran politician, with all his connections, appeared to be breaking the deadlock which had troubled the club for years. In doing so, he anticipated the findings of the working group – six months later it would score Sighthill as the most attractive site to build a new stadium on – at least if it was available and Tynecastle could not be redeveloped.

In the meantime, Foulkes offered further encouragement to supporters when he reported that the financial position at the club was not as gloomy as might have been expected, partially due to healthy season ticket sales. As such, he added, there was no immediate need to call the EGM. In fact, the meeting, which was originally expected as early as April, could now be called as late as the autumn as the board considered its options. Behind the scenes, Foulkes' priority was to ensure that nothing in the wording of any EGM motion would be 'irrevocable', at least during 2004 (an amendment later referred to by some as 'the Foulkes Clause').

The shift in direction was clearly provoking some tension between Foulkes and Chris Robinson. At a Save our Hearts meeting on 24 June, Foulkes expressed 'extreme annoyance' that he was not aware of the chief executive's business interests with the catering company, Heritage Portfolio, which had been the subject of media attention. In fairness, although Foulkes had not been aware of Robinson's other activities, there was no suggestion Robinson had attempted to conceal them. Foulkes added that he had 'got the message' about Robinson's unpopularity and the strength of feeling regarding his removal from office. During a discussion about considering all the stadium options to protect the long-term future of the club, he added, 'I'm not trying to convert the Hearts supporters – I'm trying to convince some people but not the Hearts supporters.' He also referred to the 'failings and past misdemeanours' that had afflicted the club.

Foulkes had touched on the theme of Robinson's role at the club before, although focusing on the fact his position as both a chief executive and major shareholder could raise issues of good corporate governance. Foulkes insisted it was important to avoid any conflict of interest and said there should be a distinction between those who work for the club and those who own it.

But, while speculation mounted in early July that Robinson was nearing the Tynecastle exit, the chief executive hit back at his critics. He denied there was any conflict of interest and compared his position to that of Microsoft chairman and shareholder Bill Gates. Robinson and his board colleagues were offered little reassurance from former chairman Doug Smith. In the first interviews since he left the Hearts board, Smith predicted boardroom changes and also gave his backing to more fan involvement in the running of the club's affairs. However, he also praised Robinson for his efforts in establishing the youth academy and appointing Craig Levein.

As the kick-off to season 2004–05 neared, Robinson remained resolutely in post, despite suggestions that Save our Hearts, now with 1,100 contributors to their campaign, were prepared to buy out his shareholding. Football matters provided some distraction, particularly the reports that Hearts were close to securing Manchester United's Scotland international midfielder Michael Stewart on a loan deal but the respite would prove short-lived. Once again it was the stadium issue which caused the warring factions to renew hostilities.

Just before 6 p.m. on 3 August, an announcement to the stock exchange revealed that Hearts had renegotiated their borrowing levels with the Bank of Scotland, which was conditional on 'the execution on or before 31 August 2004 of an agreement for the sale by Hearts of Tynecastle Stadium'. The fans who thought they had won a reprieve faced a new reality – the club had been given a four-week deadline to sell the ground. It was a further bitter twist that the announcement was made the day before the Stadium Working Group held its first meeting to identify a long-term home for Hearts. Robinson faced abuse from fans at the East of Scotland Shield final against Hibs at Tynecastle after the news broke but it was left to Foulkes to make an appearance after the 3–1 defeat to appease angry supporters. The chairman stressed that it was a technical announcement, which had to be made to extend the renewal date for the existing overdraft by one month to 31 August. Any increase in borrowing after 1 September would require the club to authorise the sale of Tynecastle, although no irrevocable decision would be made to do so, he added. Foulkes insisted that the sale was not being forced through and, actually, the bank had been generous in allowing the club an extra month's breathing space.

In fact, the deadline would later be pushed back further to 13 September, along with a further £3 million bank borrowing facility. But the widespread media coverage that followed further undermined efforts to build bridges at Tynecastle. For instance, Save our Hearts spokesman Gary Mackay emotively claimed in *The Scotsman*, 'They are talking about the execution of the sale of Tynecastle, and execution is the right word as this could be the death knell of this famous football club.' The paper also reported that Foulkes was unaware the statement was due to be released and memorably quoted him as being 'slightly furious' about the matter. Robinson later claimed he had not had time to inform non-executive directors about the announcement immediately. *The Scotsman* published a damning opinion piece on his stewardship of the club.

> Hearts' present position is the most grave since 1905, when, burdened with debts of £2,000, they were threatened with closure. In other words, the current guardians are responsible for the club's worst crisis in a century. They have jeopardised the very existence of the club. They should go now before any more damage is done, and leave it to Foulkes and others to do what they can to reconstruct the wreckage.

Save our Hearts responded to the announcement by deciding at a meeting on 4 August not to pursue discussions with Robinson over his shareholding. Such a move was extremely unpopular among those who did want not the campaign fund ending up in his pockets. Instead, further efforts would be made to buy out SMG while also considering action against the Bank of Scotland – which was widely thought to be driving the sale – such as closing accounts and cancelling credit cards.

But the campaigners were given one last hope shortly before the meeting closed. Save our Hearts may have given up on Robinson's shares but the rumour was that someone else had expressed an interest – it was the first suggestion that a mysterious 'East European' may soon be making an appearance at Tynecastle. Less than a week later, in a reference to Roman Abramovich, Foulkes was discussing the possibility that the club could 'find a foreign backer, as Chelsea did'. Interestingly, he also gave that as a reason for stalling the headlong rush from Gorgie.

26

SEASON 2004–05 KICKS OFF

The 2004–05 season kicked off with an entertaining 1–0 victory over Dundee at Dens Park on 7 August, courtesy of a Steven Pressley penalty. The home campaign – at Tynecastle, of course, rather than Murrayfield as originally envisaged – began in familiar fashion a week later with a combative Hearts performance, off-field controversies and a poster protest against chief executive Chris Robinson. The off-field matter involved dubious claims by some Aberdeen fans that their bus had been targeted by Hearts supporters angry at the suggestion Stewart Milne had put in a £24 million bid for Tynecastle. The poster borrowed a catchphrase from the popular reality television show, *Big Brother*, as it asked, 'Who Goes? You Decide', offering a choice of Robinson or 'Our Club HMFC'. The fact that it was the most poorly observed protest of its kind to date suggested that the tactic had almost run its course.

As usual, the game was played amid a hail of abuse and this time it was dished out equally at Robinson and new Aberdeen signing Scott Severin. Some things had changed since 2003–03, not least the sight of Severin in red rather than maroon. The 0–0 draw against an organised and determined Aberdeen proved that they were also a much-improved team on the previous season.

But, with the season barely started, attention turned once more to boardroom matters. This time it was the news all opponents of the move from Tynecastle most feared – ten developers had been approached and the club had conditionally agreed the sale of the old ground to housing developers Cala Management Ltd. The announcement to the stock exchange on 19 August revealed that the deal was worth a headline figure of £22 million, depending on planning consents and other factors such as demolition costs, although it could be reduced to a minimum price of £20.5 million, with the stadium valued at £16 million. The fact that the proceeds would be used to reduce debt was at least given more prominence than in the past. One of the headline points from the statement declared, 'Proceeds from the disposal will be used to reduce the company's outstanding debts due to the bank and SMG under the terms of its loan stock.' It later added, 'The directors believe the club's debt burden is unsustainable on a conventional basis and requires a clear action plan to redress the position.' The announcement also revealed that the club could withdraw from the Cala deal before 31 January 2005 for a penalty fee of up to £75,000 and outlined the details of an agreement which had been reached for the rental of Murrayfield.

In his position as chairman, George Foulkes was unable to be as optimistic as he appeared in his private meetings with fans. He said:

> In the current circumstances, I believe that the proposals we publish today are in the best interests of Hearts, its shareholders and supporters. The proposals have the unanimous support of the board. These are prudent and sensible actions which address two unavoidable truths – that Tynecastle is not presently commercially viable and that Hearts must agree the sale of the stadium now to ensure we have sufficient working capital to continue to trade. Our proposals include a condition which allows us to withdraw from the sale of Tynecastle before 31 January 2005 if a financially viable alternative is acceptable to us. If no preferred alternative is found by 31 January – and no one should give supporters false hope that this is possible – the sale of Tynecastle on these terms and the ground-share at Murrayfield offers Hearts the resources and further time to search for and develop a home which meets the expectations of our supporters.

With that, fans were forced to face the unpalatable truth – a housing developer had been given the green light to flatten Tynecastle and build homes on the rubble. The alternative was that 'the directors would be obliged to consider whether the company would be in a position to continue to trade'. Of course, the deal would have to be sanctioned by an EGM on 13 September but – with 46.3% of the block vote already indicating support for the sale – that appeared to be a foregone conclusion. There was also a clear warning – a vote against the proposal could lead to administration.

The get-out clause gave opponents some cause for optimism and would allow the Stadium Working Group to complete its deliberations but, equally, Cala could pull out of the deal and leave Hearts high and dry. There was also concern that the staged payments from Cala – over three years after the company had received the appropriate planning permission – would result in Hearts not receiving all the cash it was due until 2008 at the earliest. In the meantime, the club would still be carrying and servicing significant debt while also paying rental for Murrayfield. Ironically, Tynecastle could lie empty during this period with Hearts picking up the bill for maintaining the site, while any increase in land values would benefit Cala. And, while the rent figure of £20,000 per game at Murrayfield was quoted by the club, the circular received by shareholders showed that figure could more than double for bigger domestic games after fees for use of hospitality facilities and per spectator over 18,000 had been taken into account. The total could exceed £90,000 for well-attended UEFA matches. Further costs would arise for policing, stewarding, cleaning the stadium, repairing any damage done by fans and other similar expenses. In addition, the sale itself could incur capital gains tax of up to £800,000, while the process of selling the stadium would add up to almost £600,000.

The difficulties in identifying, securing and funding an alternative stadium site, with planning permission, only added to doubts about the worth of the deal. It emerged later that Hearts' biggest creditor,

the Bank of Scotland, had a 29.99% shareholding in Cala Group
Limited. There was no suggestion that the connection amounted to
anything improper but it did add to cynicism surrounding the deal.

George Foulkes, who again met with concerned supporters
outside the stadium, picked up on the issue of the possibility of
attracting a better investment offer than the Cala deal. He said,
'Whether that is a consortium of Edinburgh businessmen or
someone like Roman Abramovich, what is clear is that they would
have to make a better offer than the one we already have.' For the
third time in a fortnight or so, there had been hints about an
Eastern European backer. The fans may have been unaware of the
discussions which had taken place but, behind the scenes, it was
becoming increasingly likely that a wealthy investor was indeed
interested in Hearts. Chris Robinson said it would take something
'extremely exceptional' to halt the sell-off. Leslie Deans and Robert
McGrail insisted they still hoped to stop the sale, perhaps through
a buy-and-leaseback scheme, which would give Hearts cash
for the stadium but require them to pay rent in future years. But,
of course, it was possible that any new backer would also choose
to remain at Tynecastle.

The off-field events diverted attention from some crucial upcoming fixtures. Even former Hearts and now Kilmarnock manager
Jim Jefferies lamented the seemingly inevitable sale of Tynecastle
in his pre-match comments before the home game against the
Ayrshire side on 21 August. But even the heartfelt remarks of
someone who captained the team and made 349 appearances were
overshadowed by a new disagreement between Robinson and
Foulkes. It centred on the fact that a leaked document to *The Herald*
dismissed the possibility of a sale-and-leaseback agreement for
Tynecastle despite the fact that the chairman had publicly said any
such proposals would be considered. The document came with a
covering note which said, 'This proves Foulkes is telling lies.' An
inquiry into the leak was set up and the club clarified that it was in
fact open to the possibility of a sale-and-leaseback deal, although
no such offer had been received. Foulkes added, tantalisingly, that

it was not just Deans and Robert McGrail who could come up with an alternative to the Cala deal. 'They are not the only ones who might be interested in coming forward,' he told the Hearts website.

Later that day, almost incidentally, the team cruised to a 3–0 victory over Kilmarnock. Extra security was drafted in amid fears of trouble during and after the first game since the Cala announcement. A rumoured pitch invasion did not materialise but a group of around 400 fans gathered behind the main stand to vent their feelings.

The team then slumped to a 2–0 defeat away to Motherwell towards the end of the month after a poor second-half performance, prompting the normally composed Craig Levein to injure his hand on the dressing room wall – presumably out of frustration at the players' efforts. He was not the only one whose anger threatened to explode. A meeting of Save our Hearts during the week had agreed that the situation had become so critical that 'the gloves [were] off'. Two days later around fifty activists protested outside the Scottish Life offices in Edinburgh – the workplace of Hearts' non-executive director Brian Duffin. At the time, it was an incongruous sight in the heart of Edinburgh's financial district but it no doubt had a discomforting effect on Duffin, chief executive of the insurance and pensions company. The other board members, Foulkes excepted, would continue to be targeted with demonstrations after matches.

An organised boycott had previously been avoided but was now sanctioned given the gravity of the current situation, albeit during the relatively meaningless Festival Cup game against Hibs at the beginning of September. In addition, a second balloon protest was planned for the following match against Rangers at Tynecastle. This time the balloons would be black as a symbol of mourning for the impending loss of the stadium and possible death of the club.

But, as preparations for the protest campaign got under way, a new hope emerged. It was known that Foulkes had been involved in talks with representatives from Thailand and Ghana with a view to link-ups with Hearts but these had been concerned primarily with developing young talent. It was not known that a Lithuanian banker had held talks with Leslie Deans and Chris Robinson – who did so as a guest of Vladimir Romanov at the Chelsea–Southampton match on 28 August – about the possible purchase of all or some of their shares. Perhaps the references to Hearts' own Roman Abramovich were based on more than wishful thinking.

27

THE BALTIC BANKER

The man who stepped out of the shadows, or at least into the half-light, at the end of August and beginning of September was Lithuanian banker and businessman Vladimir Romanov. He was known to some in Scottish football after previously courting Dundee, Dundee United and Dunfermline over the past year or so, although those talks had come to nothing. However, it emerged that he also met Edinburgh's Deputy Lord Provost Steve Cardownie, a long-standing Hearts fan with a network of contacts in Ukraine and Eastern Europe, at Hampden during Scotland's 1–0 defeat of Lithuania in October 2003. It was a chance encounter which would encourage Romanov's interest in Hearts in the months ahead. Chris Robinson also took credit for identifying the foreign investor, through business advisers Vantis plc, in March 2004.

A later interview with the Lithuanian newspaper *Sport Express* quoted him as only seriously being interested in the Dundee teams and Hearts, with the latter 'better prospects in the capital of the country'. The interview added, 'I will spend any amount of money – I want this club to be the best in Scotland.'

Discussions with Hearts shareholders – including Robinson, Leslie Deans and SMG – had been taking place over the previous four months. There were concerns that Romanov's interest had 'cooled' but a tour of Westminster with George Foulkes helped to revive his enthusiasm, according to the chairman. The hints Foulkes had been dropping suddenly made some sense. Romanov may not have been in billionaire Roman Abramovich's league but his control of the Ūkio Bankas – Lithuania's fifth biggest bank – offered the possibility that Hearts' borrowings could be transferred there to appease the Bank of Scotland. Romanov also had connections in the world of football. He was described as the 'sponsor' of Lithuanian champions FBK Kaunas and was also associated with Belarussian club FC MTZ-RIPO Minsk.

In addition, Romanov was close to Lithuanian Football Federation president Liutauras Varanavicius, who was also chairman of a division of Ūkio. His talks in Scotland had involved possible injections of cash and/or a link-up which would put players brought over from Eastern Europe in the British transfer shop window. He was known to admire the passion for football in Scotland compared with his homeland, where basketball was the main sport. Also, Lithuania had joined the European Union in May 2004 and there were suggestions that Romanov hoped to expand his business empire by creating a base in one of Europe's financial centres. His credentials were checked by Foulkes' Foreign Office contacts and, indeed, the politician went as far as to urge other major shareholders to be realistic about the price they could expect to get for their stake in the club. The message was clear – Romanov offered Hearts' best hope for the future and should be given the opportunity to invest; anyone holding out for more cash should put the interests of the club first or they would never be forgiven by the fans. His comments prompted 'one or two people' to complain to the Financial Services Authority, presumably because they may have influenced the share price, although it went no further.

But there were lingering concerns about Romanov's motives and his lack of emotional ties to Hearts. Ūkio's own website listed him as a bank board member as well as shareholder and chairman of the associated Universal Business Investment Group Management. Yet a 2002 press release on the bank's website bizarrely described him as the man 'who is believed to be the real owner of Ūkio Bankas, although he holds no shares in the bank directly'. His reported friendship with the presidents of Russia and Ukraine, Vladimir

Putin and Viktor Yushchenko, has never been confirmed. Winston Churchill's assessment of Russia as 'a riddle wrapped in a mystery inside an enigma' has been used to describe the country's current premier. It could equally be applied to his Lithuanian namesake.

The possibility that veteran Ukrainian coach Anatoly Byshovets could come in as director of football posed further questions. Byshovets' track record was not in question – the former USSR player and manager of Russia had also worked in Portugal, South Korea and Georgia – but his arrival would surely cast doubt over the long-term future of Craig Levein.

The emergence of Romanov at least offered fresh promise at an otherwise gloomy time, not least because of the rumour that he would support the club remaining at Tynecastle. One man was less impressed. Levein had generally remained silent over the boardroom issues but, within days, hit out at the continuing 'off-field circus' which was proving a distraction for his players. It was something the manager would have to endure for a matter of weeks at least.

But his comments may have had some immediate impact. The Festival Cup boycott was due to take place on 4 September. The match itself was being staged in memory of Hearts and Hibs legend Gordon Smith, the talented winger who won the league with both Edinburgh clubs in the post-war era. The sombre nature of the occasion – the crowd was also asked to pay its respects to former Hearts goalkeeper Willie Duff and the 330 who died in the school siege in the Russian town of Beslan earlier in the week – may have encouraged some Hearts fans to ignore the boycott. That apart, the tactic was also deeply divisive, with many supporters insisting they would never take the drastic step of failing to support the team – in any circumstances. The boycott organisers promised they would pay tribute to Smith at an alternative protest event in Saughton Park but few turned up. The match crowd of fewer than 8,000 suggested that, while some had indeed stayed away, they had not done so in huge numbers. With the international stars on Scotland duty, the non-competitive game featured a number of fringe players on both sides and finished 3–1 to Hearts.

If there was some disappointment at the low-key nature of the boycott, the tempo, however, was certainly raised in the week before the EGM. George Foulkes called for calm amid media reports that directors and shareholders had received death threats and had their homes targeted by threatening mobs. Their families had been intimidated, incidents of graffiti had been reported and hate mail, apparently including sympathy cards, had been received. The police were called in and patrols stepped up but tensions were clearly running high.

Save our Hearts condemned the terror tactics and continued with preparations for a legitimate protest at the Rangers game on 12 September, the day before the EGM. A comprehensive statement discrediting the case for a move from Tynecastle to Murrayfield was drawn up, with plans to distribute 7,000 copies to fans on the day of the game. At the same time, 12,000 black balloons had been ordered for the demonstration during the match. Rangers fans jumped on the bandwagon by declaring that they would stage a flag protest, in the mistaken belief that the Union flag had been banned from Tynecastle by Chris Robinson. The chief executive's programme notes clarified that it was only Union flags or any other, for that matter, 'adorned with sectarian symbols' which were deemed unacceptable. Robinson at least had the backing of most Hearts supporters with that stance and, in any case, the flag protest during the interval was half-hearted and ignored by most in the Rangers end, no doubt despite the best efforts of the far-right British National Party activists leafleting at the game.

Organisers of the Hearts demonstration were disappointed that more balloons had not been distributed to fans, claiming that bags had been confiscated at the turnstiles. They later suggested that stewards had also been issued with spikes to burst them when they floated on to the pitch and trackside. Nevertheless the balloon release made an impressive sight and held up the start of the second half. The stuffy game did little to enthuse spectators further but the protest continued behind the main stand at the end of the 0–0 draw. This time the atmosphere between the 700 demonstrators and the police – some on horseback was tense – perhaps because of the presence of what appeared to be a small group of casuals. Two arrests were eventually made, although police slowly dispersed the crowd without further trouble.

28

AN EXTRAORDINARY MEETING

The scene was set for a stormy EGM the next day and so it proved. Police dog handlers patrolled outside Tynecastle and officers were on duty inside the Gorgie Suite. Yet the very organisation of the event raised questions about the club's treatment of its customers. Fewer seats appeared to have been laid out than at the AGM, despite the fact a bumper attendance was inevitable. As the 7 p.m. start time passed, 1,000 shareholders had crammed into the stifling hospitality lounge, with more standing than sitting. One fan was seen wearing a T-shirt with the slogan 'Free Hearts' and another had a more sinister message aimed at Chris Robinson: 'Kill the Pieman – Burn his House Down'. The Hearts security staff declared that they were satisfied with the chaotic arrangements, although it was bound to fuel the volatile atmosphere. So it appeared when the board filed into the room fifteen minutes late and took their seats to a cacophony of boos, shouts of 'scum' and 'Judas' and repeated chants of 'sack the board'. Several fans had to be restrained as they lunged towards the top table and stink bombs were released, presumably to represent contempt at the board's stewardship of the club.

The raw emotion on display was such that even arch-critic Gary Mackay was seen appealing for calm and eventually George Foulkes made himself heard over the din. The chairman at least had the decency to apologise for the lack of seats and late start but the suggestion of an apology from the board only prompted a round of ironic jeers. He explained that the meeting could go straight to a vote but added it was important that all views were aired and respected.

Iain Macleod, representing Save our Hearts, was the first to take the floor. He at least could expect a receptive audience. He presented a reasoned critique of the board's strategy, based on the earlier statement distributed to fans, while also appealing to supporters' obvious emotions. He described the pride and passion of the club's history and traditions, including the players who signed up en masse during the First World War because they believed that it was the right thing to do. To the loudest cheer of the evening, he then concluded:

> I believe the current chief executive should resign forthwith. If he won't resign, I'm calling on the board members to make the decision for him – it's your duty to the shareholders of this club. Brian Duffin, Stewart Fraser and David Archer SMG's representative on the board, your names will go down in history as the men who did nothing while this club was sold down the river. Think about the past generations that have played here or watched from the terracing or the stands. Think about the players from 1914 who made the ultimate sacrifice because they believed they were doing the right thing. Now it's our turn to do the right thing. But, more importantly, think about the future generations to come. Are you going to deprive them of the Tynecastle experience – never to be able to watch the Hearts in a packed stadium in Gorgie? Do the right thing and vote against the resolution to sell the stadium. Do the right thing and save our Hearts.

As the standing ovation settled, George Foulkes went on to warn that the club could go into administration if action was not taken to reduce the accumulated debt, with the stadium likely to be sold by the administrator. However, he also hinted at boardroom changes to come when he said the board was aware of its duties for 'succession planning and board enlargement'. Finance director Stewart Fraser defended his financial forecasts over the recent years – as well as those for future seasons at Murrayfield – as 'relatively spot on', insisting that accurate figures had been submitted to the board as required. One shareholder responded by accusing Fraser and the rest of the board of 'incompetence' if that was the case.

Chris Robinson became involved in proceedings for the first time when the controversial issue of the pitch size and UEFA licensing system operating in fifty-two countries was raised by a shareholder. He gave a detailed reply:

> Of those fifty-two countries, there are 420 clubs who have licences and 116 who don't meet the requirements. In Scotland, two clubs did not meet the requirements. We have only a conditional licence. The SFA, through David Findlay, made it clear to me that UEFA had issues in respect of our pitch size. He made it clear that he would do anything to allow us to play at Tynecastle. In December, after we played at Bordeaux, UEFA wrote to the SFA and said, on 3 December, that in no circumstances would Hearts receive a derogation to play at Tynecastle.

He went on to claim that the club had thoroughly investigated the possibility of lengthening the pitch by two metres to the stipulated minimum of 100 metres. However, it had been concluded that it would cost millions of pounds and the corner towers could pose a major safety hazard.

It was a surprise, then, when George Foulkes asked the stadium architect, Jim Clydesdale, to respond to Robinson. In what seemed the perfect set-up, the architect opened by joking, 'It is scary to be in a stadium that's not fit for purpose if you have designed it.' He then said the pitch could be made UEFA compliant by narrowing it from a generous 68 metres and lengthening it at the same time to 100 metres, therefore placing the corner flags further away from the floodlight towers and actually reducing the safety risk to players. He added, 'In the current circumstances, I believe there are ways of looking at it that could be finessed.' Save our Hearts representative Iain Macleod cut short Robinson's response when he chipped in, saying, 'I believe your expertise is in catering, while Mr Clydesdale's is in architecture.' That was followed by a claim that French side Auxerre had been given permission to play in the UEFA Cup despite having a pitch which did not meet the minimum width requirements. The conspiracy theorists were further encouraged when, to cheers, Foulkes then said, 'You can see why I thought Jim would be a valuable member of the [stadium] working group.'

Security staff had been required to restrain shareholders on several occasions during proceedings but the EGM ended in nothing short of mayhem. The vote was called amid a boisterous slow handclap. Shouts of 'murderers' rang out as Foulkes declared that 46.3% of the shareholding had already undertaken to vote in favour of the resolution, such a large proportion meaning that a card vote in the hall was virtually meaningless. Also, no final result would be given until the following day. Some started to trudge out without even bothering to vote but a group of around fifty surged towards the top table hurling abuse after Foulkes called the meeting closed just after 9 p.m. The angry crowd almost encircled the table but police moved in and linked arms to provide a cordon for the directors to exit through a side door. But the imminent departure of the board only enraged the baying fans further. Chairs tumbled and supporters knocked each other over as they tried to break through the police lines. The directors eventually escaped the gauntlet but not before Robinson and Brian Duffin were momentarily trapped when the line of officers briefly broke. Robinson was then forced to break into a run to reach safety. A protest continued outside the ground for some time but fans were held back as Robinson drove off.

The fury of the Hearts shareholders at the EGM had been fuelled by the stark realisation that the end of Tynecastle was in sight. But they were also venting years of pent-up anger over the stewardship of the club at the very people they held responsible. Foulkes recognised the strength of feeling when he compared the experience of chairing the meeting with working in some of the world's worst trouble spots. He told the club website:

I have been in some hostile environments before, as a councillor and MP. But that was certainly more vociferous than any of that. I've been to Columbia with two armed guards and was election monitoring in Guyana amidst an angry crowd. I've been to lots of trouble spots in the world and any human being is going to worry about what happens next.

But the meeting had been more than just rowdy. It was a turning point in the campaign against the move. Before the EGM, it had seemed inevitable that club would make the flit to Murrayfield; after it, such a move seemed almost impossible in the face of such overwhelming hostility.

The following day the result was announced to the stock exchange with a message that the motion to sell Tynecastle to Cala had been 'duly passed'. The result was given as an emphatic 62.5% vote in favour of the resolution, although this calculation did not include abstentions. When those who had abstained were taken into account the total shareholding in favour of selling Tynecastle was understood to be little more than 50%. Indeed, of more concern was that 2,957 of the 4,039 shareholders chose not to take part in the ballot, although many may have regarded the outcome as a fait accompli. In total, 153 voted for the resolution and 929 against, although the latter comprised mostly small shareholders.

29

HEARTS TRY FOR
EURO SUCCESS

Jim Clydesdale's comments at the EGM about the potential viability of Tynecastle for European competition could not have been timelier. Hearts had considered staging a derby match at Murrayfield in 1947 and the SRU agreed to the proposal but the idea of making the rugby stadium a home venue for the club was never taken further. Now, fifty-seven years later, it was a reality. Hearts were due to play their first competitive home game away from Tynecastle since moving to the Gorgie ground. And, astonishingly, the preparations were taking place amid off-field mayhem at the club. Just three days after the EGM, Hearts were due to face Portuguese side SC Braga in one of their most important European ties for years. Both sides were aware that victory over two legs would take them into the potentially lucrative group stage of the new-look UEFA Cup and the Braga coach was quick to use the stadium issue as ammunition in the psychological battle with his opponents. Rui Águas claimed he was glad the game was not being played at an intimidating Tynecastle, with its stands close to the pitch, and added that the open spaces of Murrayfield may suit his team better.

The build-up to the game was loaded with uncertainty as everyone connected with Hearts was unsure what to expect from the Murrayfield experience. The BBC website, seemingly as bewildered as the supporters, even listed the tie as taking place at

Tynecastle. The rugby stadium did not even merit a mention on the match tickets. There had been some talk of a boycott and some fans no doubt stayed away on principle but nothing was organised and ticket sales were healthy. The fans who did attend were being forced to enter the object of so much of their scorn in recent months. Yet they also realised the importance of the game and the need to support the team on the park. There was, therefore, an odd atmosphere as supporters spilled out of the pubs and made their way to the ground. The lack of Hearts 'branding' gave little sense it was a home game, with adverts for the forthcoming Scotland–Australia rugby international creating the opposite effect. In fact, the long, boisterous queues at the turnstiles – and even reports that gates were opened to avoid a crush – created an impression more of a big cup game at a neutral venue. Essentially, of course, that is exactly what it was.

Inside the stadium, the fans were in a remarkably buoyant mood, although reminders of the incongruous setting were ever present. First when the Hearts song was blasted out with, of course, the opening line of 'Away down in Gorgie at Tynecastle Park'. Then the kick-off was delayed by five minutes because of concerns about the security of the unfamiliar football nets behind the goals – this was perhaps not surprising for a ground unfamiliar with such accessories. Eventually, with the 18,769 fans still making their way into the stands, an Englishman, Phil Stamp, touched the ball to an Australian, Patrick Kisnorbo, and the first ever competitive football game at Scotland's national rugby stadium was under way.

Braga had been going well in the Portuguese league, recording a 1–1 draw with Porto the weekend before, but Hearts were sitting in fifth place on the same points as Rangers. Hearts settled surprisingly quickly but there were no goals at half-time. Then, six minutes into the second period, central defender Andy Webster met a Mark de Vries header across goal and scored the historic first goal at the home of rugby. Braga showed more positive intent after the goal but Paul Hartley put the home team two up in sixty-two minutes after the Portuguese pushed for an equaliser. Braga got one back three minutes later but Kisnorbo made it 3–1 to Hearts after crashing a shot into the net in injury time.

Most were happy with the result, although the away goal was a cause for some concern, and it was generally accepted that Hearts' biggest crowd of the season had created a memorable atmosphere. The fact that periodic chants of abuse were still aimed at the board of directors should have given some food for thought, even for those who believed the match had strengthened the case for a move away from Tynecastle. It was clear that the occasion would be very different on a wet Wednesday evening in January against Livingston or similar opposition.

If Chris Robinson was buoyed by the relative success of the Murrayfield experiment, then two official votes at a shareholders' association special general meeting on 28 September would not have given him any encouragement. An overwhelming majority, 91% of those who voted, expressed no confidence in Robinson and called for his removal from office. Committee members said the last time such drastic action was taken by the relatively conservative body was in 1993 against Wallace Mercer, then by 80% on a show of hands. A second vote opposed the sale of Tynecastle by a slightly smaller margin and called for the club to withdraw from any agreement to that effect until all options had been fully explored. Shareholder Roger Gow, who submitted the motions, said the situation facing the club was 'the biggest single issue to affect the future of Hearts since the Great War'. He spoke passionately about the sale of the stadium as 'the road to possible ruin'. He added, 'We are going to be nomads on no-man's land with massive debts. I think it's an absolute nightmare we are being drawn into.' There were few challengers to his arguments although, with under fifty people attending, the numbers were too small to send a powerful message to the board.

It was certainly true that events were moving forward and, behind the scenes, an agreement between Robinson and Vladimir Romanov was nearing completion. The Lithuanian was known to have been in Edinburgh for talks and to attend some Hearts matches. At the same time, businessman Robert McGrail, bemused that Romanov was being described as the only show in town, told George Foulkes that he was still prepared to step in and buy Hearts' debt if the Romanov deal collapsed.

The run of dreary games in the second half of September – a defeat by Dunfermline at East End Park (1–0), followed by narrow wins over Kilmarnock in the League Cup (2–1) and Inverness Caley Thistle (1–0) in the league – offered the Lithuanian little encouragement. Despite that, by the end of the month, a deal between Romanov and Robinson had been struck.

The official announcement could hardly have been timed better, coming as it did on 30 September – the morning of the crucial return match with Braga in Portugal. The statement, headed simply 'Conditional Sale of Shares by Chris Robinson', revealed that the chief executive had not held out for an inflated price. In fact, he had agreed to sell his entire holding of almost 2.5 million shares, or 19.6% of the company, for a total of £867,000 – 35p each. The day before the transaction they were trading for 34.5p, although they rose to a new recent high of 42.5p in the two weeks or so that followed. There were a number of conditions attached to the deal – for instance Romanov could pull out on payment of a £50,000 penalty. Agreements also had to be struck with Hearts' creditors and Cala. But two clauses were seized on by most supporters – first, that Robinson 'will tender his resignation as chief executive of the company' on completion of the sale and, second, that Romanov would ask Cala to allow Hearts to continue playing at Tynecastle, at least for a limited period.

Romanov also broke his silence, describing the club as a 'highly attractive opportunity for investment' and promising 'a bright future for shareholders, employees and fans of Hearts'. At first glance, it was the news many supporters had been waiting for – Tynecastle may have a future and Robinson had agreed to stand down.

George Foulkes described the announcement as 'good news' for the club, highlighting the fact that Tynecastle may be able to remain

Hearts' home. He did also caution that nothing was guaranteed in the long term and, technically, the Cala deal still remained in place but, that aside, the feel-food factor appeared to be returning to the club. Finally, attention could turn to events on the park and, with Robinson remaining in Edinburgh during the negotiations, Foulkes led the party out to Portugal. At the Labour Party conference earlier in the week, Prime Minister Tony Blair had told Foulkes he wished Hearts well in the Braga game. With that endorsement, the chairman struck an upbeat note in his pre-match interviews. His confidence was well placed as the team secured a 2–2 draw to win the tie 5–3 on aggregate and make history as the first Scottish team to qualify for the group stage of the UEFA Cup. Mark de Vries had performed the heroics on the pitch, scoring both goals, despite taking a pain-killing injection for his injured foot, but Craig Levein also deserved credit for winning the tactical battle. The 1,500 Hearts fans who congregated Braga's squares and fountains were jubilant enough at the news which broke before the game started. Now, they had further reason to make it a night to remember – some did so by taking a celebratory dip in Praça da República's Arcada Fountain.

30

LEVEIN TO LEICESTER

The supporters may have expected a return to the humdrum of league affairs after the midweek success in Europe. But the weekend of the Livingston game at the beginning of October offered yet more cause for celebration.

Vladimir Romanov had personally said very little about his intentions for Hearts and there were still doubts about his plans for the club. Given that it would seem to distance him from Hearts fans, it was odd that he chose to break his silence in the Russian newspaper *Izvestia*. Some allowances may be made for translation but the Lithuanian was quoted as suggesting that Hearts would clear their debt by the end of the year – something that, in the end, did not happen – be provided with a, presumably annual, budget of £10 million and challenge the Old Firm for honours. He may have chosen not to speak directly to his key audience, the supporters, but he did at least describe them as the 'best in the world'. Those committed to remaining at Tynecastle at all costs would have been disappointed that he planned to move to a new stadium. The fact that he was prepared to build it may have won over the more flexible supporters.

The recent developments appeared to take the impetus out of the supporters' protests. Only around 300 had taken part in a demonstration after the Inverness game and, for what must have been the first time in months, there were no signs of protest during or after the 0–0 draw with Livingston. Matters were not only moving in a more acceptable direction, they were also slipping out of the control of the ordinary fan. A handful even began to ask for refunds from the Save our Hearts share fund.

Romanov tightened his grip on the club when he agreed to buy 1.3 million shares, 10.3% of the club, from former chairman Leslie Deans for £455,000 or 35p each – taking his stake to 29.9% once the Chris Robinson deal was completed. The move, which would leave Romanov just short of the threshold requiring him make a formal takeover offer to all shareholders, had been widely anticipated but certainly reflected the seriousness of his intent.

That aside, the main focus was the draw for the UEFA Cup groups on 5 October. Some of Europe's biggest names had made it through and Hearts faced the prospect of not only some mouth-watering games but also an unprecedented and much-needed financial windfall. The draw was not disappointing, with Hearts in a five-team group alongside previous cup winners Feyenoord from Holland, the German team Schalke 04, the veteran Swiss campaigners FC Basel and the Hungarian champions Ferencváros. Rather than the traditional system of playing both home and away legs, two games would be in Edinburgh and two on the road. The first away game was just two weeks away against the Dutch giants Feyenoord – in Rotterdam. Craig Levein was not fazed by the prospect of being considered the 'diddy' team by his opponents – he was, perhaps, even hopeful that they would repeat Braga's mistake and underestimate his side.

The build-up to the big game could hardly have been worse – a comprehensive 3–0 defeat to Celtic at Parkhead. The supporters remained optimistic, however, and travelled to the Netherlands in big numbers. The 2,500 contingent certainly made themselves heard in a corner of the De Kuip stadium decked out in traditional maroon and white Saltires for Hearts' first ever UEFA league game on 21 October. Unfortunately, their efforts were not matched on the pitch and, despite plenty of possession, the players failed to rise to the occasion. The match ended 3–0 to the home team and could have been more. Hearts had not been helped by some atrocious refereeing decisions – which were understood to have been used later during a UEFA training session for referees and linesmen as examples of blunders by match officials – but nevertheless they had received a European group baptism of fire.

The team did at least make amends on their return to Edinburgh, beating Hibs 2–1 in a frenzied derby at Tynecastle three days later. That was followed by an evenly contested 1–1 draw at Tannadice on 27 October and a 3–0 defeat of United's city rivals, ten-man Dundee, the following weekend. But it was too much to expect that the month would end without Hearts' match reports being displaced by the latest breaking news and the Dundee game was played with one major absence – manager Craig Levein.

Levein had started an uncharacteristically bitter war of words after the Hibs game, accusing opposing manager Tony Mowbray of 'a lorry-load of sour grapes' and throwing 'all the toys out of the pram' for suggesting Hearts played a physical game. Levein said Mowbray had not even come into his office at the end of the match, adding, 'He got spanked and got sent home.' Levein clearly had things on his mind.

The head coach had been linked to a number of jobs south of the border, such as Blackburn Rovers and Leeds United, but nothing came of the speculation. Then, three days after the Hibs match and just before the game against Dundee United, it emerged that another English club was keen to tempt the promising young manager south – Leicester City. Levein issued a cagey denial but it was known that he had an appointment to meet Vladimir Romanov the next day and there were suggestions he may be unhappy working with a director of football, a role envisaged for Anatoly Byshovets. Levein's claim that he expected to be at Hearts for the foreseeable future appeared empty when it was confirmed the next day that he was moving to the English First Division side. He insisted in media interviews that the possible takeover by Romanov had not influenced his decision and his sole reason for leaving was an ambition to take Leicester into the Premiership, where he had always hoped to test his abilities as a manager. Yet he did refer to the ongoing uncertainty over players' contracts.

His admission that he had considered leaving for a year – which backed up his comments at the Fans' Forum meeting nine months earlier – grated with some fans, who saw him as planning his exit strategy. The fact that he would go on to tempt several key Hearts players south only heightened the anger. His suggestion that the squad wage bill halved while he was at Tynecastle was difficult to square with overall staffing costs. While there is no detailed breakdown of the figures, it is known that the total cost of players and other staff stood at £5.6 million shortly before he succeeded Jim Jefferies and was down to just over £5 million three months before he left, although that did include £140,000 in bonuses for the European successes. During that period, the average number of players and coaching staff actually went up from sixty-four to seventy-five.

The following day, Levein was on the front pages rather than the back with reports of a marriage split. It was not clear if that was a factor in moving away from home, although Romanov's advisers suggested as much in press reports. Levein may have occupied the manager's slot in the match day programme (still carping about Hibs being disrespectful and claiming credit for sending them 'back to Easter Road with their tails firmly between their legs') but it was assistant coach Peter Houston who was left in charge of the team for the visit of Dundee – before following Levein to Leicester. There was a predictably flat atmosphere at the game and some signs of anger, such as a banner accusing Levein of being a 'Judas', but the dominant performance on the park at least moved Hearts into fourth place in the league. Houston shook hands with the players and bid an emotional farewell to Tynecastle after more than eight years at the club.

Managers such as Motherwell's Terry Butcher were mentioned as possible replacements but, in reality, there was one outstanding candidate – record league goal scorer and true Hearts legend, John Robertson.

31

ROBBO STRIKES AGAIN

The big managerial news on 1 November was the resignation of Scotland manager Berti Vogts, apparently because of the abuse he received from the media and others. He even cited an incident when he was spat on. It was not clear who did this, although it was presumed to have been a Scotland fan after the dreadful 1–1 draw with Moldova in October. But it was not long before the Hearts managerial merry-go-round hit the headlines again. The Leicester director of football, Dave Bassett was ditched, leading to suspicions that Craig Levein did have concerns about working with Anatoly Byshovets in a similar role – and installed Peter Houston alongside him at Leicester. Levein also chose to speak out about the situation at Tynecastle, backing his friend John Robertson for the top job.

Sure enough, Robertson was unveiled as the new Hearts head coach on 3 November 2004 after the club agreed to pay a six-figure compensation fee to Inverness Caledonian Thistle. His assistant Donald Park, another former Hearts player, also made the trip south to the capital.

Robertson had been a coach at Livingston and had guided Caledonian Thistle into the SPL, where they were exceeding most people's expectations. Robertson gave up on payments he was due to smooth the deal, which was completed just in time for the next big European match – Schalke at Murrayfield. At his first press conference, Robertson confessed that he had hoped to return to Tynecastle since the day he left in 1998. The former player, who had been known as 'Ceefax' by his Hearts team mates because of his detailed knowledge of the game, added, 'My playing record does bring added pressure but I am here because of my coaching ability . . . I would manage the guys if they played on a public park, such is my affection for the club.'

It was odd, then, that Robertson's first game in charge was not in familiar Gorgie surroundings but across the railway line at Murrayfield. Coach John McGlynn selected the team for the match against the high-flying Bundesliga outfit, although he discussed his choices with Robertson, who took his place in the dugout. He must have been impressed when he looked around at the 27,272 crowd filing into the stands – despite the fact that the stadium remained more than half-empty because of Murrayfield's cavernous capacity. Nevertheless, it was Hearts' biggest attendance against continental opposition since 29,500 packed Tynecastle for the 1960 European Cup tie against Benfica in 1960, with some, no doubt, turning up because of Robertson's appointment.

Ironically, though, it seemed to work against the team. With so many neutrals and rugby fans in the crowd, the atmosphere remained flat from start to finish. Not that the players did much to lift their spirits. They competed well enough in the first-half without ever looking threatening. But Patrick Kisnorbo's soft sending-off for a second yellow card after diving in the box at the start of the second forty-five minutes turned the game against the home team. It was no surprise when the side sitting second in the Bundesliga scored seventeen minutes from time with a 30-yard drive. Another appalling European referee did not help but, in truth, Hearts had looked second best.

In post-match interviews, Robertson admitted the Germans deserved their win, despite some histrionics and an inconsistent referee, but he promised to attack in the final two UEFA matches to try to secure the third place which would take Hearts into the next round. Schalke coach Ralf Rangnick praised Hearts' passion and organisation but claimed his side deserved the points. Interestingly, the former Stuttgart head coach, who had visited

Gorgie four years before, added, 'It would have been tougher for us at Tynecastle – I'm absolutely convinced about that. The atmosphere was good tonight but, from my memories of Tynecastle, I can tell you that it is much worse for an away team.' It was more ammunition for the Murrayfield doubters, although there was the not insignificant consolation of the estimated £1 million raked in from ticket sales, hospitality and German television fees. The takings were double that made from the Stuttgart match in 2000, then the most lucrative game in the club's history.

On 7 November, before the team got back to league business, a number of those associated with the club – including Hearts players and supporters – first attended the unveiling on of a memorial to the men of the 16th Royal Scots who signed up to fight in the First World War. The long-overdue cairn at Contalmaison, in France, was erected after the Hearts Great War Memorial Appeal raised the required £50,000. Soldiers from the battalion had advanced further than any others on the first day of the Battle of the Somme in 1916, reaching the hamlet of Contalmaison. George Foulkes later followed up that ceremony by tabling an early day motion in the House of Commons recognising the sacrifice of the Hearts players in the war.

The same day the cairn was unveiled, the team travelled north to Aberdeen, where they picked up a valuable but hard-fought three points with a 1–0 victory and moved into third place. Robertson picked up his second win three days later with a 3–1 defeat of Dunfermline at East End Park in the League Cup, which set up a semi-final in February. Another league point was picked at Kilmarnock the following weekend after a 1–1 draw before Robertson faced his first Tynecastle outing. Unfortunately, the Motherwell match did not follow the script and Hearts were edged out 1–0 after Alan Maybury gave away a dubious penalty and received a red card in the process. The disappointment was compounded by the fact it was Hearts' first home defeat to a team outside the Old Firm for two years. Robertson's frustration was obvious when he was drawn into a public spat with referee John

Rowbotham, claiming the match official lied when he accused the Hearts boss of swearing. He was later fined £500. But there was at least the excitement of a make-or-break trip to Basel in midweek to lift players and supporters alike.

Almost 2,000 Hearts fans followed the team to the Swiss city on 25 November after Basel provided 300 extra tickets to meet demand. With Basel top of the Swiss league, the journey was made more in hope than expectation but the supporters quickly made themselves seen and heard in and around the Barfusserplatz before making their way to St Jakob Park. The Saltire flying outside the town hall in place of the Swiss flag suggested that the fans could expect a warm welcome and so it transpired.

The Basel supporters within the stadium had a cheekier message, on the Scottish Braveheart theme, when they unfurled a banner that declared, 'Brave enough to break Hearts'. But they would be proved wrong. The defence was rock solid, particularly Craig Gordon in goals, and a positive attacking set-up allowed Hearts to take the lead from a Dennis Wyness goal after half an hour. Basel equalised thirty minutes into the second-half but Hearts continued to scrap for the winner and the unlikely figure of fullback Robbie Neilson crashed the ball into the net on the verge of full-time to score his first goal for the club from open play and make it 2–1. Craig Levein sent a text message to his successor saying he almost dropped his glass of wine in disbelief when he heard on the radio that Neilson had scored. It just about summed up the feelings of most fans.

The travelling supporters were understandably ecstatic but the Basel fans were also remarkably magnanimous after a result which left them struggling in the group. The good humour between the two sets of supporters continued after the game at bars across the city, with the Swiss hailing 'the excellent Jocks' as the biggest and loudest away support to visit St Jakob Park, despite being drawn against the likes of Celtic, Manchester United, Inter Milan and Juventus in recent years. Indeed, such was the bond that Basel fans would make an exchange visit to Edinburgh and take in an SPL encounter in the months ahead. Hearts had arguably secured their best ever result in Europe and made some lasting friends in the process.

Three days after returning from Switzerland, a narrow 3–2 defeat to Rangers, after taking the lead at Ibrox, seemed to confirm that Hearts were ready to compete with Europe's big guns. Unfortunately, the competitive display in Glasgow was somewhat overshadowed by more off-field distractions. It emerged that, despite having no official position with the club, Anatoly Byshovets had gone into the victorious dressing room after the Basel triumph and told the players to turn down the celebratory music. There were also claims he had criticised the performance of some players, although it was never made clear if that was the case. The attitude seemed harsh on the players, who had achieved a memorable result and, more importantly, could have been seen to undermine Robertson's position as head coach. The incident at least resulted in the enigmatic Eastern Europeans launching what could loosely be described as a charm offensive.

Byshovets denied he had been a 'spoilsport' but said the players were told to be professional and remain focused on the next game. He also insisted that Robertson was the man in charge of the squad. At the same time, Vladimir Romanov staged a meet-the-press event where he outlined his vision for the club. Speaking through an interpreter, he extravagantly predicted that Hearts could overtake the Old Firm, with bigger crowds and a better stadium – at Tynecastle or elsewhere. His ambitions seemed bold but fanciful to most, including Hearts fans. Some of that could be put down to a lack of understanding of Scottish football and the vice-like grip Celtic and Rangers have exerted on the game for a combination of sporting, commercial and religious reasons. But he could certainly not be accused of lacking in either aspiration or inspiration.

Romanov also gave some personal details for the first time, even handing out old family photos to journalists. He described how he grew up in Russia, with his family caught up in the

900-day siege of Leningrad which German troops began in 1941 in an effort to bring the country's second city to its knees. He added that his father fought in the war and was one of the Soviet troops who reached Berlin in 1945. Romanov himself worked on a nuclear submarine in the Soviet navy, cruising around the British coast during the Cold War. As an adult he was reputed to have stood up to the Russian mafia and Lithuanian underworld and he was said to have suffered business disappointments as well as successes. His message was clear – hardship is sometimes unavoidable but also 'change isn't always the worst thing'.

However, he was coy about providing any financial details. Questions about how much he would invest in Hearts, what he would do about the club's debt mountain and how the year-on-year trading losses could be reversed remained unanswered. The fate of fourteen players whose contracts were due to expire at the end of the season was also not clear. The interrogation was timely. Earlier that day, the club had announced yet another set of huge losses, this time £2.4 million up to 31 July 2004. Net debt, meanwhile, had reached a staggering £19.6 million. Taking part in the UEFA Cup had at least brought in £1 million, helping turnover to reach £7.2 million. Yet, despite repeated claims of savage wage cuts, staff costs had dropped by a mere £72,000 when drastic reductions were surely needed more than ever before.

Romanov was not the only one to break his silence the day the financial results were released – Chris Robinson also took the opportunity to speak expansively for the first time about the Lithuanian. But, before doing so, he also passed comments on the club's finances, claiming in a BBC Radio Scotland interview that, despite the latest losses and barely significant fall in overall staff costs, '[we] are moving in the right direction. Year by year, we have been cutting back on costs, particularly the cost of the playing squad, and also trying to increase the revenue.' When asked what his place would be in Hearts' history, he went on to compare the recent sequence of record losses with other eras, while having the decency to exempt the most successful period in the club's history and added:

I think [that, during] the ten-year decade (*sic*), the club's results have been as good as many of the decades, with the exception of the 50s ... There were lots of mistakes made but there were a lot of very good things over those ten years and it's very easy to forget them.

He claimed credit for identifying Romanov during a 'succession-planning' exercise he started up to eighteen months before, adding:

I sat down and decided that ten years was enough for anyone at the frontline in the job that I was doing but, to be honest, the club needed freshness and change and we set out to find someone who could take on the reins ... I'm very pleased that it's someone who has deep pockets as far as we can ascertain and, importantly, a love of football and that's all you can ask of anyone coming in to your football club.

With deep pockets and a love of football, Romanov appeared to be the man capable of transforming Hearts. But the latest results underlined the pressing need for action and it remained to be seen if the man from the former Soviet Union would be the one to lead the much-needed revolution at Hearts.

The boardroom circus continued without let-up in December, not least because the deadline for the completion of Vladimir Romanov's buy-out of Chris Robinson had been set for 8 December. It quickly became apparent that the deal was unlikely to be completed on time and would be set back, to the frustration of the chief executive's harshest critics. As predicted, the date for an agreement to be reached was put back to 28 January 2005, to 'allow sufficient time for those discussions', while the actual transaction had to be completed by 4 February. A similar extension to the Cala deadline, from 31 January to the end of February, followed shortly afterwards.

Hearts fans pointed the finger of blame at SMG for the hold-up, even picketing the company's Glasgow headquarters. SMG denied stalling the negotiations and were even understood to be prepared to sell at the same price as Chris Robinson and Leslie Deans – 35p a share. It was less clear what proposals were on the table for repaying the £4.5 debt to the media company.

The backdrop to these developments was the approach of Hearts' most important game for years: the make-or-break European decider against Hungarians Ferencváros. The build-up was encouraging enough – a 3–0 defeat of Dunfermline on 4 December for John Robertson's first win at Tynecastle. It was followed the next Saturday by a less impressive 1–1 draw with Inverness Caledonian Thistle as Robertson returned to his former club. Robertson did not, however, return to Inverness as the game was actually played at their SPL-compliant rented home, a sparsely attended Pittodrie Stadium in Aberdeen.

Robertson used Jim Jefferies' 1998 motivational message by telling the players that they would become legends if they won the Ferencváros game and took Hearts through the group stages of the UEFA Cup. Indeed, the team already had the unusual honour of being the last club representing Scotland in Europe, with Celtic tumbling out earlier and Rangers exiting after playing Auxerre the night before. The last time a club outside Glasgow had outlasted the Old Firm in Europe was during Hearts' great run in the same competition in 1988–89. The occasion certainly captured the imagination of the fans, with another healthy crowd of 26,182 turning up at Murrayfield on 16 November. Unfortunately, that enthusiasm failed to translate into atmosphere as another flat night in the huge rugby stadium began to unfold.

The team started strongly enough, and even had the ball in the net after twelve minutes, but the goal was ruled out for handball by Paul Hartley. It was an uphill struggle after the Hungarian champions scored against a flat-footed Hearts defence on thirty minutes. The tie ended as a contest as news filtered through that Basel had scored against Feyenoord. A 1–0 win for the Swiss was the single scoreline which would take both teams through to the next round and few were surprised when it ended that way. Ferencváros, too, finished with a 1–0 victory, though they did little else to endear themselves to Hearts fans and neutrals alike. It had been a bad-tempered match. Visiting coach Csaba László was sent to the stand for complaining when Hearts refused to give his team the ball back after it had been kicked out to allow treatment for a Hungarian who claimed to be injured. However, his players did themselves no credit with their cynical challenges, play-acting and time-wasting. The sixty free kicks awarded in the match reflected the scrappy nature of the encounter as much as it revealed the scattergun approach of yet another ineffectual European referee.

Hearts were out of the UEFA Cup and they went with a whimper rather than the big bang that had been promised. Then events took a nasty turn after the final whistle. Robertson and his opposite number later disagreed on exactly what happened but the angry exchange between the two men was witnessed by those heading for the exits and was caught on camera. László accused Robertson of kicking him after he complained about the incident which saw him banished from the dugout. The outspoken Robertson, who had been involved in a worrying series of post-match spats, told the club website, 'He called my team cheats. I told him that was his opinion and then he stood on my foot. I just got him off my foot; it's as simple as that. If I'd kicked him, he wouldn't still be standing.' László retorted, saying, 'There are almost 30,000 people here who have come to watch football and two coaches are fighting at the side of the pitch. It's crazy ... Hearts are a good team; maybe they just need a new coach.' Whatever the truth, and it was reported to UEFA although Robertson escaped punishment, the incident was an unsavoury way to end Hearts' European challenge. They finished bottom of their table, with Ferencváros faring little better – one place above but also out of the tournament. The venture had been commercially successful – indeed, it would later be estimated to have brought in around £2 million. But the uninspiring games against Schalke and Ferencváros had led even some supporters of Murrayfield to ask if the team would not have benefited more from playing at Tynecastle. It was an argument which would soon be developed further by the Stadium Working Group.

32

TYNECASTLE STADIUM: FIT FOR PURPOSE

The Stadium Working Group, set up by George Foulkes to examine all possible stadium options, finally reported on 21 December, the day after the Cala deadline had been extended. And it certainly did not disappoint the critics who opposed the move away from the club's spiritual home.

It concluded that the deal with Cala should be scrapped as it was 'not in the best interests of the club' and Hearts should remain at Tynecastle. The main stand could be improved and the pitch lengthened (with its width also altered to allow the players enough of a run-off area) at an estimated cost of £100,000. That would allow the club to stay at Tynecastle for up to five years while the value of the land accrued to Hearts. It was estimated the value could top £30 million by 2009. Murrayfield could remain an option for European games if there were difficulties with Tynecastle. The club should then apply for planning permission for the redevelopment of the Gorgie ground and, thereby, establish the true value of the site. Finally, the working party recommended that Hearts should work with the City of Edinburgh Council to explore the possibility of redeveloping Sighthill Park with a new stadium as part of the scheme.

The expert group had systematically dismantled the arguments put forward by the Hearts board. Just twelve months earlier Tynecastle had been declared 'not fit for purpose' – the working party had found the precise opposite to be the case with some alterations. In doing so, it echoed many of the views of Save our Hearts and most ordinary supporters. The report's summary struggled to contain its disdain for the financial difficulties at the club and board's proposed solutions for tackling those problems. It began:

> The club finds itself in a position with an unacceptable level of debt in relation to its turnover and projected future turnover. The disposal of the principal asset, while providing a short-term fix, gives huge concerns for the future. Projections by the club indicated that Murrayfield will suddenly see the club turning in a profit in 24 months. The assumptions made to reach this position are founded in increased ticket sales, increased income from sponsorship and corporate-day entertainment. Nothing we have uncovered will suggest that these will occur. Indeed, an alternative scenario could be painted where the club find themselves with poor match results, falling crowds, drops in season ticket sales and higher revenue costs in playing at a stadium which is ill-suited to crowds of circa 8,000 . . .
>
> The working group are not opposed to Hearts moving to an alternative venue but believe that this should be done under a controlled set of circumstances where the future is planned and the requirements of the supporters and the long-term well-being of the club are considered paramount.

Some of the detail in the report was equally critical. One passage suggested a working group should have been set up two years previously to consider all the stadium options, while it added the club had been 'less than helpful' in releasing information.

But, most damning of all was the passage which roundly dismissed the argument about Tynecastle's suitability for European competition – a primary reason given for the stadium sale when the announcement was officially made in the 2003 annual report, then in the 'Not Fit For Purpose' report and later in the disposal document circulated to shareholders in August 2004. The document had misled the supporters over this issue, it claimed, and, in any case, the 'aspirational' pitch size of 105 metres by 68 metres had been withdrawn two years before because it was felt too many clubs would not be able to meet the regulation. The report said:

> The club have published a document indicating that Tynecastle is 'not fit for purpose'. This in many ways is misleading. It makes assumptions regarding pitch sizes that may not be satisfied by 83% of SPL clubs. Regulations governing pitch sizes set at 105 metres x 68 metres were introduced in 2000 by UEFA who had to withdraw them in 2002 since it was quite clear that many of the clubs in Europe could not comply without huge expense of meeting this aspirational standard with a five-metre run-out space. The problem was thus not unique to Scotland.

The report flatly contradicted the suggestion that 'any examination of the structure of Tynecastle, taking into account the position of the corner towers, will show that it is simply not possible to create even this minimum pitch size'. In fact, the report said the UEFA issues were 'capable of resolution'.

The working party also accused the club of not making 'sufficiently strenuous efforts' to set up a meeting with the SFA to allow a discussion of the pitch problem. The report added, 'After discussion it was clear that within the interpretation of the regulations laid down by UEFA, Tynecastle stood a very good chance of being made capable for use to host club matches in competitions.' A formal visit from an appointed UEFA delegate was required to resolve the matter once and for all, it urged. The document concluded, 'After this visit and dialogue directly with UEFA, the club could balance the benefits of large supporter turnouts at Murrayfield v the intimidating cauldron of Tynecastle.'

The working group had done its homework. In 1999, UEFA had originally proposed introducing a club licensing system to ensure high sporting standards, quality infrastructure, sound financial management and effective youth development among the Continent's clubs. As Chris Robinson said, consultation took place before the idea was approved in June 2000. Eight national associations around Europe – Scotland, England, Netherlands, Spain,

Sweden, Norway, Slovenia and Luxembourg – were chosen to pilot the scheme and report back to the powers that be. It was at this time that Robinson announced plans to move from Tynecastle, suggesting at the 2000 AGM that it was too small. In 2001, he told the BBC that Hearts would soon be subject to a new European licensing regime, adding, 'We are able to get some relaxations, but we have been advised by UEFA that, by 2010, a pitch of the size of Tynecastle will be outwith the criteria for all European matches.' A draft report was drawn up by UEFA in June 2001. After feedback from the national associations, a final UEFA Club Licensing Manual was produced in March 2002. That document contained no mention of a 2010 deadline for the licensing requirements but it had been discussed as a possible cut-off point. It stressed that some flexibility would be built into the scheme, which would be operated by the national associations using the UEFA report as a template to develop their own National Club Licensing Manuals.

The UEFA manual recommended that pitches should measure 105 metres by 68 metres but offered alternative minimum dimensions of 100 metres by 64 metres. The reason for the leeway was that UEFA 'recognised that in some stadiums, for technical reasons of a construction-related nature, it is impossible to increase the field of play to the required dimensions'. The manual added that national law would have to be taken into consideration when attempting to meet the licensing criteria. In other words, a hemmed-in stadium with no room to develop, not least for legal reasons, would be exactly the type which could apply for an exemption.

However, the waters were muddied when the UEFA Cup regulations for 2004–05 were published. They stated that 105 metres by 68 metres were indeed the required pitch dimensions for teams competing in that competition. However, the rules added that national associations could apply for 'exceptions', something which, for now at least, is regarded as a formality for any stadium meeting the minimum licensing requirements.

Indeed, UEFA have since confirmed that they received exception requests from twenty-three national associations for season 2004–05, with five of those granted to clubs in relation to their pitch size. Three of those were English – Arsenal, Chelsea and Liverpool – while one, FC-Matáv Sopron, was from Hungary and the other, KSK Beveren, was based in Belgium. UEFA said, 'Their requests for exception have been accepted because the dimensions were still within the dimensions set by the Laws of the Game (minimum of 100 metres x 64 metres), which is not the case for Tynecastle.' In other words, none were as small as Tynecastle. Interestingly, UEFA said 'official information' from Auxerre and the French Football Association gave the club's pitch size as 105 metres by 68 metres, adding, 'For further questions, I kindly refer you to the FFA.' Neither Auxerre nor the FFA has responded to enquiries. At least one website – stadiumguide.com, which claims to be the 'largest and most complete guide on the internet dedicated to the football stadia of Europe' – lists Auxerre's pitch dimensions at the Stade de l'Abbé Deschamps as 100 metres by 60 metres.

In fact, every exception was granted in 2004–05 and Hearts were the only club in Europe forced to play their games for that season in an alternative stadium because of pitch-size criteria. It is true that Hearts failed to meet even the 100-metre minimum pitch length but it was by such a small margin – just two metres – that surely the required alterations could be made. The run-off area may, in places, have been reduced in size but that particular licensing requirement was considered 'best practice' rather than mandatory. It was also true that the rules could change but, equally, there was nothing to suggest they would.

It seems no coincidence that the first rule of world football, under FIFA's 'Laws of the Game', is that the field of play for 'international' matches, which includes clubs from different countries, can be a minimum of 100 metres by 64 metres. It has never been explained how UEFA hoped to insist on a pitch size bigger than that deemed suitable in the fundamental rules of the sport – or how they could do so in the future without FIFA agreeing to amend its own 'Law 1'. If FIFA failed to do so, a club prevented from competing on these grounds could, presumably, launch a legal challenge.

Reflecting on the UEFA episode now, Chris Robinson still insists that a larger pitch size may yet be required by UEFA. However, he also admits that the club did not consider the possibility of narrowing the pitch' to meet the minimum criteria regarding pitch length. He says:

> The 2000 document set us down a road which – along with debt levels, the financial position of the company and the state of the stadium – led to a strategy of trying to find a new stadium. What we weren't trying to do was find a technical solution for Tynecastle as we didn't believe that would have any long-term viability.

The working party report, however, was concerned with more than the UEFA compliance issue. It looked at nine sites in total, scoring each on a broad range of criteria such as availability, access, suitability, planning considerations and wider community issues. Any new stadium was expected to cost around £25 million. Three of the sites examined were discounted immediately. Ingliston was unavailable and Saughton Park was a well-used public park which had traffic and possible construction problems associated with the Water of Leith flood plain. The third option to receive no further consideration was Peter McGrail's Gorgie redevelopment scheme. The working party reported that the club failed to indicate a formal interest in the scheme to the local authority, despite a request to do so. As a result the council, working to strict deadlines, was forced to enter into a deal with the private sector to deliver an alternative project

The report expressed disappointment at the collapse of Peter McGrail's scheme before it had even had a chance to succeed. It said, 'The SWG formally asked the club to enter into such discussions with City of Edinburgh Council. The club declined to do so.' The decision was taken despite an agreement among working group members at their first meeting that the plan should form the benchmark by which all other options would be judged. Senior council officials privately described the plan as a 'neat solution' which could meet the needs of both Hearts and the local community. Even at that early stage, however, Peter McGrail, had doubts that the club would co-operate in pushing the scheme forward. He was right to be sceptical.

Much of the flak was directed at Chris Robinson over the collapse of the plan. He, in turn, launched a vehement attack on Peter McGrail. He accused the businessman of producing a plan which could never be delivered because it did not fit the site and called on him to apologise to the fans for giving them false hope. Robinson claimed that he had never been formally asked to take the plan forward by the working party. That version of events, however, was later disputed by group member Derek Ferrier. The chartered surveyor told a fans' meeting how he had gone to Robinson's office to present the plans. 'Halfway through the meeting, I could tell by the way he was looking out the window and looking at his shoes that he wasn't interested,' Ferrier said. Peter McGrail, meanwhile, defended his plans. He had always recognised there were difficulties in his scheme but blamed Robinson for failing to take it seriously. He said later:

> What my development plan did was give something concrete for the troops to rally round. Chris called it giving them false hope but I totally believe that it was a viable proposition. It also kept the window open for someone like Romanov to come in.

David Murray's land at Hermiston was initially considered by the SWG but also ruled out because of insurmountable planning difficulties. However, because of the furore over Peter McGrail's doomed plan and the conclusion that Tynecastle was viable, it almost escaped notice that it was actually Sighthill which had received the highest evaluation score (184 points). The area was first identified by Hearts in the 1930s, had more recently talked up by both Robinson and George Foulkes and would later receive tacit support from John Robertson. The site studied by the working group was already earmarked for an athletics stadium by the city council and Edinburgh Rugby was in discussions about using the facility. Despite potential planning problems, a separate football stadium alongside the athletics venue 'could be the best long-term option for the club if the obstacles can be dealt with'. In addition, the three new existing stands at Tynecastle could be dismantled and re-used at the site. However, three months earlier, Edinburgh had lost out to Glasgow as Scotland's candidate city for any potential Scottish bid to host the 2014 Commonwealth Games and, in the same month as the SWG report, doubts were cast over the city council's ability to fund its ambitious sports facilities strategy, with each project to be re-examined for possible cutbacks.

Tynecastle was placed second in terms of overall suitability with a rating of 178 points, losing some marks for the shortcomings outlined by Robinson many times in the past. According to the report, 'The group worked conscientiously towards overcoming the understandable emotion that would make Tynecastle the favoured choice while quietly ignoring its shortcomings.' But the ground had potential to earn more revenue – for instance, by creating business units in the vacant space under the stands at a cost of around £500,000. The report said:

> The club has promoted a view that Tynecastle is 'not fit for purpose' and used these arguments to justify the plan of moving to Murrayfield. The SWG believes not all of the arguments listed in the 'not fit for purpose' promotion stand close scrutiny ... The entire site is at the centre of a major change in the area. If the club does not explore fully the options to achieve a better end result than selling and moving out then a valuable opportunity is being ignored.

Perhaps surprisingly, the next ranked site was Murrayfield (168 points). It was praised for its proximity to Gorgie, as well as its facilities and playing surface, but it was considered too big and there were concerns that any insecurity of tenure could leave Hearts homeless at some point in the future. It was also warned that most SPL games would not be as attractive as big European nights and, therefore:

> The influence of three well-attended UEFA Cup games should not be taken as a template for the future success of Murrayfield. Grave concerns exist that the club will enter into a situation where there is a downward spiral and no escape route.

Essentially, the move to Murrayfield, with no alternative options in place, could lead to relegation and ultimately receivership.

Two parcels of land at Straiton received little backing from the experts with a score of 142 points because of the area's 'many problems', including distance from the core Hearts support, potential traffic chaos on match days and the existence of mine workings in the area. The lowest evaluation mark (124 points) went to Braehead because it was located on poor-quality ground over a rubbish tip and quarry and was accessible by only a single, narrow road.

George Foulkes welcomed the report, which was passed to the board for its consideration. Chris Robinson criticised it for failing to understand the financial realities of the club, although its remit had not been specifically to deal with such matters. To the bemusement of some working party members, he seemed to suggest that the stadium was the root of the club's financial difficulties rather than those charged with its stewardship. Robinson later went further, adding that the working group was 'just full of Hearts supporters and came to an obvious conclusion'. At best, his comments were ungracious to those who had given hundreds of hours of their time free of charge. At worst, they were an insult to the group's independence. Foulkes had the good sense to 'completely and unequivocally disassociate [him]self from the remarks'. He added that the board had unanimously agreed the composition of the group and any objections should have been expressed when it was being set up.

But, even as the last journalists left the press conference to launch the report, full copies of which had still not arrived by taxi, events had moved forward with breathtaking speed. Before 1 p.m., Vladimir Romanov had audaciously seized the initiative in the stadium debate. Emboldened by the findings of the working group, he had used his right as a shareholder to call an EGM. The last such meeting was held to approve the sale of Tynecastle. This one would seek to do precisely the opposite and withdraw from the deal. Action was being taken to implement the main recommendation from Lord Macaulay's working party before the media copies of the report had even arrived at Tynecastle.

It was a move Romanov must have been considering for some time and it shifted the power struggle firmly in his direction. The banker had his own 10.3% stake and could rely on the votes of Leslie Deans and Robert McGrail, which amounted to around 20% of the company. But, in what even Foulkes later described to fans as 'a wonderful irony', Robinson was also obliged, under his share transfer agreement, to use his 19.6% stake to vote in accordance with Romanov's wishes. The man who championed the sale of Tynecastle and move to Murrayfield was being forced to help to overturn that same grand plan.

George Foulkes rightly insisted that financial guarantees would have to be in place before the board could be expected to withdraw from the Cala sale at the EGM, which was to be held at the same time as the AGM on 10 January 2005. The chairman recognised 'the growing tide' of support for remaining at Tynecastle but warned that working capital must be in place if administration was to be avoided.

33

TYNECASTLE HOUSING PLAN DEMOLISHED

The festive season had not been overly generous to Hearts. The team was comprehensively outplayed when they were defeated 2–0 by Celtic at Tynecastle on Boxing Day and had to fight tooth and nail for a point in the 1–1 draw with Hibs at Easter Road in the New Year derby. A toothless 0–0 draw away to Partick Thistle in the Scottish Cup the following weekend suggested all was not well among the Hearts squad.

The fact that the January transfer window had opened and so many players were out of contract in the summer appeared to be distracting some key team members. Defender Alan Maybury and striker Mark de Vries were tipped to follow Craig Levein to Leicester, which they did, with Patrick Kisnorbo following close behind. Then, Scotland international Stevie Crawford looked certain to sign as a replacement striker, only for the deal to founder over his wage demands. For once, the board received some praise for standing firm in the face of claims that it would cost up to £100,000 to sign the thirty-one–year-old from Plymouth on a three-and-a-half year contract and that he wanted £4,000 a week in wages. To most fans it simply did not seem to represent good value for money at a time when attempts were being made to bring the wage bill under control. Commenting on the saga later, Chris Robinson defended the decision but also appeared to acknowledge that similar errors had been made in the past. He admitted, 'We have quite rightly been accused of financial profligacy in the past, but the club is more important than one signing.' In a rare show of support for the beleaguered chief executive, one fan even posted on the Hearts Kickback chat forum that 'this is potentially one of the best decisions the current board has ever made'. However, it was also suggested that the uncertainty over Hearts' future had put the player off a move to Tynecastle before he finally opted to sign for Dundee United, who disputed the wage demands quoted for Crawford.

The departure of Maybury and de Vries had cut up to £7,000 a week from the wage bill but, despite that, John Robertson still did not know his budget. With such uncertainty, the head coach appeared helpless to reassure his distracted players or attract new signings to the club. Around twenty Eastern European players identified by Anatoly Byshovets were due to arrive in Edinburgh for a training camp, funded by Vladimir Romanov, but there was a danger that their arrival would devalue the promising youngsters already at the club.

Romanov must have been mindful of that instability when the AGM was convened at Tynecastle's Gorgie Suite on 10 January. The second EGM in four months was tabled to follow directly afterwards, although it was expected to be adjourned for two weeks while Romanov continued his discussions with Hearts and their creditors about the club's future.

And so the routine business of the AGM got under way with little fanfare. The 11 a.m. start had been deliberately moved from the evening slot to allow 'more sensible discussions', although it was also seen as a ploy to reduce numbers by making attendance difficult for shareholders with work commitments. The fact that it would not allow for pre-meeting drinks was suspected but never acknowledged. In any case, around 500 shareholders still turned up for the meeting and the mood was noticeably lighter than the tumultuous EGM four months earlier. There was even a hint of humour about the proceedings. Several fans directly in front of the top table wore Russian hats, while George Foulkes compared his possession of the casting vote with sitting in on a meeting with Prime Minister Tony Blair and Chancellor Gordon Brown, who were embroiled in a much-publicised power struggle.

In fact, the only notable business was the re-appointment of Chairman Foulkes, who received what appeared to be unanimous backing from those in the hall, and Director Brian Duffin, who got no more than five votes in a show of hands. Both were re-elected due to proxy votes in any case, although Duffin was the subject of more barbed humour when one shareholder asked if he was the type of person who invited himself to parties when no one wanted him there. There was also anger at SMG's absence, with the media group's board representative David Archer unable to attend because of 'other engagements'. One shareholder said it was only common decency to turn up at such an important meeting. Even Foulkes said he believed the media company should have been represented. Campaigners blamed SMG for trying to force through the sale of Tynecastle to ensure they received the cash for their loan stock and had privately suggested that we have to 'focus on making sure David Archer never wants to step into Tynecastle again in his life'. The fact that Archer was said to rarely attend matches at Tynecastle did little to endear him to supporters, although the media group would argue that he was on the board of Hearts as a representative of its biggest institutional shareholder rather than to turn up at games.

Then, after the routine business of the AGM, Foulkes dramatically announced that Romanov had decided he did now want the EGM and ballot to go ahead, to end the uncertainty surrounding boardroom affairs at the club. At midday – or 'high noon' as some had it – the surprised shareholders looked on as Romanov's adviser Sergejus Fedotovas was invited to the top table to deliver a speech on behalf of the Lithuanian banker. His opening lines certainly struck a chord with those in the hall:

Hearts, Hearts, Glorious Hearts – it's down at Tynecastle they bide.
I have spent a lot of time in Edinburgh in the last six months and I

have learned that bide means to stay, remain or live. As the song says, Hearts bide at Tynecastle. Mr Romanov intends that Hearts will continue to bide at Tynecastle . . . Home is here – home is at Tynecastle. Home is where matches have been won or lost; heroic tackles and saves have been made; spectacular goals have been scored; and home is where the memories linger and where we find comfort in times of downheartedness. Home is Tynecastle.

After a burst of applause, Fedotovas went on to stress that, for Hearts to challenge the Old Firm, it was crucial for the club to retain its most valuable asset. He then explained why Romanov wanted to invest in the club:

Vladimir Romanov believes that there is a passion for football in Scotland which is unmatched in the vast majority of countries worldwide. He is a real football fan who revels in the passion which is generated by the arena of football. In Hearts, the premier side in Scotland's capital city, he believes that there is huge potential and he believes he has the ability to unlock that potential to meet the challenges ahead. He believes that Hearts is the only club in Scotland which has the potential to overtake Celtic and Rangers . . .

Vladimir Romanov wants to make sure that Hearts is no longer perceived as a selling club and, when he talks of Hearts as not being a selling club, that phrase is extended to mean that it will not sell its stadium and its birthright either. And he is prepared to put his personal wealth at the disposal of Hearts to achieve this . . .

The building blocks are there for your club to break the Old Firm stranglehold on Scottish football and, once that has been achieved, to look for greater recognition and glories on the wider European stage. Financial support is forthcoming. I give you Mr Romanov's personal undertaking that he aims to make this club hugely successful. All that remains is to ensure the future of Tynecastle.

Fedotovas explained that Romanov intended to assume part of the debt due to the Bank of Scotland and provide working capital, at least on a medium-term basis. He added, 'This financial package could be worth several million pounds to Hearts over an initial three-year period.'

The speech, which also backed the findings of the Stadium Working Group, had no doubt played on the emotions of the shareholders, although some later nit-picked over its flowery language. It had also provided some outline financial details, however vague. But its ambition, as before, was certainly bold and unambiguous. At that point, Fedotovas turned to the audience, who shared a collective sense of occasion when he said:

> From the information we have received regarding voting intentions, it would appear that the vote on this resolution will be very close. In fact, it may well boil down to whether or not you, the people in this room, are prepared to raise your hands in support of the vision for the future of Hearts which is presented by Vladimir Romanov. The alternative is to move to Murrayfield, a stadium which, at times, could be operating with crowds of less than 10% of capacity for some home matches, with no guarantee of security of tenure beyond five years and, consequently, with no guarantee of the continued existence of this 130-year-old club.

The address was warmly received but shareholders nevertheless faced a difficult decision. Many may have possessed small stakes in the club but, to one degree or another, its fate lay in their hands. The board, including popular chairman George Foulkes, had recommended voting against Romanov's motion to scrap the Cala deal. After all, the club's creditors could pull the financial plug if the cash they were owed was thought to be in jeopardy. Yet Fedotovas had warned that selling up and moving to Murrayfield could spell the end of the club.

Former chairman Leslie Deans gave Romanov his and Robert McGrail's backing, saying the banker offered the 'best and only way forward'. And, as shareholders considered how to cast their votes, Romanov was asked to introduce himself to the gathering. He did so with some embarrassment, encouraged by the standing ovation and loud cheers, saluting the fans as he walked from the front row to the top table and taking time to shake hands with those wearing the Russian hats. He made some brief remarks through his interpreter but the reassurance was in simply seeing the man who controlled the destiny of Hearts. When the polite applause faded, Foulkes declared the EGM at an end.

This time there were no scuffles and surprisingly few angry shouts. At the last EGM, the board had been the focus of the fans' fury but, this time, Romanov – who posed for cameras with a Hearts scarf proudly held aloft as he left the Gorgie Suite – was the target for their acclaim. The Lithuanian did not linger – after all, he had an appointment with the creditors. He appeared to have convinced the ordinary shareholders; now he had to do likewise with a fellow banker. For the rest, it was time to vote on perhaps the most important issue in the history of Hearts.

The result was declared twenty-four hours later, after the EGM ballot papers and proxy votes had been counted. And it was certainly convincing. The small shareholders had clearly decided to back Romanov, despite effectively voting blind. The big investors allied to Romanov may have been privy to some additional background or personal information but the ordinary fans with a stake in the club had been asked to go with their gut instinct as much as anything else. In the event, significant numbers put their faith in Romanov, also realising the lack of any real alternative, rather than follow the advice of their own board. A total of 70.2% of votes cast supported the resolution to withdraw from the Cala sale. It was a fatal blow for the controversial deal.

Romanov declared himself delighted with the 'tremendous' level of support but the Hearts board still insisted it could not cancel the sale until financial guarantees were received. Talks with all the interested parties were said to be going well. The supporters, for now at least, could concentrate on their real concern – the team on the park.

The signing of former Falkirk striker Lee Miller on loan from Bristol City helped to concentrate the minds of fans. And the new man did not disappoint, scoring a goal after less than three minutes of being brought on against Dundee United at Tynecastle on 15 January, with what must be one of the fastest debut goals ever scored in maroon. Hearts went on to win 3–2 in an odd game that ebbed and flowed between boredom and excitement. A tough 2–1 win against Partick Thistle in the Scottish Cup followed four days later, amid a swirling Edinburgh wind, and was followed by a similarly competitive 1–1 draw with Dundee at Dens Park the next weekend. The proof that a renewed sense of spirit was returning to Hearts, if such was needed, arrived with a battling 2–1 victory over Livingston at Almondvale on 25 January and then a 1–0 defeat of Aberdeen at Tynecastle at the end of the month. The former was notable for the Hearts side having eleven Scots in the starting line-up for the first time in an incredible eight years. However, both games also witnessed the arrival of promising foreign players – Icelandic striker Hjalmar Thorarinsson came on in the Livingston game and Lithuanian winger Saulius Mikoliunas looked tricky against Aberdeen. Less encouraging was the speculation linking Hearts' top scorer and player of the year the previous season, Paul Hartley, with Celtic. It was obvious that Hartley, who had just been named in his first full Scotland squad, was keen on a move to his boyhood heroes but the 'derisory' offer of £200,000 from Celtic was hastily rejected by the Hearts board. The suspicion was that Romanov had intervened to shake off Hearts' reputation as a 'selling club' – or at least an 'underselling club'. The fans could only hope this was a sign of things to come.

During the month, former manager Craig Levein was quoted as having reversed his previous position and admitting the uncertainty at the club was a decisive factor in his decision to leave. He also suggested he would not have tolerated the trialists' training camp. But, those unhelpful comments aside, some semblance of order appeared to have been restored at Tynecastle. There was even the boost of signing former Celtic striker Mark Burchill and experienced Lithuanian international midfielder Deividas Cesnauskis. Off-field events would soon dominate again at the beginning of a frenetic February, however.

34

THE ROMANOV REVOLUTION

A consortium of Edinburgh businessmen had made what seemed like a last-ditch attempt to invest in the club before the Romanov era finally dawned. Plumbing business owner Pat Munro and spokesman Fred Wood insisted their offer, reported to be in the region of £30 million, was deadly serious. The deal – which involved investors from Russia, Switzerland and Iceland – included a sale-and-leaseback of Tynecastle, an increased players' budget for John Robertson and an improved offer for Chris Robinson's shares. The club did little to encourage the consortium but the Edinburgh businessmen did indicate a willingness to work alongside Romanov at some point in the future if it proved in the best interest of the club.

Behind the scenes it may have proved a minor distraction but negotiations were going well between Vladimir Romanov and Chris Robinson. Days after the reports of a rival consortium entering the fray, the deal was finally sealed, with the transfer of shares and cash taking place on 1 February. Perhaps the powers that be were waiting until after the keenly anticipated League Cup semi-final clash with Motherwell at Easter Road that night to publicise the transaction. Maybe it was hoped the news would allow fans to enjoy a double celebration. If so, they would have been disappointed by the outcome of the game. Hearts tumbled out of the cup in cruel fashion despite having a huge crowd packed into their Edinburgh rival's stands. The team fought back bravely from 2–0 down after an uncharacteristically shaky defensive performance.

Two goals in the last five minutes, including one in time added on, ensured thirty minutes of extra time and, despite a number of chances for Hearts, Motherwell broke away and scored the winner with thirty seconds remaining. The Lanarkshire team and its supporters were understandably jubilant at reaching their first League Cup final for almost fifty years – their last appearance had resulted in a defeat by Hearts. It was a crushing disappointment for Hearts. But there would be some cause to celebrate the following morning, when the announcement about the finalised share deal was finally made.

A section of the Hearts support believed the ousting of Robinson was even more important than the stadium issue. They argued that he, after all, was the chief executive in charge as the club teetered on the brink of oblivion. Debts were at a massive £19.6 million and the proposed escape route involved selling the family silver and moving into a rented home. The stock exchange statement that Robinson had resigned as part of the agreement was therefore met with the kind of glee not normally associated with the morning after a semi-final defeat.

The buy-out involved Romanov becoming the largest shareholder, with 3.8 million shares or 29.9% of the company. Despite resigning as chief executive, Robinson would remain on the board as a non-executive director. Sergejus Fedotovas, Romanov's most public aide, was appointed interim chief executive in his place while a permanent replacement was recruited. Director Brian Duffin, who had so recently been re-elected by block votes without the backing of the shareholders at the AGM, also resigned after eight years at the club, indicating that it was time for new board members to take Hearts forward. Perhaps surprisingly, two other Lithuanians were brought in as non-executive directors – Romanov's son Roman Romanov from Ūkio and Lithuanian Football federation president Liutauras Varanavicius, who was also linked to Ūkio.

Even Robinson welcomed the revolution, while also claiming some credit for its completion. In an interview for this book, he reflects on his time at the helm:

People claimed I didn't have a Plan B, but I did – Romanov was Plan B. I had already taken the decision to pass on the reins to someone else and one of my hopes was that he would be able to find a way through the treacle. I was impressed with Romanov because, apart from anything else, he appeared to be someone who was genuinely interested in football. In some ways there was even a Plan C because I was also trying to put pressure on the council to open up a site such as Sighthill for development and that might yet happen. I have no regrets about the club moving from Robinson to Romanov because it was what the fans wanted. Not only that but, if we had continued to operate with such a high level of debt, we would have faced administration and there's no doubt in my mind that that would have ripped the heart out of the club.

I accept responsibility for my part in that but I also think it was one of the most successful decades in the club's history because of the cup win, regularly competing in Europe and consistent league performances with exciting players. Hindsight is a wonderful science and if several things had happened differently – such as the downturn in the media and football industries, Bosman and SMG's decision not to convert – it might have been even better. Looking back, it was probably the worst possible time in the club's history to adopt a speculate-to-accumulate policy. But we didn't know that then, of course.

Almost exactly 100 years after one Russian-born financial expert was brought in to help turn the club around, another had arrived, charged with the same task. Arguably the situations facing Elias Furst in 1905 and Romanov a century later are the worst financial crises Hearts have ever faced. History, it seemed, was repeating itself.

Fans' representatives and others associated with Hearts lined up to hail equally the end of one era and the beginning of another, while also insisting that Robinson should sever all ties with the club. As the supporters had come to expect, no precise sums of money were mentioned but the message was that the debt could be gone in two years and money would not be a problem, for the right players. The aim was simple – to challenge Celtic and

Rangers before the end of the decade. One cynical Lithuanian journalist suggested that might mean a Hearts team composed of eleven of his countrymen but the new directors insisted Hearts would always retain their Scottish identity. A UEFA announcement the same day that squads in European competitions would have to include at least four home-grown players by 2006 ensured Hearts would remain true to their roots, at least to a limited extent. At the same time, Liutauras Varanavicius seemed to have grasped the enormity of the task ahead. 'Once you enter football, you never go away – it is like a swamp,' he told the club website.

Less than a week after the transfer of shares had gone through, Hearts emerged from the quagmire of the long-running stadium debate. A statement to the stock exchange on 8 February began simply by saying, 'The board of Hearts announces that it has today exercised its right to withdraw from the agreement for the sale of Tynecastle Stadium to Cala Management Limited.' And with that – the deal was dead.

The announcement went on to add that, after discussions with Vladimir Romanov, the board had 'received the comfort it has been seeking as to the financial position of the company going forward'. In addition, the debt had been transferred to Ūkio, relieving the Bank of Scotland of any concerns about recovering its cash. According to George Foulkes, the Lithuanian bank had offered better terms to Hearts, there was no pressure to sell-up and the threat of administration had disappeared. The Bank of Scotland would continue to provide only day-to-day services and a 'modest' overdraft option for Hearts.

The chairman also paid credit to Romanov, describing him as 'a white knight' who had saved Hearts from losing their home. It was quickly established that the first priority was to examine ways of redeveloping Tynecastle to make it more commercially successful. Essentially, the board intended to follow the recommendations of the Stadium Working Group, which included making Tynecastle UEFA-compliant at a cost of £60,000. Two rows of seats would have to be removed from each of the end stands, reducing capacity by 500, but the authorities had agreed that a slightly reduced run-off area of four metres would be acceptable. Hearts applied for permission to make the changes and their proposal was granted. Murrayfield would still be an option for European matches, because of its increased capacity, but Hearts would do everything possible to remain in Gorgie. Foulkes told the club website:

> It's a great time as a very big shadow has been lifted as far as the club's future is concerned. We can now look confidently ahead and discuss the possible redevelopment of Tynecastle to make it more commercially viable. This is the preferred option for us all and one that I'm sure Hearts fans everywhere will agree is a fantastic prospect.

There was still a possibility of relocating to a new stadium if, as the working party said, a better case could be put for such a move. No doubt the much-touted Sighthill site figured prominently in everyone's thoughts. But Foulkes' comments were a stark contrast to Chris Robinson's assertion in the 'Not Fit For Purpose' document a year or so before that to 'consider continuing at Tynecastle set against the UEFA compliance position is not one which directors of any plc could ever take'.

On the contrary, Foulkes described the withdrawal from the sale of the old stadium as the last piece of the jigsaw. If he was right, attention could at last turn to the players on the park. After all there were the small matters of qualifying for Europe and challenging for the Scottish Cup to consider.

Four days after the disappointment of the League Cup exit to Motherwell, Hearts lined up against Kilmarnock in the Scottish Cup. Unfortunately, it was to be another disappointing day. Again the team dominated but failed to take its chances and again the opposition scored with just seconds to go. At least this time it had been to claim a draw (2–2) rather than a victory but it was hardly more palatable for that. With a league game coming up against the Ayrshire side and a replay the following midweek, it would mean three games against Kilmarnock in twelve days.

The following weekend, Sergejus Fedotovas and Vladimir Romanov made a fairly low-key appearance on the pitch before the game to greet the fans. They held Hearts scarves aloft and returned the applause of the supporters but chose not to address them directly. It was a pity then that there were only 9,220, the lowest home league crowd of the season, to witness the occasion. Hearts dominated the game, with good performances from Saulius Mikoliunas, who scored his first goal, and a debut for his countryman, Marius Kizys, in the 3–0 victory Kilmarnock. There were signs that a more cohesive and dangerous style of football was coming together.

The two teams faced each other for the third time in twelve days, with Hearts looking better with each outing. The third Lithuanian at Hearts, Deividas Cesnauskis, made his debut during the Scottish Cup tie and took the man-of-the-match award after a great all-round performance and the third, decisive goal. Lee Wallace must have entered the record books as the first player to play his initial three games against the same opposition, scoring his first goal after a 70-yard dash from defence and finishing after a fine one-two. Saulius Mikoliunas joined his countryman as the best men on the pitch – on Lithuanian Independence Day. Later in February, Hearts lost again to Motherwell, this time 2–0 at Fir Park, but at least then went on to defeat Livingston 2–1 at Tynecastle in the Scottish Cup. The reward for that would be a semi-final against Celtic at Hampden.

The day of Livingston's 2–1 defeat, the Heart of Midlothian Supporters Trust had held its second annual general meeting. The occasion, justifiably, merited some backslapping for the achievements of the fans' organisation. Trust chairman Martin Laidlaw said:

> To say it has been an eventful year is clearly an understatement. The last year has witnessed what became the most successful football supporters' campaign of recent years ... In effect, the Heart of Midlothian Supporters Trust along with our partners, the Federation of Hearts Supporters Clubs, have saved the club.

At the same time, there was official acknowledgement of what was widely expected by those close to the campaign. A report by trust board member Jane Lewis credited Save our Hearts with meeting many of its original objectives, not least 'halting this insane charge into oblivion' by moving to Murrayfield. An initial delay of one year had been achieved, Chris Robinson was no longer chief executive and an apparently more receptive board and majority shareholder were in place. With that in mind, it was agreed that there 'will eventually be a winding down of the organisation that is Save our Hearts'. A notice was posted on the window of the Save our Hearts shop in Gorgie Road announcing that it would close by the end of April due to the success of the campaign. The next letter to trust members said the campaign group would cease to exist by the end of the season. It was time for peace to break out.

35

STANDING UP TO
THE 'BULLIES'

George Foulkes had called the redevelopment of Tynecastle 'the final piece in the jigsaw' – as had his predecessors. Now, any such work would be overseen by a new chief executive.

With the Chris Robinson era over, Hearts announced on 3 March that the new man at the helm was to be former SRU chief executive Phil Anderton. It was yet another bizarre twist in the unfolding Hearts saga. The executive who had occupied an office in the rugby stadium during the negotiations to allow Hearts access to Murrayfield now took up the hot seat at Tynecastle, the ground which would have been reduced to rubble as a result of the same agreement.

The appointment itself was not surprising. Anderton, a Hearts supporter as a boy, was highly regarded in Edinburgh business circles after performing well during a difficult time at the SRU. He worked for Coca-Cola before taking up the post first of commercial and marketing director at the SRU, and then chief executive. Before resigning amid a Murrayfield power struggle, he was credited with organising Scotland's most lucrative sporting event ever – the 2004 match between Scotland and England which brought in £2.4 million. During his time at the SRU he earned the nickname 'Firework Phil' after the extravagant displays staged before rugby internationals. George Foulkes described him as 'number one' on the club's wanted list. Anderton, in turn, said it was an honour to take up the high-profile position at a club with such potential. It was just as well he did not do so until 21 March – otherwise the whirlwind of controversy which erupted as the announcement was being made may have led him to question just what he had taken on. At least this row related to football.

The day before, on 2 March, Hearts squared up to high-flying Rangers at Tynecastle. Indeed, Anderton was one of those who took up his seat in the stands along with his fellow supporters. The game was an evenly matched affair and heading towards a 1–1 draw after Hearts scored a late, but deserved, equaliser. There had been a number of potentially controversial incidents, such as Hugh Dallas's decision to wave away Hearts' penalty claims when Andy Webster was scythed down in the box by Sotirios Kyrgiakos. But nothing could match the events of the final tumultuous minutes. With injury time ticking away, Rangers floated a speculative free kick into the Hearts box. Kyrgiakos, again, and Lee Miller jumped for the ball as it looked to be heading out for a goal kick. No one appeared to believe anything was amiss, until linesman Andy Davis waved over the referee and told him that Miller had committed a mysterious infringement on his opponent. Such was the shock when the award was then given by Dallas that Saulius Mikoliunas rushed over to the linesman to protest. Unfortunately, his momentum carried him into a chest-to-chest barge on the official. Dallas flourished a red card. Mikoliunas swore in disgust and duly received a second sending off for his troubles. Rangers' Dado Prso also got a red card for wrestling the ball from Craig Gordon. When calm was restored, Rangers converted the penalty. The full-time whistle went seconds later. In an unsavoury final act, missiles were thrown in the direction of the referee and linesmen as they left the pitch. Three arrests were made by police.

Hearts had lost out on a deserved point but, more importantly, their most creative player of recent weeks was likely to be in serious trouble with the SFA.

It was perhaps the most talked-about incident of the season to date and Hearts were quick to respond. The following day, Foulkes apologised for Mikoliunas's actions – indeed, he had already written as much to the match officials. He added that disciplinary action against the Lithuanian would also be considered.

But the loyal MP also told how the main talking point of the current Labour Party conference had been the injustice of the penalty award rather than the Prime Minister's keynote speech that day. Similar indignation was expressed elsewhere. Such was the popular reaction that Hearts were almost forced to make a stand.

And so it was that the club made the unprecedented, at least in modern times, request for an inquiry into the 'integrity of the decision' to award the penalty. Hearts and Celtic chat rooms had been swamped with conspiracy theories about the linesman's inclinations, although nothing was ever proven to that effect. But Hearts insisted they were not accusing the assistant of cheating, rather they were trying to establish why such an unlikely call had been made. More than anything else, it appeared to be an attempt to stand up to what most fans outwith the Old Firm regarded as an institutional, if not intentional, bias towards the two Glasgow clubs. The SFA virtually disregarded the request before even considering it but perhaps Hearts had made their point already. A new regime was in place at Tynecastle and it could not be relied on to follow the unspoken conventions of Scottish football. Despite a venomous media reaction and a warning from the SFA that they would consider charging Hearts with 'bringing the game into disrepute' for even requesting an inquiry, it was clear they would not be pushed around by the Old Firm 'bullies' and the football establishment.

There was no surprise, then, when the SFA did reject Hearts' request or when Saulius Mikoliunas was handed a five-match ban, on top of the automatic three-game suspension, for exceptional misconduct relating to his double red card. But still Hearts refused to accept their fate and announced that they would appeal against the extended ban for Mikoliunas.

The club received the backing of the main Hearts fans' organisations, which wrote to the SFA asking that referees and assistants be required to declare any allegiance to a football team, as happens in England. The groups also suggested that a study of refereeing decisions should be undertaken to establish if there was any bias towards the Old Firm. The notion was given short shrift. The following day the SFA's head of referee development, Donald McVicar, was reported as describing the row and the reaction of the supporters as 'pathetic'.

Almost inevitably, Hearts were on the receiving end of a disputed penalty in their next game. Paul Hartley scored from the spot kick to earn a 1–1 draw away to Dunfermline on 5 March. A week later the club once again issued a challenge to the Scottish football authorities – this time the SPL. Up to twenty-three first-team squad players had been laid low by a flu virus and Hearts asked for the forthcoming Inverness Caledonian Thistle game to be postponed because of this. But the league judged that Hearts still had sufficient players available to fulfil the fixture. The weakened team of youngsters and fringe players meekly surrendered to a 2–0 defeat. Normal service was resumed the following weekend when Hearts, boosted by the news that captain Steven Pressley had signed a new three-year deal, coasted to a 3–1 win over Livingston at Tynecastle. After a break for international fixtures – with Walter Smith's Scotland competing well in a 2–0 defeat to Italy – the players recorded a far more memorable victory two weeks later. The well-deserved 2–0 win over Celtic at Parkhead on 2 April should have been the perfect preparation for the Scottish Cup semi-final against the same opposition the following weekend. Unfortunately, the day out at Hampden was to be remembered for all the wrong reasons.

The death of Pope John Paul II at the beginning of April had caused widespread mourning around the world. Naturally, the grief was most keenly felt in Catholic communities but others also recognised the significance of events. Yet there had been a delay in deciding whether or not to hold a minute's silence at the two semi-finals due to be played a week later. Presumably, there had been some concern that it would be disrupted, with bigoted

Hearts fans and assorted hangers-on the most likely suspects. Before the game on 10 April, Hearts had issued an appeal to their 15,000 supporters to 'observe and respect' the tribute. The futility of that quickly became apparent after the teams lined up around the centre circle and referee Stuart Dougal blasted his whistle to call for quiet. Unfortunately, such was the volume of boos and jeers which rang out around the national stadium from the Hearts end, he was forced to cut the minute's silence short after around twenty seconds. It was true that some simply sought to antagonise the opposition supporters and others resented being forced by the unpopular SFA to comply with a tribute which offended genuinely held beliefs but the same could be said for any similar event. In truth, there was no excuse. It was a shameful lack of respect which reeked of anti-Catholic bigotry and Hearts rightly issued an apology after the game. Sadly, by then, the actions of a minority of Hearts supporters had been beamed around the world on television and subsequently covered by newspapers across the globe.

The tasteless behaviour also seemed to hand Celtic an immediate advantage, although the mindless few in the crowd appeared not to have considered such a possibility. Their supporters were incensed but their moral indignation seemed hollow when they resorted to their own sectarian chants and inflammatory songs. It can also have done nothing to inspire Hearts' contingent of Catholic players to fight for the cause. The result was a fevered Celtic onslaught, driven onwards by their furious fans, leading to goal number one after just three minutes. A second just after the restart pushed the game beyond Hearts, despite the fact they pulled a goal back on the hour mark. Six arrests were made at the game for sectarian breach of the peace. Later reports suggested they included both Hearts and Celtic fans.

The day after the semi-final, chief executive Phil Anderton expressed his anger at the disruption to the minute's silence and said fans who behaved in such a way had no place at the club. He said, 'I am angry because this great club has been dragged through the mire by the actions of a few people ... Let's be absolutely clear – we have an issue there that we have to deal with.' He also warned that the actions of the mob at Hampden could discour-age potential supporters and investors, the very people the chief executive was trying to attract to Hearts, from becoming involved with the club. Anderton promised that action would be taken to provide a safe and comfortable environment for everyone at Tynecastle. His words were welcomed by the vast majority of supporters. The creeping claims that this section of the support represented Hearts' 'traditions', despite the fact there was little or nothing to support this, only increased the need for urgency. It was time that the bigots associated with Hearts were banished once and for all. One contributor to a Hearts chat forum said the fight for the future of Hearts appeared to have been won with the success of Save our Hearts, only for 'the enemy within' to open up a new front. The supporter also claimed to have discussed the potential disruption to the minute's silence with Anderton before it even happened. His impression from that meeting was that any such behaviour would prove to be 'the death song of dinosaurs'. The announcement, a week later, that the club was to set up a working party to stamp out sectarianism and racial abuse suggested he may have been right.

But while many connected with Hearts expressed genuine shame at the events of the semi-final, it seemed others were less inclined to take responsibility for bad behaviour at Scotland's football grounds.

Almost 18,000 crowded into Tynecastle for the derby sell-out three days after the Hampden disappointment, an indication of the continuing lure of football when live television cameras are absent. The atmosphere was predictably tense but there was no excuse for the Hibs supporters who booed, jeered and sang during a half-time tribute song to McCrae's sporting battalion. The attempt to drown out 'Hearts of Glory', performed live by Craig Herbertson, was all the more ignorant and unnecessary because the First World War battalion contained 150 Hibs supporters, in addition to the well-publicised Hearts contribution. It was the second act of mindless disrespect by Edinburgh football fans in four days, this time by those following the team from Leith.

The game itself offered little in the way of entertainment, with few clear-cut chances. In the end, the match was decided by three defensive lapses – the first justifiably leading to a goal for the home side, the next two going Hibs' way. For the second time in four days, Hearts had lost two decisive goals through slack defending. On the first occasion, it cost them a place in the Scottish Cup final. The second time, with Hibs eight points clear and only six games to go, it virtually killed off their chances of qualifying for Europe. The season, which had so recently offered so much, was effectively dead in the space of those four days. Painfully, their great rivals had not only struck the killer blow, the result also put them in pole position for a third-place finish.

Despite the opportunity to make up ground on their rivals in the final round of matches before the top-six split, Hearts lost 2–1 to relegation strugglers Dundee United at Tannadice on 16 April, with the home side scoring a stunning last-minute winner. It was the third such scoreline within a week. In a worrying indication of mounting behind-the-scenes pressure, John Robertson told the club website after the match, 'People have to stand up and be counted. It's not players who lose their jobs through mistakes, it is managers and coaches who do.' With his contract up for review at the end of the season, he had cause to be anxious.

Hearts had the satisfaction of scoring a late goal when they faced rivals Hibs for the second time in ten days on 23 April, Andy Webster heading home with three minutes to go to earn a 2–2 draw. In reality, it was a hollow cause for celebration as Hibs edged ever closer to European qualification. A week later the sums finally added up – Hearts could only manage a 0–0 draw with bogey team Motherwell at Tynecastle and they were mathematically eliminated from the race for a European place. The game, which featured a typically disjointed performance, was almost forgotten amid a flurry of speculation about the future of John Robertson. At least a section of fans offered their support as they chanted 'Robbo must stay'.

The month of April had been truly miserable. The team was out of Europe and the Scottish Cup, with some disgrace along the way. The position of the manger, a genuine club legend, appeared increasingly vulnerable and there were no signs of the onset of the Romanov revolution. In addition, the club had been found guilty of bringing the game into disrepute over the Rangers penalty affair, fined £5,000, severely censured and warned about its future conduct. The SFA also launched an investigation into a coin-throwing incident at the Tynecastle derby match after referee John Rowbotham was hit on the head by a missile. There was the minor consolation that Saulius Mikoliunas's five-match ban was reduced to three games but, with no chance of qualifying for Europe, the decision was of little consequence.

The six-monthly figures up to 31 January 2005 gave some cause for optimism, suggesting the club's finances were at least moving in the right direction. Thanks to the UEFA Cup games, turnover had increased by £1.1 million, although the cost of renting Murrayfield had reduced profit margins to little more than would have been expected at Tynecastle. Meanwhile, staff costs and losses were both down – but the latter still stood at £221,000 before taxation.

The day the interim results were issued, 29 April, was also the 100th anniversary of the club's registration at Companies House. In an interview on the club website, George Foulkes looked forward with optimism, declaring that the coming season could be 'one of the most exciting and successful in our history'. He added, 'I feel we have weathered the storm successfully and are about to set sail on a much fairer course.' However, he admitted that the previous eighteen months had been 'among the liveliest in our entire history'.

36

THE END OF AN ERA

The issue of John Robertson's future refused to fade as the team attempted to prepare for the game against Rangers at Ibrox on 7 May and the manager was even being forced to publicly deny rumours about his private life. A board meeting had been scheduled to take place the day before the Rangers match and, with Robertson increasingly unsettled by the uncertainty surrounding his job, the matter was placed at the top of the agenda. Unfortunately, the board failed to come to a decision, announcing at 8 p.m. that discussions would continue after the game in Glasgow. The board meeting, however, went on until after midnight. It was clear there was much to debate. The uncertainty had not disappeared – it had intensified.

Somehow the manager and players remained focused enough on the Rangers match to come away with a creditable 2–1 defeat at the hands of the championship contenders. But the question of Robertson's future took centre stage again just two days later. The fact that he had not been given a vote of confidence at the original board meeting suggested his position was extremely vulnerable and so it turned out. Robertson was offered a job at the club but it was effectively a demotion. He could remain as assistant head coach but a new manager and possibly a director of football would be appointed. Robertson took some time to consider the offer because of his strength of feeling for the club. But, given his pride, he was never likely to accept. And so it was that Robertson, with a first-team career spanning sixteen years behind him, walked away from Hearts on 9 May after just six months in the manager's seat.

At least he did so with remarkable dignity and his reputation broadly intact. The former striker even held a press conference side-by-side with the chief executive who had to deliver the board's verdict – poignantly below one of his own framed Scotland shirts. Some mistakes had been made but Robertson defended his record, highlighting the wins in Basel and at Celtic Park and the fact the team had reached two semi-finals. However, he was gracious enough to accept the board's decision under the terms of his contract, which had been drawn up to avoid payment of full compensation. In an illustration of his affection for Hearts, he also wished the new head coach well, urging him to lead the club 'boldly into this new era'. But he believed the new man would also need 'substantial funds' to achieve that success. Robertson added that he had no regrets about moving to Tynecastle and even refused to rule out a return with the words 'never say never' and, with that, he headed for the golf course. Assistant coach Donald Park soon followed him out the door.

The club, meanwhile, insisted the decision had been based on ambition. Robertson had shown promise and, in 'normal' circumstances, he would probably have been retained. But a proven coach was needed to bring success. Vladimir Romanov added some telling detail when he was quoted on the BBC suggesting the team wasn't 'playing right'. It was a high-stakes gamble by the Lithuanian. He may have been reluctant to hand his cash to a relatively young coach and one he did not appoint but, given his ambitions, there would be no excuses for not providing a hand-picked appointee with a sizeable budget. Romanov's counterpart at Chelsea, Roman Abramovich, had, after all, dismissed the popular and relatively successful Claudio Ranieri and replaced him with the highly-rated José Mourinho, who duly wrested the Premiership from the control of Arsenal and Manchester United at the first time of asking. The parallels would surely end there. Romanov had promised to invest in the playing squad but it would be nowhere near the cool £100 million available to Mourinho.

The reaction to the latest bombshell was mixed. At best, Robertson had engineered some memorable performances and brought through a handful of exciting young players in difficult circumstances. Recent results showed only two wins in eleven games but, overall, his record was no worse than inconclusive and more time was needed to judge his abilities. It was the failure to win a UEFA place or reach a cup final which appeared to have sealed his fate. Nevertheless, the decision prompted a good deal of anger towards the board. Predictably, Chris Robinson was singled out for criticism amid rumours that he had been a staunch critic of Robertson, although the board as a whole had passed judgement rather than any individual. There were even suggestions that Robertson's vocal support for Save our Hearts may have contributed to his downfall, although there was no way to verify any such claims.

There was, however, some good news for Robinson's critics – it was confirmed he would sever all ties with the club at the end of the season. Phil Anderton reportedly received a death threat, despite taking the time to write to supporters and explain the reasons behind the decision. The first hints of a backlash against the Lithuanians also emerged. Worryingly, even Anatoly Byshovets was reported as considering the removal of Robertson as a mistake. Of greater concern, it also emerged that the Ukrainian, a widely tipped replacement for Robertson, was no longer advising Romanov on football matters.

Threats of a protest at the last home game of the season the following Sunday soon followed. It was ironic that the match, against Celtic, would have been the last ever played at Tynecastle had Romanov not stepped in and bought his stake in the club. Anderton reminded the fans of this when he told the pre-match press conference that Tynecastle would be 'a demolition site' by now if the Lithuanian had not intervened.

Such thoughts must have been on the minds of Hearts supporters as they set out for Tynecastle on 15 May. In different circumstances, it would have been a historic final day at the old stadium. The fans took their seats in glaring sunshine as Hearts lined up against Celtic, the 2003–04 champions desperate for three points to regain the initiative in the title race. The bad blood between the two sets of supporters only heightened the sense of impending drama. Hearts, with coach John McGlynn and captain Steven Pressley temporarily sharing managerial responsibilities, certainly opened the match with what seemed to be a renewed fervour. Despite the fact the team also appeared well-organised, gaps at the back allowed Celtic to score with their first attack of any real menace. But Hearts staged a spirited fight back and equalised with twenty minutes to go, only for the visitors to then score the winner seven minutes later. There was to be one further twist before the end. The last time Hearts had been involved in a major penalty controversy, they had been playing Rangers at Tynecastle. Now it was Celtic's turn. With the home side streaming forward in search of an equaliser, Pressley found himself in the opposition box with the ball at his feet. Celtic substitute Craig Beattie lunged in and the Hearts skipper clattered to the ground. Not only did referee Willie Young fail to award the penalty kick, and it was a reasonable claim, he also booked Pressley for diving. It was his second yellow card. In his first taste of management, Pressley was forced to take a premature walk up the tunnel. For the second time, Hearts had potentially lost out on a point against the Old Firm due to a last-minute penalty decision. The fact that Celtic's Stan Varga was not cautioned for a similar 'offence' earlier only added to the sense of injustice.

It was little wonder then that the travelling supporters were the ones celebrating at the final whistle. In fact, despite an announcement that the Hearts squad would perform a lap of honour, most home fans drifted quietly out of the stadium. A presentation due to take place in appreciation of George Foulkes' part in the recent turnaround in the club's fortunes had been cancelled as it was not thought appropriate 'in the present circumstances'. The threatened demonstration – or show of support for John Robertson, depending on opinion – never materialised and there was no widespread anger directed at the board during or after the game. Indeed, those behind the protest plans had formally called off the action when reports emerged that Chris Robinson would not attend what was to be his last home game as a Hearts director. So the players returned to the pitch to take the acknowledgement of those who remained in the sparsely populated stands. A muted rendition of the Hearts song followed and then several dozen young fans staged a mini pitch invasion. The subdued mood was perhaps not surprising. There was an overwhelming sense of fatigue among supporters drained after an emotional roller coaster of a season.

The moment so many fans had dreaded – when they walked out of Tynecastle for the last time – had been averted. Even memories of the fight to stay in Gorgie seemed to have faded. What previously promised to be a tearful, defining day now stuttered towards a forgettable and inconsequential anticlimax but at least, when the announcer hopefully declared, 'See you next season' to the departing stragglers, he meant at Tynecastle rather than Murrayfield.

Season 2004–05 ended as season 2003–04 had begun twenty-odd months before – with a 2–0 scoreline against Aberdeen. Only this time, Hearts were the vanquished rather than the victors. In many ways, it was a fitting end to a season which seemed to have drained everyone connected with the club. It showed in the results – the last win was way back at the beginning of April, almost two months before. The small band of Hearts supporters who had made the trip to Pittodrie watched as the team put in a lifeless second-half performance. Players and supporters alike wearily applauded each other as the final whistle blew on season 2004–05.

The only meagre consolation was that all the teams involved in the 1986 league 'loss' suffered worse fates. The champions that day, Celtic, lost out to Rangers in equally dramatic circumstances, losing two late goals to Motherwell to surrender the title to their rivals. Like Hearts all those years ago, Celtic lost the killer goal with seven minutes to go and then a second in injury time.

Dundee, who had struck the fatal blow nineteen years before at Dens Park, were relegated and even Celtic's feeble opponents in 1986, St Mirren, had just announced the need to sell their Love Street ground to 'save' the club. But it was little genuine consolation.

The fact was the team had finished a distant fifth in the league and missed out on a European place. The club had no manager and a number of players were out of contract in the summer. The protracted transfer negotiations with new-found star striker Lee Miller gave little cause for optimism. Before any new players could be brought in, a new head coach would have to be identified. Until then, the club ran the risk re-entering the perpetual state of uncertainty it so recently appeared to be escaping. It was the end of two turbulent seasons. Hearts supporters could only hope that a third would not follow.

SUMMARY

Throughout the past 130 years, Hearts have generally been good enough to compete at or near the top of Scottish football yet never strong enough to dominate. A historical analysis ranks them best of the rest in terms of league success – wins and points – and fourth behind the Glasgow two and Aberdeen on trophies won. A closer look at Hearts' triumphs shows that almost all were achieved during two golden ages, each lasting around ten to fifteen years. They occurred in the early years and the post-Second World War era. But, for a number of reasons, Hearts failed to fully grasp and build on those opportunities.

In fact, Hearts have failed to consistently break the duopoly of the Glasgow giants despite persistent attempts to do so. And the barren periods, with no success to celebrate, have been extensive. The first spanned forty-eight years, the second lasted thirty-six years. During those lean times, the club has suffered agonising near misses and, worse, the calamity of repeated relegation.

The previous pattern of trophy success would suggest Hearts were due a new golden age around the turn of this century. Yet the boom and slump of the club's earlier history, on and off the field, has continued. Relegation and failure to win promotion were followed by a painful league 'loss' and a handful of cup finals and runners-up places. Performances improved but resulted in only one Scottish Cup, the memorable 1998 victory. By the time a new golden age beckoned in modern times, it was too late. The club was no longer durable enough to maintain the challenge.

Football factors, such as the strengthened position of Rangers and Celtic and the broadening of horizons to focus increasingly on European competition, have played their part in those failures. The Hillsborough tragedy and subsequent Taylor Report resulted in huge stadium costs for Hearts and others. In recent years, the fluctuation of television income and the Bosman ruling have also had an impact. External events, too, have proved pivotal, not least the outbreak of the First World War and the sacrifices made by all the Hearts players. Changes in society at large since the 1950s have generally benefited the biggest teams at the expense of others, including Hearts. More recently the club has struggled first through a recession but then had the 'luxury' of spending against a backdrop of booming Edinburgh property prices, which inflated the value of its own land.

It is also an often-overlooked reality that Hearts, unlike almost all the other major clubs in Scotland, have never enjoyed the luxury of a super-rich benefactor. Local worthies certainly bailed the club out after it was wound up in 1905 and Wallace Mercer took control in 1981, offsetting a similar demise. Chris Robinson and Leslie Deans bought a controlling stake in 1994 and Vladimir Romanov became the major shareholder in 2005. But, throughout the past 131 years, there have been no sugar daddies prepared to throw huge sums of money in Hearts' direction regardless of the return. With little margin for error, therefore, the combination of a successful manager, support staff and, preferably, boardroom has been a prerequisite to putting a winning team on the park. Unfortunately, some or all have been missing for lengthy, unfulfilled periods of Hearts' history.

However, there are indications that the finances of both Scottish football, in general, and Hearts, in particular, are currently improving. The latest PricewaterhouseCoopers annual review, for season 2002–03, found that total SPL losses fell by £10 million to £53 million, the combined wage bill decreased, as did transfer fees, while turnover increased. On the other hand, total debt actually rose by £41 million to £186 million and attendances fell by 3%. Over half of the clubs, including Hearts, were technically insolvent, it said. Author and PwC partner David Glen said that further action was being taken to reduce debt levels but he singled out the Hearts situation as a note of caution, stressing, 'The emotion that surrounds football can also not be underestimated as evidenced by the extreme level of debate generated at Hearts over the stadium sale.' He later concluded that '[overall], there is a long way to go but the signs of financial recovery for the SPL are there and growing – losses are falling and the debt mountain is being tackled, principally by cutting back on squad sizes, players' wages and transfer fees'. Indeed, Hearts' latest six-monthly figures, up to January 2005, bear that analysis out, with debt, losses and staff costs all down. However, this period did include an unprecedented UEFA Cup windfall.

Those latest interim results contained a health warning that Romanov could not be expected to 'cure all of our ills' – it remains to be seen how the remainder of the SMG debt will be paid by September 2007 – but he is reputed to have deep pockets. He may even have a fortune – in assets and investments at least – running into hundreds of millions of pounds. If true, he could be Hearts' first sugar daddy. The most meagre of slices of his wealth would no doubt improve the chances of glory in the future, although it comes with no guarantees. Any football club – and Hearts should know this better than most by now – must also manage its finances and its ambitions wisely if it is to achieve long-term success.

Romanov's early public statements suggest he aims to be the man who finally inspires Hearts to scale new heights. Such visions are alluring but fanciful to most Hearts fans, particularly those reared on a diet of lower league football and brushes with financial disaster. Romanov's ambitions may well not be fully realised; Hearts supporters would tolerate as much. After all, they have been condemned in the past to a worse fate than success. After the past two turbulent seasons some would settle for guaranteed survival, preferably in the top league.

However, the ill-conceived plan to sell Tynecastle and move to Murrayfield has, for now at least, been abandoned. The building workers moved into the Gorgie ground during the close season but with orders to develop rather than demolish. The bad feeling and uncertainty created by the departure of John Robertson has been replaced by a renewed sense of optimism following the appointment of highly regarded manager George Burley. The former Ipswich Town and Derby County boss, who won the Premiership Manager of the Year award while with the Suffolk side, promised, on his first day, that he had targeted players who would 'excite the fans' and hopefully challenge the Old Firm. His first signings suggest that he has been provided with a budget to make that dream a reality.

Romanov must be commended for that and more, although only time will reveal the true worth of his commitments. Others deserve credit for their part in the turnaround, not least George Foulkes and all those associated with the Save our Hearts campaign. But the club's vulnerability had once again been exposed. Those who guard Heart of Midlothian's destiny today should take heed of the club's past perils, recent and distant.

There must never again be any need to save our Hearts.

BIBLIOGRAPHY

BOOKS

Aitken, Mike, *Glorious Hearts* (Edinburgh: John Donald Publishers Ltd, 1986)

Aitken, Mike and Wallace Mercer *Heart to Heart: The Anatomy of a Football Club* (Edinburgh: Mainstream, 1988)

Alexander, Jack, *McCrae's Battalion: the Story of the 16th Royal Scots* (Edinburgh: Mainstream, 2003)

Conn, David, *The Football Business: Fair Game in the 90s?* (Edinburgh: Mainstream, 1998)

Docherty, Gerry and Phil Thomson, *100 Years of Hibs 1875–1975* (Edinburgh: Donald, 1975)

Fairgrieve, John, *The Talk of the Toon Are ... the Boys in Maroon: Heart of Midlothian, the Authorised Inside Story of an Unforgettable Season* (Edinburgh: Mainstream Publishing Co Ltd, 1986)

Gallacher, Ken, *Slim Jim Baxter: the Definitive Biography* (London: Virgin Books, 2002)

HMFC (compiler), *Images of Scotland: Heart of Midlothian Football Club* (Stroud: Tempus Publishing Ltd, 1998)

Jardine, Sandy and Michael Aitken, *Score and More: the Sandy Jardine Story* (Edinburgh: Mainstream, 1987)

Jefferies, Jim, with Jim McLean, *All Heart: the Jim Jefferies Story* (Edinburgh: Mainstream, 1998)

Jordan, Joe, with James Lawton, *Behind the Dream: My Autobiography* (London: Hodder & Stoughton, 2004)

Joyce, Philip and Fraser Gibson, *Evening Times, The Wee Red Book 2004–2005 Football Annual* (Glasgow: Newsquest Ltd, 2004)

Mackie, Albert, *The Hearts: The Story of the Heart of Midlothian FC* (Edinburgh: Stanley Paul, 1959)

Hepburn, Ray, Wallace Mercer, et al, *Ten of Hearts: the Heart of Midlothian Story 1980–90* (Edinburgh: Mainstream, 1990)

Mackay, Dave, with Martin Knight, *The Real Mackay: the Dave Mackay Story* (Edinburgh: Mainstream, 2004)

Mackenzie, Roddy, Hearts: the Official Illustrated History of Edinburgh's Oldest League Club (Derby: Breedon Books Publishing Company Ltd, 2001)

Mackenzie, Roddy, *Hearts Official All-Time Greats* (Edinburgh: Lomond Books, Grange Communications Ltd under licence from Heart of Midlothian FC, 1999)

McIlroy, Gwen and Alan MacPherson, *That'll Be the Day: the Story of the Day that Hearts won the Scottish Cup* (Dundee: David Winter and Son Ltd, 1998)

McPherson, Dave, with Derek Watson, *A Tale of Two Cities: the Dave McPherson Story* (Edinburgh: Mainstream, 1996)

Morrow, Stephen, *The New Business of Football: Accountability and Finance in Football* (Basingstoke: Macmillan Business, 1999)

Murray, William J, *Bhoys, Bears and Bigotry: the Old Firm in the New Age* (Edinburgh: Mainstream, 1998)

Murray, William J, *The World's Game: a History of Soccer* (Urbana: University of Illinois Press, 1996)

Murray, William J, Football: a History of the World Game (Aldershot: Scolar Press, 1994)

Murray, William J, *Glasgow's Giants: 100 Years of the Old Firm* (Edinburgh: Mainstream, 1988)

Murray, William J, *The Old Firm: Sectarianism, Sport and Society in Scotland* (Edinburgh: Donald, 1984)

Price, Norrie, *Gritty, Gallant and Glorious: a History and Complete Record of the Hearts 1946–97* (Aberdeen: Norrie Price, 1997)

Reid, William, *The Story of the Hearts: A Fifty Years' Retrospect 1874–1924* (Edinburgh: HMFC, 1924)

Scottish Football League (compiler), *The Scottish Football League Handbook Season 2003–2004* (2003)

Scottish Football League (compiler), *The Scottish Football Review 2003–04: the Official Handbook of Scottish Football* (24th edition) (Epsom: PPL Sport & Leisure, on behalf of The Scottish Football League, 2003)

Speed, David, Bill Smith and Graham Blackwood, *The Heart of Midlothian Football Club: A Pictorial History 1874–1984* (Edinburgh: Heart of Midlothian FC plc, 1984)

Szymanski, Stefan, and Tim Kuypers, *Winners and Losers: the Business Strategy of Football* (London: Viking, 1999)

BOOKLETS

McCartney, John, *The Hearts and the Great War* (includes 'The 'Hearts' and the Army') (Edinburgh: Bishop and Sons, 1917)

Tales from Tynecastle (Edinburgh: The Simmath Press Ltd, 1929) season)

NEWSPAPERS

Edinburgh Evening News
Daily Mail
The Daily Mirror
Daily Record
Daily Telegraph
The Herald
Scotland on Sunday
The Scotsman
Sport Express (Lithuanian paper)
The Sun
Sunday Herald
Sunday Mail
Sunday Times
The Times

Selected Magazines, Fanzines and Other Publications
Hansard (1914)
Heart of Midlothian Football Club Stadium Working Group Report
Heart of Midlothian Supporters Trust Annual Reports
Hearts: the Official Monthly Magazine
Hearts Annual Report
Hearts Official Matchday Magazine/Programme
The Jambo: Official Magazine of Hearts FC
No Idle Talk
PricewaterhouseCoopers Financial Review of Scottish Football
Still, Mustn't Grumble
Tynecastle Stadium: Not Fit For Purpose

Websites
www.afc.co.uk
www.bbc.co.uk
www.celticfc.co.uk
www.dundeeunitedfc.co.uk
www.fifa.com
www.heartsfc.co.uk
www.hibernianfc.co.uk
www.le.ac.uk
www.londonhearts.com
www.londonstockexchange.com
www.queensparkfc.co.uk
www.rangersfc.co.uk
www.scotprem.com
www.scottishfa.co.uk
www.scottishfootballleague.com
www.scottishleague.net
www.stadiumguide.com
www.uefa.com

INDEX